Community
Engagement
Abroad

Community Engagement Abroad

PERSPECTIVES AND PRACTICES ON SERVICE,
ENGAGEMENT, AND LEARNING OVERSEAS

Edited by Pat Crawford and Brett Berquist

Michigan State University Press | East Lansing

♾ The paper used in this publication meets the minimum requirements
of ANSI/NISO Z39.48-1992 (R 1997) (Permanence of Paper).

Michigan State University Press
East Lansing, Michigan 48823-5245

LIBRARY OF CONGRESS CATALOGING-IN-PUBLICATION DATA
Names: Crawford, Pat, editor. | Berquist, Brett, editor.
Title: Community engagement abroad : perspectives and practices on service,
engagement, and learning overseas / edited by Pat Crawford and Brett Berquist.
Description: East Lansing : Michigan State University Press, [2020] |
Series: Transformations in higher education : the scholarship of engagement
| Includes bibliographical references and index.
Identifiers: LCCN 2019022081 | ISBN 9781611863482 (paperback)
| ISBN 9781628953855 (epub) | ISBN 9781609176235 (pdf)
| ISBN 9781628963861 (Kindle edition)
Subjects: LCSH: Foreign study—Case studies. | Service learning—Case studies.
Classification: LCC LB2376 .C63 2020 | DDC 370.116—dc23
LC record available at https://lccn.loc.gov/2019022081

Book design by Charlie Sharp, Sharp Des!gns, East Lansing, MI
Cover design by Shaun Allshouse, www.shaunallshouse.com
Cover art by Pat Crawford

Michigan State University Press is a member of the Green Press Initiative and
is committed to developing and encouraging ecologically responsible publishing
practices. For more information about the Green Press Initiative and the use of
recycled paper in book publishing, please visit *www.greenpressinitiative.org*.

Visit Michigan State University Press at *www.msupress.org*

Transformations in Higher Education: Scholarship of Engagement

The Transformations in Higher Education: Scholarship of Engagement book series is designed to provide a forum where scholars can address the diverse issues provoked by community-campus partnerships that are directed toward creating innovative solutions to societal problems. Numerous social critics and key national commissions have drawn attention to the pervasive and burgeoning problems of individuals, families, communities, economies, health services, and education in American society. Such issues as child and youth development, economic competitiveness, environmental quality, and health and health care require creative research and the design, deployment, and evaluation of innovative public policies and intervention programs. Similar problems and initiatives have been articulated in many other countries, apart from the devastating consequences of poverty that burdens economic and social change. As a consequence, there has been increasing societal pressure on universities to partner with communities to design and deliver knowledge applications that address these issues, and to co-create novel approaches to effect system changes that can lead to sustainable and evidence- based solutions. Knowledge generation and knowledge application are critical parts of the engagement process, but so too are knowledge dissemination and preservation. The Transformations in Higher Education: Scholarship of Engagement series was designed to meet one aspect of the dissemination/preservation dyad.

This series is sponsored by the National Collaborative for the Study of University Engagement (NCSUE) and is published in partnership with the Michigan State University Press. An external board of editors supports the NCSUE editorial staff in order to ensure that all volumes in the series are peer reviewed throughout the publication process. Manuscripts embracing campus-community partnerships are invited from authors regardless of discipline, geographic place, or type of transformational change accomplished. Similarly, the series embraces all methodological approaches from rigorous randomized trials to narrative and ethnographic studies. Analyses may span the qualitative to quantitative continuum, with particular emphasis on mixed- model approaches. However, all manuscripts must attend to detailing critical aspects of partnership development, community involvement, and evidence of program changes or impacts. Monographs and books provide ample space for authors to address all facets of engaged scholarship thereby building a compendium of praxis that will facilitate replication and generalization, two of the cornerstones of evidence-based programs, practices, and policies. We invite you to submit your work for publication review and to fully participate in our effort to assist higher education to renew its covenant with society through engaged scholarship.

HIRAM E. FITZGERALD
BURTON BARGERSTOCK
LAURIE VAN EGEREN

Contents

Preface

The stories shared in this volume came together through an authentic desire to communicate with others the strengths and weaknesses/celebrations and struggles of the authors' experiences with study abroad and community engagement in diverse international settings. While the sharing was initially an internal exercise, we quickly recognized that we have kindred spirits across universities in the United States and abroad. Our goal is for readers to connect with our commonalities and perhaps find something of value they can apply to their own work. The volume dives into the history of international engagement within the context of Michigan State University in order to frame the context of our stories. Readers are encouraged to think about how their own institutional context has or has not framed their own stories.

The reflective process takes time, and sometimes distance, to unpack the wealth of things we learn through our doing. As a community of learners, we also benefit from listening to others and then looking for how their stories connect to our own. We test out others' observations and conclusions on our experiences, looking for what fits and what does not. Exploring existing and creating new models, frameworks, and schemas aid us in our attempts to organize what can seem like disparate thoughts and experiences into a rigging that makes sense within our own context. We encourage readers to borrow, test, modify, and extrapolate from our experiences to articulate their own ways of knowing the world and how they define their practice. From this iterative cycle we all advance through sharing back with the broader community. Please accept our stories for what they are (full of insights and limitations), and we look forward to learning from yours.

Michigan State University and International Engagement

Michigan State University (MSU) has a long history of international engagement, beginning with the country's first dean of international studies and programs, appointed in 1956. For several decades, MSU has engaged in capacity building in higher education, most notably in Africa. MSU is known for three distinctive components of experiential education: The Center for Service

Learning and Civic Engagement serves more than twenty-seven thousand students each year participating in community engaged learning or community service, more than ten thousand students are active in undergraduate research activities, and nearly three thousand study abroad. More than 1,400 faculty members engage in international research, and a significant number of these seek to share their experience with undergraduate students. From the 1980s, MSU developed a model for education abroad that grew through faculty engagement. The institution provided a strong vision, resources, incentivization, and accountability for programming originating with the academic unit and college. The MSU model was based on faculty leadership rather than administrative program development and took the institution to rapid growth in participation that resulted in the highest study-abroad enrollment among public universities for nearly a decade (2004–2012).

Short-term faculty-led programming was unfashionable when MSU adopted this model but it has subsequently become the driver behind study abroad growth in the United States nationally for the past twenty years. Of the more than four hundred faculty members actively recruiting students to the education abroad programs they lead, a growing number offer the students the opportunity to learn with a community overseas. A strong culture of international development and service, coupled with an entrepreneurial approach to study abroad, resulted in an environment conducive to a broad continuum of engagement abroad. The university's strategic plan "Bolder by Design" calls for even more efforts to focus on "global resilient communities" as a platform for research and mutual learning.

The present volume offers scholarly reflection on several decades of practice at a public university that is uniquely positioned to shed light on the wide range of practice in the intersection between service learning and study abroad.

Faculty Learning Community for Community-Based Learning Abroad

The volume shares a wide variety of practice rather than a normative model. Each author brings their perspective, experience, and philosophical orientation to community engagement and develops these through ways that are appropriate to the needs of the community and project they have chosen to work with. This book shares these perspectives and approaches within a general framework and offers takeaways germane to the broadest range of higher education institutions. This ranges from models for community development over multiple sustained years of strategic planning and implementation to microengagement projects as part of a larger education-abroad program. Writers present their perspective and motivation, ranging from curricular efforts linked to professional training and development to larger multiyear projects for community development overseas.

The authors initially came together through an invitation from the study-abroad office to share practice and frameworks for several decades of programming. This effort sought to strengthen understanding and synergy among different approaches and to focus the university's emerging strategy to leverage faculty engagement and research through work on "global resilient communities." The high level of interest among faculty leaders led to the present book project, developed through a Bailey Scholars Faculty Learning Community (FLC) at MSU. It is built on the strengths of two key units that are national leaders in their fields: Education Abroad, and Outreach and Engagement.

The FLC strives to attract a wide readership audience for the book by including diverse representation of countries, types of engagement ("big E to little e"), length of programs, and a range of voices. The stories offer value to experienced as well as early career practitioners from the fields of service learning, experiential education, community engagement, and education abroad. Chapters include contributions from nineteen authors representing administrators, faculty members, students, and international partners.

The book begins by setting the context of engagement and service learning at Michigan State University (Frank A. Fear and Karen McKnight Casey) and positing four core principles that have directly or indirectly shaped the institution's engagement-abroad programming:

1. Reciprocal relationships with community-based partners will characterize MSU's work.
2. Community voice and expertise will be recognized and respected.
3. Students will be educated about the reasons that led to establishing the partnership and why the effort is important from a community point of view.
4. Benefits will be bidirectional and balanced—for the community and for the university.

In chapter 2, Brett Berquist and Joy Milano review the literature on service learning and education abroad to find the intersections for creating a framework to serve as scaffolding for readers to review the subsequent program cases, as well as to reflect on their own engagement-abroad programming activities or planning.

Seven unique program cases are then developed from the scholarly perspective of the authors' home discipline.

Chapter 3 outlines the thought process of a unique husband–wife academic team leading programs to India. Keri and Daniel Dutkiewicz's "engagement ecology" focuses on programming design to maximize student learning through intense guided community interaction, which also leads to sustained service engagement back home for the community causes initiated while overseas. The authors also address the institutional barriers for community learning intended to continue beyond the period abroad.

In chapter 4 Zenia Kotval, Christiane Ziegler-Hennings, and Anne Budinger bring a welcome perspective from an overseas partner to share their experience designing programming that intentionally combines theory and practice to enhance professional planning training for American and German students. In this particular program, the U.S. and German universities are themselves the "community" in the engagement programming.

Chapters 5 and 6 offer different angles from the institution's medical schools. Christina Dokter and Gary Willyerd reflect on a qualitative approach to improve program design and learning outcomes through supervised medical clinics through the College of Osteopathic Medicine. Rae Schnuth and Cheryl Celestin situate the College of Human Medicine's catalog of several overseas destinations within a clear strategy to develop personal learning and career choices. The different foci of these colleges' programming is a useful illustration of the continuum of engagement developed in chapter 2.

One location for Dokter and Willyerd's program has been a location high in the northern Andes of Peru, and Rene Rosenbaum (chapter 7) relates the philosophical underpinnings of his work there. He posits the program as a platform to explore the depth of faculty commitment to provide these experiences in a university context. Experiencing two university programs working in different ways with the same community was an eye-opening experience for Berquist, leading to his reflection with Milano (in chapter 2) on a continuum of engagement and the need for rubrics to reflect a broad range of programing choices rather than a prescriptive approach. The three final cases (chapters 7–9) are fairly aligned in the philosophy behind the programming efforts and the faculty motivation to undertake the significant workload to make such intense learning experiences possible.

The final two chapters (8 and 9) are situated within a new model for civic engagement, a required core component of the Residential College of Arts and Humanities. Working on ecotourism projects with a network of communities in Costa Rica, Vincent Delgado and Scot Yoder (chapter 8) encourage students to face the challenge of dissidence to deeper understanding of self. Stephen L. Esquith concludes the cases with a masterful reflection on the ethical impact of his years working with a community in Mali, including a postwar reconciliation effort. His program aims to help students develop their global perspective, embracing the positive as well as the negative toward a deeper understanding of their own culture.

Each of the authors brings a unique voice to the discussion of community engagement abroad. The volume concludes with a weaving of the stories together from their intrinsic and extrinsic value perspectives and lessons learned. The personal and disciplinary lenses are expressed through their epistemology (ways of doing), ontology (worldview), axiology (values and preferences), and methodology (ways of doing).

CHAPTER 1

The Story of Place: What We Learned About Engaged Study-Abroad Work at Michigan State University

Frank A. Fear and Karen McKnight Casey

U nderstanding a circumstance depends on knowing a story—the unique circumstances that characterize a situation. Understanding is grounded experientially when those in a story take time to sense-make. Insiders have important information to share, as long as they disclose openly and without self-serving intent.

The contributors to this volume are insiders to a story. They decided, one after the other, to organize and offer study-abroad programs using some form of community engagement. They all did their work at the same institution of higher education, Michigan State University (MSU).

The MSU administration recognized that a number of faculty members were involved in engaged study-abroad efforts. Faculty members were invited to form a learning community—to share and learn about similar work being done on campus. Conversations led to writing this book.

Part 1. The Emergence and Spread of Engaged Study Abroad at Michigan State University

Engaged study abroad emerged (recognizably) across campus in the 1990s. In predominant form, it fused service learning and study abroad, an interpretation that is explored by Berquist and Milano in chapter 2.

An intriguing aspect of the MSU experience is what influenced the development of engaged study-abroad work—work that was undertaken years before the term "engaged study abroad" was used on campus. Even though MSU is well known for international work, the genesis of engaged study-abroad work was faculty and student involvement in social activism (initially) and, later, in experiential education and service learning.

Social Activism and Domestic Service Learning

MSU was fertile ground for social activism long before there was anything known as engaged study abroad. From the early 1960s through the late 1970s, faculty members and students were engaged actively in various efforts, including protesting the Vietnam War, condemning local housing restrictions, and urging that economic penalties be levied against apartheid South Africa.

Racial and social justice were areas of keen interest on campus. Robert Green and Maxie C. Jackson were two campus leaders. In the 1960s, Green worked closely with Martin Luther King Jr. in Green's role as national education director of the Southern Christian Leadership Conference. In the 1970s, Jackson was appointed by then-governor William Milliken to chair the Governor's Commission for Volunteerism in Michigan. Green later became dean, with Jackson serving as assistant dean, of MSU's College of Urban Development.

Another prominent name during those days was H. Frank Beeman, who served as the university's tennis coach and director of Intramural Sports and Recreation Services. Beeman was concerned about what was happening in South Africa. Frank and his spouse, Patricia, organized the South African Liberation Committee. For this and other efforts, the Beemans received the first Peace and Justice Award from the Peace Education Center of Greater Lansing.

John S. Duley is another notable figure from that era. Duley, who served as a campus minister and faculty member in MSU's Justin Morrill College, was a campus pioneer in experiential education and, later, in service learning. Well known for his civil rights work, during 1965–1968 Duley brought MSU undergraduates to Mississippi to help students succeed academically at a local African-American college. Duley was also active in the peace movement of the time, advocating for peace and justice, and lobbying for an end to the production and distribution of nuclear weapons.

The work of these and other faculty members helped reform MSU's institutional policies and practices. Most notable on the policy side was the decision in 1978 to divest university resources from apartheid South Africa. New programs were established, such as the Student Education Corps and the Volunteer Income Tax Assistance program (VITA).

The biggest step programmatically came in 1968, when MSU established the Office of Volunteer Programs. The office carried the title "Volunteer" because the prevailing thinking at the time was that this work resided outside of the academic purview of faculty and students. That interpretation changed over time as the experiential and service-learning movement spread nationally. The title of the center changed accordingly, renamed "The Service-Learning Center."

The center was directed ably for years by Mary Edens, who established a national reputation as a founder of the service-learning movement. Edens, a campus mainstay, helped numerous faculty members organize service-learning courses and offer cocurricular experiences. The center that she built—renamed "The Center for Service-Learning and Civic Engagement" in 2003 to reflect the emergence of engagement nationally—is the oldest continuously operating service-learning center in the United States (Center for Service Learning and Civic Engagement, 2008).

The authors of this chapter can speak personally to how Duley and Edens influenced their careers and work. Duley and Edens helped Frank A. Fear incorporate community-based work in his teaching, research, and outreach program. In the 1990s, Karen McKnight Casey (as community partner) and Fear (as faculty member) collaborated with Rex LaMore (Urban Affairs Programs) and David Horner (Office of International Students and Scholars) on a domestic service-learning program for international students, dubbed "the reverse Peace Corps." Later, Casey came to campus and played a variety of student-support roles, eventually assuming (in 2000) the directorship of the center that Edens had built.

Fear, Casey, and many other faculty members also benefitted from the support that earmarked John DiBiaggio's tenure as MSU president (1985–1992). That support included active, hands-on leadership from presidential assistant MaryLee Davis. A well-respected figure on campus and off, Davis represented MSU ably through public speaking engagements and by serving on local boards and participating in civic initiatives. Davis also convened faculty from across campus to share service-learning innovations and discuss issues. The meetings were held in the university's Board Room, a location that signaled to faculty the importance of the work. Service learning was becoming a priority at MSU.

Service Learning as a Form of University Outreach

Service learning gained significantly from the contributions made by a university committee launched in 1991 during DiBiaggio's tenure. The committee was charged by then-provost David Scott and overseen by Vice Provost James Votruba.

Votruba was the last administrator at MSU to hold the title assistant provost for Lifelong Education. Then, in 1991, he became the first MSU administrator to hold the title vice provost for University Outreach. The title change—from assistant to vice, and from Lifelong Education to Outreach—was significant. It signaled the university's intent to become more active than ever in "reaching out" to share knowledge with external audiences through faculty scholarship. With Votruba's leadership, MSU became an institutional leader in a national outreach movement. The committee's work contributed to that stature.

Chaired by Fear, the committee defined outreach as "a form of scholarship that cuts across teaching, research, and service. It involves generating, transmitting, applying, and preserving knowledge for the direct benefit of external audiences in ways that are consistent with university and unit missions" (Provost's Committee on University Outreach, 1993, p. 1).

By articulating outreach as *scholarship that cuts across the mission*, committee members asserted that initiatives such as service learning should be understood as scholarship, specifically, "engaged teaching." It was a landmark designation for MSU. In 2000, engaged scholarship was adopted formally into the university's promotion and tenure process (National Collaborative for the Study of University Engagement, 2009).

Service Learning in International Contexts

Another major boost came in the mid-1990s when then-president Peter McPherson sought to expand study abroad by repositioning a heretofore domestic program—the university's Alternative Spring Break (ASB)—as an international option. Carlos Fuentes (MSU's Service Learning Center) and Luis Garcia (Office of Racial and Ethnic Student Affairs, now named the Office of Cultural and Academic Transitions) teamed up to offer a not-for-credit, week-long, service-focused ASB program in Mérida, Querétaro, and Amealco, Mexico.

Then, in the early 2000s, Fuentes and Garcia (in his new program, the College Achievement Migrant Program) partnered with Professor Rick Paulsen (College of Agriculture and Natural Resources) to offer a credit-bearing, service-based, ASB opportunity in the same Mexican cities. The fieldwork was completed in a concentrated week, but the experience included a semester-long seminar, which included prefield preparation and posttrip reflection.

Those efforts are early examples of what today is termed "engaged study abroad." Another early program was codesigned and refined in the early 2000s by Fear and two of his doctoral students, Margaret Desmond and Diane Doberneck (now with the Office of University Outreach and Engagement). In "Community Engagement in Rural Ireland," students engaged collaboratively with village leaders in designing and undertaking projects associated with a regional development plan in the west of Ireland. The program was designed with assistance from staff members in service learning and study abroad using seed funding from the Michigan Campus Compact and the Office of University Outreach and Engagement.

Another example was an Africa-focused program designed and offered by Jeanne Gazel, entitled "Building Partnerships for Orphaned and Vulnerable Children." This program was one of the first efforts at MSU to integrate a development priority (Africa focus) with undergraduate engaged learning. MSU students worked with local partners to address youth issues.

Fitting the Work to Institutional Priorities

An extremely important part of this story is when the work was included in a comprehensive plan for university priorities and directions. That happened when Lou Anna K. Simon became MSU president in 2003. Simon launched an executive initiative called "Boldness by Design." The plan articulated strategic imperatives, including the intent to enhance the student experience; enrich community, economic, and family life; and expand international reach (Michigan State University, 2003). In Boldness by Design, service learning and civic engagement were positioned as highly desirable practices with impact: They enhance the student experience and enrich community, economic, and family life. Furthermore, engaged study abroad expands MSU's international reach.

President Simon further accentuated the importance of this work in her 2007 Founder's Day comments. She set a goal of having 50 percent of MSU's undergraduate students involved in service learning by the year 2012—the 150th anniversary of the Morrill (Land Grant) Act. This commitment was expressed with renewed vigor in Simon's Bolder by Design, the university's strategic imperative for 2013–2020 (Michigan State University, 2013). Service learning was set as a goal for *all* undergraduates. Additionally, the university sought to increase the number of undergraduates participating in community-engaged study-abroad efforts.

Another administrative move—a structural change—bears mentioning. For years, the Service Learning Center had been administered solely by the vice president for Student Affairs and Services. A second reporting line—the Office of University Outreach and Engagement—was added in 2007. The administrative realignment gave further recognition to, and support for, service learning as a scholarly enterprise.

Emerging Principles of Engaged Practice

What does the body of work look like after all those years? First, and very importantly, models at MSU for engaged study abroad and domestic service learning vary. Through a "thousand flowers blooming" motif, MSU embraces and supports diversity of expression.

However, four characteristics are associated with engaged programs across the university— domestic and international. These points of emphasis operate informally as principles of engaged practice.

- Reciprocal relationships with community-based partners will characterize MSU's work.
- Community voice and expertise will be recognized and respected.
- Students will be educated about the reasons that led to establishing the partnership and why the effort is important from a community point of view.
- Benefits will be bidirectional and balanced—for the community and for the university.

Part 2. Dramatic Growth and Expansion of Study-Abroad Programs

For years, MSU undergraduates had participated selectively in study-abroad programs. The office MSU designated to coordinate the programs was established in 1970 as the Office of Overseas Study, located in the Office of International Extension in the Continuing Education Service. Even though MSU had become a mega-university by 1970—with nearly forty thousand students, including more than thirty-one thousand undergraduates—only about two hundred students participated in overseas study that year (Gliozzo, 2012).

Growth and development started when Charles A. Gliozzo assumed responsibility as director, a position he served ably during 1973–1993. Among many things, Gliozzo revised the program's name to "Office of Study Abroad" to signify an emphasis on international education. He promoted faculty engagement in study-abroad efforts, most notably through short-term programs held around the world, and he worked hard to diversify the student body participating in study-abroad programs.

Administrative responsibility for the office was also adjusted during Gliozzo's tenure. It migrated from the Continuing Education Service to a campus-wide coordinating structure for internationally focused work—a deans-led unit—called International Studies and Programs (ISP).

Participation in study abroad expanded significantly during the time Gliozzo led the office, from about 50 programs in 15 countries and 900 students in 1984 to nearly 90 programs in more than 20 countries and about 1200 students by the time Gliozzo left the office in 1993 (Gliozzo, 2012).

But while study abroad had become a solid, respected program under Gliozzo's leadership, it was not considered to be a campus priority. Enrollments ebbed up and down as a result. According to *Open Doors*, an annual report of the International Education Exchange (and the gold standard reporting system), approximately 1460 MSU undergraduates participated in study abroad in 1980–1981. Nearly fifteen years later, in 1994–1995, the number was about 1025 students.

Study-abroad programs became a focus of institutional attention when Peter McPherson came to MSU as university president in 1993. McPherson was keen on expanding and deepening MSU's commitment to international work. As an MSU alumnus and former administrator of the U.S. Agency for International Development (USAID), McPherson was well aware of MSU's prominent standing as an internationally focused university.

McPherson saw an opportunity in study abroad. He advanced a plan, and the landscape at MSU changed quickly. His idea, simple in concept, was big in design: Expand study-abroad offerings significantly so that most (theoretically all) MSU students could participate in at least one study-abroad experience during their MSU academic careers. The corollary goal was to make MSU number one in rank among American public universities in terms of the number of students participating in study abroad annually.

A clarion call rang across campus—*More students, more programs, more faculty members, and more locations.* Expectations were put in place and the campus geared up to deliver on presidential aspirations. A "monthly scorecard" was prepared and shared publicly to evaluate progress across MSU's departments, schools, and colleges.

The cornerstone for the ramp up was MSU's new study-abroad funding model, designed by then-dean of ISP John Hudzik. The model offered financial incentives to participating units and faculty members. Tuition return was a key element in the model. Study abroad made it possible for some faculty members to earn a summer salary. It also opened up teaching opportunities for academic specialists and nontenure faculty (called "fixed-term faculty" at MSU).

MSU delivered many of its offerings using a "May-mester" model—so called because a good share of MSU's study-abroad programs began in early May, immediately following the end of the spring semester. The programs were led predominantly by MSU faculty members, organized typically as six- to eight-week offerings.

With programmatic adjustments and administrative persistence, McPherson's vision became reality. According to data from *Open Doors*, MSU was the top-ranked American public institution in terms of undergraduate study-abroad enrollments every year for nearly a decade, from 2003–2004 through 2010–2011.

Taking Stock of Growth

Despite the achievements made in a relatively short period of time, some on campus felt that the pressure to deliver a high-volume study-abroad program would wane in the long term. For one thing, the emphasis on study abroad was perceived to be person-identified with McPherson, a declaratively oriented chief executive who liked to set stretch goals, announce them publicly, and "compel the troops" to charge forward. McPherson favored quantitative targets and announced several "guarantees" during his tenure as president, including a much-publicized "Tuition Guarantee" (no tuition increase for undergraduate students over four years).

At issue was whether the priority emphasis on study abroad would survive McPherson's presidency. Some answered yes. They believed MSU had developed a delivery system with the capacity to engage large numbers of students in study-abroad programs. Others said no. They felt study abroad would be replaced with new administrative priorities.

Both groups were right, at least in part. Because MSU had scaled up its capacity, student participation remained high over the years. For example, nearly 2500 MSU students studied overseas during 2013–2014. But complimentary priorities, quality and embeddedness in the undergraduate experience, would accompany size as characteristics of MSU's study-abroad portfolio.

Leadership Transitions and the Evolution of Study Abroad

Achieving quick and steady increases in numbers was a nonnegotiable matter, given McPherson's mandate to expand the study-abroad portfolio quickly. But was that achieved at a cost? Some said yes. They felt quantity took precedence over quality.

It was not surprising, then, to witness an evolution in the way study abroad was conceived and organized. The evolution began when Simon—having previously served as MSU provost—succeeded McPherson as MSU president in 2003.

Simon, an MSU faculty member and administrator with more than thirty years of campus experience, had solid roots at MSU: She knew the place well and understood its culture. Simon recognized that MSU's international work represented a comparative advantage for MSU as it competes with peer institutions for national–global standing and prestige.

To help achieve her vision, Simon turned administratively (among others) to Jeffrey Riedinger for leadership. Riedinger, who had succeeded Hudzik as ISP dean in 2007, shared Simon's strong commitment to the land-grant university philosophy, particularly in extended form—"Global Grant," as Simon declared during her early years as president. Both Simon and Riedinger are champions of work to advance the economic and social standing of people, especially those "left behind" in developing areas around the world. Those convictions set the stage for yet another transition in study abroad.

That transition accelerated in 2009 when Riedinger appointed Brett Berquist as executive director of the MSU Office of Study Abroad. Berquist's mandate was to maintain and improve management systems necessary to support a large-scale study-abroad portfolio and to enhance the academic profile of study abroad.

Implicit in this challenge was the need to better connect study-abroad programs with faculty scholarship. This interest was reinforced, if not compelled, by Simon's successor as MSU provost, Kim Wilcox. Among many other things, Wilcox sought to better align MSU's international research-outreach work with its study-abroad offerings. Wilcox asked that a map be prepared locating MSU's research-outreach presence internationally and MSU's study-abroad locations. The map did not reveal a high degree of overlap.

Creating an Engaged Study-Abroad Learning Community

What might be done to close that gap? Berquist studied MSU's study-abroad portfolio. He found more than thirty programs (about 10 percent of the portfolio) that included some form of community engagement—as community service, community development, disciplinary knowledge application, and professional outreach. The programs were scattered throughout the university, situated in a variety of professions, disciplines, and fields.

With a list of programs and faculty leaders in hand, Berquist picked three programs to study in more detail. He made field visits to experience the programs in operation and to discuss issues with program leaders, students, and community partners.

With grounded experiences and interpretations in hand, Berquist returned to campus and invited the thirty-plus program leaders to a group meeting. The purpose was to create awareness about the work being done across campus and to foster collective learning from that work. The inaugural meeting was largely a "meet-and-greet" exchange because many participants met for the first time. At subsequent meetings the program leaders talked extensively about their work. Those conversations revealed commonalities and differences in philosophy and approach, but no program or approach was depicted as "the standard" to emulate. At the end of each session Berquist asked participants whether they wanted to meet again. "Yes" was the answer each time. Berquist had established a faculty learning community.

Over time the conversations turned to conceptual and operational issues, such as how to recruit and select students. The discussions also included matters pertaining to MSU's culture, including academic and faculty issues. One matter stood out: Doing this work, participants recounted, "did not always count" during times of annual evaluation and "RTP" (i.e., faculty reappointment, tenure review, and promotion).

At issue was a way to enhance the academic profile of the work. The idea of a book project emerged because relatively few of those around the table had published their work. Dr. Patricia Crawford, an associate professor of landscape architecture, offered to coordinate a book-writing project. Crawford was then director of an undergraduate program that offered several engaged study-abroad options, the Liberty Hyde Bailey Scholars Program.

Part 3. Seven Cases of Engaged Study Abroad at MSU

Seven cases are included in the book that developed. Consistent with MSU's culture of encouraging diversity, the cases that follow represent a fascinating mix of perspectives and approaches. Engagement is a motif for these authors, interpreted and applied in various ways but with similar intent—to advance their work. With experimentation, there is a sense of discovery, too: a new tool is being used to plow familiar turf.

Implications for How Engaged Study-Abroad Programs Are Conceptualized

An India-based experience led by spousal team Dutkiewicz and Dutkiewicz (chapter 3) was designed to address common deficiencies in study-abroad programs. The authors contend that programs do not always provide students with cultural immersion opportunities or cultivate long-term relationships with local partners.

To address those deficiencies, the Dutkiewiczes designed a program with twin centerpieces. First, they engaged successive generations of MSU students in community development work in India. The students worked to enhance daily living circumstances of vulnerable children and families. Alumni of the program created a group—Students Advancing International Development (SAID)—to raise funds in the United States for the program's work. Second, on-the-ground efforts were undertaken in collaboration with a local nonprofit organization. That organization seeks to improve living conditions among India's most disadvantaged citizens.

How Do You *Really* Learn to Become a Planning Professional?

"Book learning" and lecture courses have their place, Kotval et al. (chapter 4) assert, but learning those ways is insufficient for enabling a planner to plan effectively. "Planning depends upon the assembly of a group of persons actively, cooperatively, and in concert, to achieve a unified goal," they write. Service-learning and engagement are valuable approaches because they enhance students' "ability to work with community members in developing a plan that suits the needs of a community—meshing academic knowledge and social skills."

Drawing on a mix of literatures (service learning, active-experiential learning, engagement, and field-based analyses from the planning field), the authors describe and analyze an academic collaboration in urban and regional planning between MSU and a German-based university, a partnership that spans thirty years. The collaboration enables German students to have community-based practice experiences in the United States and for MSU students to have similar experiences in Germany.

The authors describe the curriculum and discuss challenges and opportunities. Among other things, they emphasize how important it is for faculty to become conversant with literature in cooperative learning, service learning, and group dynamics.

Improving the Professional Education Model

Studying engagement through case analysis is the focus of attention in Dokter and Willyerd's chapter (chapter 5). A phenomenological approach is used to study the participation of osteopathic students in an international medical service elective, a program that involves students in one of two Latin American locations: Guatemala and Peru.

The researchers draw on literature in experiential, transformational, and intercultural learning to study the effects of the international experience on students' professional development. Attention is given to studying potential enhancements in students' critical thinking capacity and potential contributions enabled by reflective learning.

The study protocol includes using pre- and postexperience assessments, conducting individual and focus-group interviews, analyzing students' reflective journals, and evaluating critical incidents associated with the engagement experience. Study data are framed and interpreted by core competencies associated with medical practice, including medical knowledge, professionalism, patient care, and communication skills.

The study revealed a variety of positive outcomes resulting from the international engagement experience, including "stretch learning." Stretch learning occurs when, for example, students become more comfortable with perceived disorganization of a local medical system.

Engendering Cultural Sensitivity in Professional Education

Those responsible for medical education have become increasingly declarative about the need to include opportunities for culturally diverse practices in physician education programs. That interest includes how "good experiences" should be organized and offered. Those issues are addressed in MSU's "Leadership in Medicine for the Underserved" (LMU) program, a certificate program discussed in Schnuth and Celestin's chapter (chapter 6). The program is designed and conducted using a service-learning frame.

Among other things, LMU is designed to help students better understand the relationship between health and poverty, reveal health care barriers faced by historically underserved populations, and improve students' ability to communicate effectively with diverse people.

An important feature of the program is tracking the impact that the experience has on participants' knowledge, attitudes, and career choices. Schnuth and Celestin report that MSU participants in the program are more likely to select primary care as a field of practice when compared to non-LMU participants. Many students come away from the experience with a commitment to work with underserved populations.

Engagement for Faculty Development

How might engaged study-abroad experiences influence how faculty members think about and approach their work? Rosenbaum (chapter 7) gives considerable attention to that question.

Educated as a labor economist, Rosenbaum's work focuses on issues associated with economic and social justice, with emphasis on "the people left behind." His work is grounded in critique, layered with concern about people and their well-being, and infused with hope about the future.

The case report and analysis of Rosenbaum's work in Huamachuco, Peru, is as much about his academic and personal journey as it is about an engaged study-abroad experience per se. His treatment focuses extensively on meaning: what the work means to him, to his Peruvian partners, to MSU, and to "citizen champions of the work," which in this case are members of a Michigan-based service organization who endorse and support the work taking place in Peru.

Deepening an Understanding of Context

Ethics "in" and "of" development represent frames of reference for the engaged study-abroad program undertaken by Delgado and Yoder (chapter 8). The initiative is conducted under the auspices of the university's Residential College in the Arts and Humanities.

"The need for a new approach" emerged in the early phases of the program, a realization that emanated from issues and questions raised by students. A new framework was designed and put in place, an approach that unpacked and extended what the coauthors see as the traditional model: that is, university faculty establishing a partnership with professionals associated with one or more community-based organizations. The new approach includes students and community residents as partners and differentiates "partnerships" from "relationships."

That shift in approach precipitated a shift in program emphasis—per the authors, "from an exploration of the ethics of tourism and sustainable development that utilizes engaged partnerships to one that is about engaged partnerships using the subject of tourism and sustainable development to help students ground their work."

Civic Engagement's Challenges

The words "highly self-reflective" capture the essence of Esquith's chapter (chapter 9). Drawing on engagement experiences undertaken by MSU's Residential College in the Arts and Humanities, Esquith offers commentary on what he calls "perplexities, dilemmas, and illusions." The commentary is designed to enhance (in the author's words), "the achievement of the values of self-awareness and responsibility that the college's civic engagement study abroad programs strive to embody."

Perplexity (from Jane Addams's classic work of the early twentieth century) refers to puzzlement that comes when we make assumptions that disallow us "to transform a troubling situation into a less harmful and violent one." *Dilemmas*, among many things, pertain to "the tension between trust and truth."

Esquith also addresses the matter of promise-making, that is, when and how much can we promise community partners. His treatment of *illusion* connects to Vaclav Havel's interpretation of the environment in which Czech citizens lived in the 1970s and 1980s. Havel called it "living within a lie." The appellation is used to discuss the college's work in Mali. It underscores the importance of understanding work as it takes place in a sociopolitical context.

Esquith's chapter represents a portal into what he calls "the harsh realities of democratic politics." Engagement is not always considered a democratic practice, but it is. Thinking of it that way—and the practice that results from it—can go a long way toward improving university work undertaken under the rubric "community development."

Part 4. Commentary About the Michigan State University Cases

What did we learn from our analysis?

First, there is considerable diversity in perspective and approach across the chapters. That is to be expected, given the broad frame of reference for community-based engagement at MSU.

Second, the work is taking place in a variety of international locations with a variety of partners, and for a variety of purposes. That outcome is illustrative of MSU's approach of encouraging work in places, ways, and approaches that faculty members prefer.

Third, most of the work is technical assistance to communities, that is, generating and/or applying knowledge for the purpose of improving local circumstances. Very little of the work is being undertaken as social activism for the purpose of transformational change—that is, designed to fundamentally change or replace social systems and structures.

Fourth, there is an overarching emphasis on student and professional development. Because the work is undertaken through curricular auspices, we would expect there to be a prevailing emphasis on students. Among other things, students grapple with perplexing issues—academically and personally.

Fifth, most of the work blends disciplinary, interdisciplinary, or professionally based under-standing with concepts/approaches from service learning and other forms of community-based pedagogy. That approach blends "what" (the subject matter) with "how" (the means to organize and conduct a student-focused field experience).

Sixth, "community" is always a setting for work and, less so, a focus of attention. While the work is always done in community settings, community development is not always at center stage.

Seventh, a good share of the work appears to be either academic service to communities and/or outreach from MSU to communities. An important and provocative question involves the extent to which the work being undertaken is actually "engagement" as a unique form of university work vis-à-vis service and outreach, which are more traditional forms of university work.

Finally, some of the work is being done by faculty members who consider themselves to be "engagement scholars." The rest of the work is being undertaken by faculty members who draw on engagement to do work in their discipline, profession, or field.

Part 5. Final Comments

What is our overall conclusion?

The idiomatic expression, "It is what it is," seems relevant.

That position is less judgmental, more supportive, as long as there are ongoing conversations about the work—not only within projects, but across projects, so that those involved can learn more deeply about the work. Leading questions include the following: What are the major issues and challenges? What have we learned? What will we do differently next time? Answers will guide decisions about fundamental choices: How should we engage? Where should we engage? With whom should we engage? When do we engage? When do we not engage?

Answers to these and other questions need to be documented and shared to advance practice, build a knowledge base, and make informed judgments and choices both programmatically and institutionally. It will be fascinating to see what the future holds.

REFERENCES

Center for Service Learning and Civic Engagement. (2008). 40th Anniversary celebration. Retrieved from: http://www.servicelearning.msu.edu/events/past-events/40th-anniversary-celebration.

Gliozzo, C. A. (2012). Looking back, looking forward at the education of study abroad in the United States. Retrieved from http://studyabroad.isp.msu.edu/history/interview_gliozzo.pdf.

Michigan State University. (2003). Boldness by design. Retrieved from http://boldnessbydesign.msu.edu/imperatives.asp.

Michigan State University. (2013). Bolder by design. Retrieved from http://bolderbydesign.msu.edu.

National Collaborative for the Study of University Engagement. (2009). Reappointment, promotion, and tenure study, 2001–2006. Retrieved from http://ncsue.msu.edu/research/reappointment.aspx.

Provost's Committee on University Research. (1993). University outreach at Michigan State University: Extending knowledge to serve society; A report by the Provost's Committee on University Outreach. Retrieved from http://outreach.msu.edu/documents/ProvostCommitteeReport_2009ed.pdf.

CHAPTER 2

Intersections Between Service Learning and Study Abroad: A Framework for Community Engagement Abroad

Brett Berquist and Joy Milano

Chapter 1 provides an analysis of the institutional context that allowed an ecology of engagement to flourish through institutional prioritization of the values of student learning overseas and the individual priorities of dedicated faculty members working within their disciplinary perspectives. This has led to community engagement on a global scale, aligning faculty service to the community with faculty members' pedagogical practices in the classroom. In this chapter, we identify the overlap between the substantial bodies of literature from community engagement, service learning, and education abroad. This is not intended as an exhaustive review of the literature; rather, we identify useful concepts to develop a new framework that captures the intersections of engagement, service, and learning in international settings. We believe the framework will be useful for the readers to review their existing practice or to guide their institution's engagement in this space. The focus in this chapter is on Michigan State University (MSU) as a case study in the hope that, due to the institution's long history in community engagement and education abroad, what is discussed here will be of value to others interested in enhancing or initiating community engagement in their education-abroad programming.

Service and Engagement at Michigan State University

Michigan State University's 2006 "community engagement" designation by the Carnegie Foundation (Carnegie Foundation, 2014) provided an "imprimatur" to the service-learning and community outreach and engagement work with its external constituents that had been developing in its ecology of engagement for many years, as outlined in chapter 1. This evolved from the previous view of the public service, outreach, and engagement mission of higher education at its founding as one of the first land-grant postsecondary institutions—one-way dissemination of the knowledge generated in higher education through short courses, extension services, and faculty consultations. As Weerts and Sandmann (2008, p. 74), describe it:

While traditional conceptualizations of public service and outreach emphasized a "one-way" approach to delivering knowledge and service to the public, higher education leaders began using the term engagement to describe a "two-way" approach to interacting with community partners to address societal needs (Boyer, 1996; Kellogg Commission, 1999). The new philosophy emphasizes a shift away from an expert model of delivering university knowledge to the public and toward a more collaborative model in which community partners play a significant role in creating and sharing knowledge to the mutual benefit of institutions and society.

For several decades, MSU has been "looking at voluntary service as purposeful, planned and reciprocal contributions to the community and for the public good" (Center for Service Learning and Civic Engagement, 2014). This high level of community engagement permeates both its service-learning pedagogy and its outreach mission. To further understand the current engagement emphasis, the following section reviews the evolution of service learning in the United States into the more explicit two-way community engagement of today.

The Roots of Service Learning in the U.S. Context

According to Campus Compact's Annual Membership survey, 58 percent of all students attending a member institution engaged in some form of community participation before graduation (Campus Compact, 2016), such as cocurricular programming, service-learning courses, service-learning option courses, or other forms of engagement with the community.

The service and outreach missions of colleges and universities and their expression through service learning and community engagement can trace its roots back to the historical mission of higher education (Thelin, 2011), through the Morrill Act that created land-grant institutions in the 1860s and the resulting extension education practices, and to the more progressive education efforts of the 1960s. Higher education historians note the prominent role of community and society beginning with the earliest colleges, formed with an eye toward educating future citizens and leaders (though, as Thelin points out, education was intended particularly to benefit those [men] of the upper class). As the new nation was formed, the focus shifted to educating for nation-building and democracy, as well as preparing citizens to engage in nation-building through needed trades and industry (Thelin, 2011; Jacoby, 1996). The land-grant act "inextricably linked higher education and the concept of service, specifically related to agriculture and industry" (Jacoby, 1996, p. 11). Normal schools to train teachers are another long-standing form of civic engagement for U.S. tertiary institutions (Cucchiara, 2010). Service has been woven throughout the missions and philosophies of historically black colleges and universities (HBCU) and special-focus colleges and universities (SFCU) (Brotherton, 2002).

Service learning is a unique pedagogical strategy because it balances service to the community with learning in a more typical classroom style, connecting the existing body of knowledge with hands-on practice. The learning, however, is intended to be reciprocal. An integral part of service learning is engagement with community partners, who identify the needs to be addressed during the service. Guided critical reflection connects the service to the learning, with an end result being the development of civic knowledge and skills (Stanton, Giles, & Cruz, 1999; Jacoby, 1996; Clayton,

Bringle, & Hatcher, 2013). Similarly, the community gains from the university's engagement in several ways, including fresh energy, new perspectives, and the specialized knowledge gained from scholarly activity. In this way, service learning, when done appropriately, is more than just a pedagogy, it is also a way to engage the faculty and the institution in the scholarly mission of outreach, according to Jacoby. Community here indicates not just the local neighborhoods surrounding institutions of higher education but "the state, the nation, and the global community" (Jacoby, 1996, p. 5). There is a broad range of possibilities for service-learning activities, for example, urban community gardening, assistance in filing tax returns, building homes for low-income families, and so on. From the faculty perspective, service learning potentially brings "new life to the classroom, enhances performance on traditional measures of learning, increases student interest in the subject, teaches new problem solving skills" (Bringle & Hatcher, 1996, p. 222). Other positive student outcomes include development in critical thinking skills, civic and social responsibility, and personal development (social justice, self-efficacy, etc.) (Bringle & Hatcher, 1996; Markus, Howard, & King, 1993).

Philosophically, service-learning moves students away from thinking of service in the context of volunteerism or charity. Rather, it moves participants to a social justice and policy stance in which the community and the students learn from each other. Charity tends to be paternalistic, with one group controlling the knowledge and resources and "charitably sharing" them with the other group (Stanton et al., 1999, p. 3). Robert Sigmon (quoted in Stanton et al., 1999, p. 3) identified three principles for service learning in 1979 that encapsulate this perspective:

- Those being served control the service(s) provided.
- Those being served become better able to serve and be served by their own actions.
- Those who serve are also learners and have significant control over what is expected to be learned.

As a pedagogy, service learning is grounded in experience, drawing on many different philosophical epistemologies (see Bandura, Kolb, Coleman, Argyris & Schön, Freire, and particularly Dewey). In the southern hemisphere, particularly South America, Freire's emphasis on solidarity adds a dimension of social justice to service learning that might not always be the case in the northern hemisphere. Morris Keeton characterized this experiential learning as transforming "the individual, [revising and enlarging] knowledge, and [altering] practice. It affects their perceptions and interpretations of the world" (quoted in Stanton et al., 1999, p. 4). Dewey believed that education must encompass not only the historical "great books" but the application of learning to contemporary issues. Service learning, then, "is the various pedagogies that link community service and academic study so that each strengthens the other . . . the interaction of knowledge and skills with experience is key to learning" (Ehrlich, 1996, p. xi).

Service learning is reciprocal; it gives the power to the community to identify its needs and collaborate with those serving to meet them. Additionally, as a part of the reciprocal relationship, students should not be placed into a community service–learning partnership simply to fulfill learning outcomes or provide services that "do not meet actual needs or perpetuate a state of need" but should seek and address "the causes of need" (Jacoby, 1996, p. 7). Student outcomes include self-knowledge, improving skills (e.g., teamwork, problem solving), development of civic and social responsibility, and career preparation (Bonar, Buchanan, Fisher, & Wechsler, 1996; Gray, Elizabeth, Fricker, & Geschwind, 2000; Ward & Wolf-Wendel, 2000). Notably, the outcomes for service learning are not limited to enhanced student learning or addressing the cause of community needs; faculty members also gain an opportunity to "explore teaching and learning in ways that have implications for all pedagogies" (Clayton et al., 2013, p. 335).

Known as the "third mission" of higher education, service and outreach has gone through an evolution from a unidirectional expert model to a two-way model that unites colleges and universities and their communities. Especially for land-grant institutions, the service tradition initially took the form of providing practical knowledge via extension services, short courses, and faculty consultation, as explained in the preceding (Weerts & Sandmann, 2008). As service and outreach continued to evolve into the twenty-first century, it evolved into a more recipro-cal relationship "serving the community, to extending and reaching out to it, to engaging it in bidirectional relationships and interactions" (Weerts & Sandmann, 2008, p. 76). While service learning is intended to provide a "service" to the community from which the students learn, community engagement is a collaborative, cooperative effort to come alongside a community as an equal partner to decide what the needs and goals are and what each will do, bringing the students along in the effort, through which they learn. Stemming from the same epistemologies, community engagement is the next step of service learning.

International Service Learning

We have reviewed the development of service learning in the American context as a first step in understanding the development of community engagement as a philosophy and a pedagogy; in this section, we review the overseas context of this movement. The history of international service learning, as outlined by Hoffa (2007), details the precursor to formal service-learning education in an international context as an evangelical call to "help" people through missionary and volunteer service in the latter half of the nineteenth and early twentieth centuries, mostly through works projects like building roads, bridges, hospitals, schools, and so on. In areas other than Europe, this not only represented a religious impulse, but also "represented an overt dimension of some overseas activities sponsored by the US government and educational institutions" (p. 37). This evolved into what Hoffa labels "nonacademic overseas programs"—as students worked with vol-unteer and humanitarian programs after the end of World War I to provide relief services. Some of these agencies later became pioneers of international education. International work camps also came out of this period, in which American students worked with former allies and adversaries to rebuild the war-torn areas of Europe (a concept that continues to the present day). Similar ideas led to establishing the Peace Corp in the 1960s—as a way both to tap into the American youth's deep interest in volunteerism, and "to address international development issues but also as a means to internationalize the outlook of all Americans" (p. 125). Much of the international development that took place during the Cold War era was largely one-directional—the United States coming in to use its expertise to help others—even though it did broaden the country's international outlook.

Service learning as a pedagogy, including in international contexts, began to take root in the experiential learning movement of the 1960s and 1970s, and flourished in the 1980s with the founding of organizations like Campus Compact, Campus Outreach Opportunity League, and International Partnership for Service-Learning and Leadership. Participating in an international service-learning opportunity utilizes the pedagogical goals of a traditional, domestic service-learning course while providing outcomes derived from studying abroad—immersing oneself in another culture while experiencing both the practical and theoretical aspects of the course(s) in which students are enrolled (DeWinter & Rumbley, 2010). Internationalization as an organizing principle or concept emerged in the mid-1990s as "the process for integrating international/intercultural learning into the teaching, research and service functions of an institution" (Olson & Peacock, 2012, p. 305). This global view eventually bridged the education goals of shared values, shared nature of work, student learning outcomes, and an international outlook; international engagement in the form of service learning fulfills all of these goals of globalization of education as enumerated in the early twenty-first century (Edwards & Teekens, 2012). As institutions struggle with pedagogies that will introduce an international and intercultural view into traditional classes across the disciplines, service learning remains a pedagogical strategy that, by its nature, is uniquely positioned to address the goals of internationalization.

For MSU, the university's focus on engagement locally and internationally was reinforced through 2005 strategy statements and again in 2013 (see chapter 1) that posited strategic imperatives for increasing engagement and international reach (Fitzgerald & Simon, 2012; Simon, 2009). This was the impetus for the creation of a community of practice to celebrate the range of practices and to support program leaders interested in adding this dimension to an existing program, or developing a new program, to identify approaches that contribute to the university's strategy and vision of community engagement abroad.

Intersections of Service Learning and Education Abroad

Service learning in an international context brings with it extra challenges versus service learning completed within the community in which the institution lies. It requires significant preparation for faculty and risk-taking on the part of all constituents. Gòkè-Paríolá and Smith-Paríolá (quoted in DeWinter & Rumbley, 2010) caution that "Faculty must take special care to bring to light and confront both their own and their students' preconceived notions of the place where they are studying and the people they find there and to replace those notions with more respectful and accurate understandings" (p. 80). Global citizenship (which urges a vision of worldwide respect, responsibility, and common humanity) is at the intersection between service learning and study abroad and differentiates international service learning from domestic service learning, which often focuses on citizenship in a local community, state, or even learning opportunities to benefit another country without overtly connecting that citizenship to international contexts. Opportunities to reconsider citizenship roles, along with notable contributions to cross-cultural understanding, are unique contributions to student learning found in the intersection of service learning and study abroad (Bringle & Hatcher, 2011). Similarly, when viewed through the lens of international education, service learning provides a distinctive opportunity to evaluate the North American perspective with an international perspective on disciplinary and citizenship issues.

Community Engagement at MSU

As noted in chapter 1, MSU's long tradition of international development provides the backdrop for growing student interest in service learning overseas and bottom-up faculty-led programming initiatives, with more than four hundred faculty involved in delivering education-abroad programming, consequently favoring diversity of programming approaches over a top-down articulation of program models. The university uses the term "community engagement abroad" to encompass a range of programming types and orientations, from activities focusing on maximizing delivery of service (such as medical care) as the primary output, to programs that require competence in the community's language as a prerequisite, with home-stays for lodging and a philosophical focus of learning with the community. In chapter 1, Fear and Casey discuss how several core values have contributed to form an ecology of engagement, with a broad range of focus in working with communities, as illustrated in figure 1. Toward different learning goals, program leaders and their sponsoring academic unit make program design choices that can be situated on a continuum of engagement with a community overseas. Program leaders undertake such programming from various angles; for example, faculty members with a community engagement focus may initiate programming with a particular engagement vision or a long-standing program leader may elect to add a community engagement component to an existing education-abroad program. These can range from a weekend focused on community needs assessment or an intervention, such as building a small facility, on one end, all the way to a decade-long commitment to assist a rural network of communities to organize, design solutions to their needs, and bring students into multiyear projects in consecutive summers in Ireland (Doberneck, Lally, & Chalou, 2015), on the other end. While the learning potential in such programs is high, there are many pitfalls to reflect upon in order to avoid potentially reinforcing negative assumptions and the inequalities between the Global North and the Global South. Grusky challenges us to reframe such programs from "life-enriching" to "complacency shattering" or "soul-searching" and an opportunity to move the learning from the "(well-meaning but simplistic) desire to serve" to a "more solid foundation for global understanding and action." (Grusky, 2000, p. 866).

Ideally, as the program continues and the relationship with the community deepens, the reciprocity factor also increases and the programming moves further along a continuum toward deeper sustained engagement. At one end of the spectrum, similar to traditional study-abroad programs, the focus is on the learning benefit to the student/volunteer and the relationship with the community is "transactional." On the other end of the spectrum, the community works with the faculty leaders and student volunteers to analyze need, design sustainable solutions, and implement them together, and the relationship with the community can be "transformative" (Enos & Morton, 2003). Programs pursue a range of learning objectives and can focus primarily on student learning or, to some extent, also include community benefit. They are not mutually exclusive but the particular program's learning objectives, the disciplinary practice of the program leader's area of study, and their individual views on community work inform program design

FIGURE 1. Service-based experiential learning continuum of engagement.

choices within this ecology of engagement; "service learning" occurs when there is a balance between learning goals and service outcomes (Furco, 1996). In his 2016 book *Liberating Service Learning*, Stoecker proposes that the core concept of the sequence of service learning—(1) learning, (2) service, (3) community, and (4) change—should be reversed. Our continuum is an oversimplification of complex relationships and we do not suggest that each program and community relationship will always fall neatly into one category. There are a number of other illustrations in the literature that describe the potential evolution of these relationships over time. Our intent with this visualization is to illustrate the range of practices in order to facilitate overseas program design choices. The chapters that follow in this volume illustrate this range of practice. The relationship with each community is different, as is the background and perspective of the program leader designing the engagement.

Service-Based Experiential Learning Continuum of Engagement

The education-abroad literature offers several decades of examination of the value of overseas learning experiences during postsecondary education, but relatively little analysis of this particular type of learning abroad within a community project and how it compares to more traditional program types. Several decades of large-scale studies focus on the potential benefit of education abroad on these outcomes. (For an overview of the major studies in the literature see Potts and Berquist [2014] and Twombly, Salisbury, Tumanut, and Klute [2012] for a critical review of the literature on learning outcomes of study abroad.)

The field of international education has a solid foundation for the claim that education abroad may enhance participants' personal, social, intercultural, and academic skills. Most of the literature, however, examines traditional education-abroad program types, primarily enrolling in regular classes at a host university or studying with a professor from the home university where the learning environment is moved overseas. As the demand for more highly experiential programming rises, for example, internships, service learning, and so on, we need to know more about the learning outcomes of these programming types, and whether a short service and engagement experience is added to a traditional program or the majority of the experience focuses on service and engagement.

In 2003, Lilli and John Engle published a framework to analyze education-abroad program components and compare differences in gains in target language fluency as well as intercultural competence. Their work is a strong example of the practitioner research undertaken in education abroad (Streitweiser & Ogden, 2016). At the time, they were managing a study-abroad center in France for U.S. students and wanted to find out whether certain program components produced stronger learning outcomes, primarily in language fluency. Starting from an analysis of the range of practice in their study-abroad center, they identified seven "defining components" and mapped these across five study-abroad levels ranging from "study tour" to "cross-cultural immersion programs" (Engle & Engle, 2003). The framework has had a major impact on the discourse in the education-abroad field and continues to inform program design. This classification has helped many education-abroad faculty and administrators analyze different programming options and consider how certain components may impact the learning outcomes they seek.

As Fear and Casey have outlined in chapter 1, community engagement and education abroad have a long tradition at Michigan State and, not surprisingly, approximately 10 percent of MSU's three hundred programs demonstrated overlap between these fields. As the faculty learning community that became the vehicle for this book shared its program experience, Berquist often asked members to discuss their philosophical stance on development work and how they interact with their overseas communities. In other settings (e.g., the faculty learning community and workshops coordinated by the education abroad office), faculty leaders and program administrators were asked to reflect on not only program choices as they related to the learning goals of the course curriculum but also how the overseas setting would impact the learning experience. Berquist found it challenging to provide guidance for program leaders wanting to develop a new program focusing on community engagement or to incorporate a component of this to their longstanding program. With a central strategic focus on building global resilient communities, the need for tools to support faculty and administrators engaging with this type of programming was pressing.

In his early efforts to understand the range of practice in this area, Berquist encountered a dilemma in a sense similar to that which Steve Esquith refers to in chapter 9—the ethical challenges of this particular type of programming. He traveled to Huamachuco, Peru, high in the Andes in the north of the country, to observe firsthand two very different MSU programs working with the same community. In chapter 7, Rosenbaum describes a program that requires Spanish fluency, deep cultural and linguistic preparation, and an extended period of time living with families and working on projects that have been designed with the community and a commitment to continuity and sustainability. For example, an engineering student on the program had worked with one of the program's founding leaders to build solar water heater systems. During his site visit, Berquist saw that the maternity ward at the local hospital was still using the structure built by previous students but that the subsequent group was training local people in how to design and install the systems in order to reach more remote health care posts. The level of cultural integration was tangible in the respect with which the students spoke of their hosts. The programming had been designed with the community as an equal peer, and students felt they were learning more from their hosts than the students were offering them.

On the other program, one of MSU's medical colleges brought a team of advanced students as well as doctors from Michigan communities for a two-week intensive treatment clinic with the same community, as outlined in chapter 5 by Dokter and Willyerd. The participants' primary goal was to provide as much care as possible during their time in-country. They stayed in a guesthouse for travelers, took their meals together, spoke relatively little Spanish, and were not studying the culture, language, and history of their host region the way the students on the twelve-week program were. Their learning goals were very different from the longer program but equally legitimate.

As an administrator, Berquist had to reconcile these very different perspectives. As outlined in chapter 1, he believed that all MSU community engagement programming would seek to adhere to four core principles:

1. Reciprocal relationships with community-based partners will characterize MSU's work.
2. Community voice and expertise will be recognized and respected.
3. Students will be educated about the reasons that led to establishing the partnership and why the effort is important from a community point of view.
4. Benefits will be bidirectional and balanced—for the community and for the university.

As he interacted with participants and program leaders on these very different programs working with the same community high in the Andes, Berquist encountered a similar strength of vision and clarity regarding the objectives of their project. Later, he realized that there were significant differences of vision for such programming even between two of the medical schools at the same university. What was needed was a tool to help process different programs and identify how various components may contribute to the learning goals of the sponsoring unit. His role was to support the academic objectives of the seventeen academic colleges at Michigan State, with a wide range of priorities and learning objectives.

Taking inspiration from Engle and Engle's 2003 framework, we have identified twelve components of community engagement programming abroad and measure these across three levels of engagement, as illustrated in table 1. We have reviewed the programming behind the cases presented in chapters 3 through 9 and used them to illustrate the concepts, from our perspective, within MSU's ecology of engagement. Each program leader, administrator, department, and institution will make choices on designing programs that are optimal to the learning outcomes sought. However, the components listed in the following interact in specific ways to support desired outcomes. For example, service activity length, the language used in coursework and/or service work, the type of student housing, and the provision for guided/structured cultural interaction all impact depth of engagement.

Program

LENGTH OF PROGRAM AND SERVICE

The link between duration of study and learning value has been the subject of discussion for several decades, with recent findings focusing on the value of program design and learning support over duration (Twombly et al, 2012; Vande Berg, Paige & Hemming, 2012; Potts & Berquist, 2014). Service-learning activities can be as short as a weekend or the main focus of a program of several weeks.

Table 1. Framework for community engagement abroad program design

BERQUIST AND MILANO COMMUNITY ENGAGEMENT ABROAD FRAMEWORK	LEVEL 1	LEVEL 2	LEVEL 3
Program components	Low	Mid	High
PROGRAM			
Length of program and service	1–4 weeks	5–8 weeks	>8 weeks
	Chap. 3–5	Chap. 9	Chap. 6–8
Language used in coursework and/or service work	English	English and host language	Host language
	Chap. 3–5	Chap. 6, 8, 9	Chap. 7
Type of student housing	Hotel or guesthouse	With local students	Homestay
	Chap. 3, 5	Chap. 4	Chap. 6–9
Guided reflection	Student initiative	Weekly facilitated reflection	Min. 3×/week individual or group guided reflection
	Chap. 5	Chap. 3, 4, 6	Chap. 7–9
Provisions for guided/ structured cultural interaction	Only as part of service interaction	Combination	Cultural interaction organized in addition to service
	Chap. 6	Chap. 3, 5	Chap. 4, 7–9
SERVICE			
Level of self-determination by the community for service undertaken	Minimal	Negotiated	Initiated by community
		Chap. 3–6, 9	Chap. 7–9
Reciprocity with host community and academy	One direction	Some hosting and some connection with local academy	Reciprocal visits, joint publishing of reports or proceedings
	Chap. 3, 5–7	Chap. 8, 9	Chap. 4
Sustainability of community relationship/partnership	One-time projects	Multiyear commitment but only during project work	Sustained long-term commitment including communication with community outside service delivery
		Chap. 3, 5	Chap. 4, 6–9
ACADEMICS			
Connection to home curriculum	Service described in syllabus of the overseas section only	Community engagement is reflected in institutional strategy	Community engagement is a component of the core curriculum
			Chap. 3, 4, 6–9
Interdisciplinary focus and/or leadership	The program leader's discipline is the primary lens	Two different disciplines are combined in the pedagogical design	Three or more disciplines are included in the program with a minimum of two different leaders from different disciplines
		Chap. 5	Chap. 7–9
Faculty role	No leader or simple coordination	Facilitator with some expertise in development and/ or culture of region	Owner of community relationship, facilitator with expertise in development and culture of region
		Chap. 3, 5, 6	Chap. 4, 7–9

LANGUAGE USED IN COURSE WORK AND/OR SERVICE WORK

Foreign language acquisition was a primary driver behind study-abroad programming for many years (Hoffa, 2007), but the rise of short-term and faculty-led programming has seen even traditional destinations develop semester or short courses delivered in English, particularly for the study-abroad market. Programs here range from the Peru program in chapter 7, where students are required to have a minimum of four semesters of Spanish study, begin the program with an intensive Spanish course, and conduct their projects in Spanish, to the medical program with the same community described in chapter 5, where no language prerequisite is required and most activities are conducted in English with the assistance of translators for the duration of the short program.

TYPES OF STUDENT HOUSING

With the same community in Peru, chapter 7 describes a program where students are housed with community families, whereas participants in the medical program in chapter 5 stay in a guesthouse where social interaction is primarily with other participants. The landmark Engle and Engle study identified the impact of housing type on foreign language gains. In this context, it would be more directly related to the type of cultural interaction, including linguistic.

GUIDED REFLECTION ON CULTURAL EXPERIENCE

Study-abroad programming often includes guided reflection, journaling, and other techniques to ensure the students are actively processing their learning. The cultural intervention approach developed by Vande Berg et al. builds on the initial findings of the Engle and Engle study. There are multiple ways of approaching this, but the majority of the case studies in this volume reflect the general trend in faculty-led programming to include debriefing sessions and guided reflection with some frequency.

PROVISIONS FOR GUIDED/STRUCTURED CULTURAL INTERACTION

Some programs position this as a core component, while others focus on the delivery of service and may organize additional cultural interaction outside of the service project. Many programs include service project teamwork with the host community.

Service

LEVEL OF SELF-DETERMINATION BY THE COMMUNITY FOR SERVICE UNDERTAKEN

As discussed earlier in this chapter, there is a general expectation that the community should have some level of self-determination for the service. This includes identification of community needs, potential impact, and the available resources to support the projects. Chapter 8 describes relationships with communities in Costa Rica through a program focus on sustainable ecotourism led by a faculty member who feels the community should determine the service projects. Chapters 3, 4, 5, 6, and 9 illustrate a negotiated approach to determining service projects.

Because most U.S. programs of this nature work with communities in the developing world, re-ciprocal travel is often a challenge. One exception in our collection of case studies is the hosting that took place with the Mali community described in chapter 9. After several cycles of work with an expanding group of communities in Costa Rica, the authors of chapter 8 received institutional funding to stage a learning conference with several additional leaders from the home institution to gather with leaders from the communities in one location to review their work and agree on future goals. This rubric also includes the extent to which faculty connect with faculty at universi-ties in the host country. In some institutions with a long tradition of faculty-led programming, where the coursework is delivered by home institution faculty, it is challenging to establish robust linkages with local academics, as is the case for most of the program cases described in this volume. A particularly useful indicator of this collaboration is coauthorship of reports and academic papers reflecting on the programming efforts, such as illustrated in chapter 4, where the lead authors are from the partner institution overseas.

SUSTAINABILITY OF COMMUNITY RELATIONSHIP/PARTNERSHIP

Community assessment of the impact of projects undertaken through the program may differ from the program's assessment. A long-term commitment may help navigate these differences, particularly in the early iterations of the program. Program leaders in chapters 4, 6, 7, 8, and 9 have demonstrated a sustained long-term commitment to the community partnership, includ-ing communications and activities outside the period of student service delivery. For example, Esquith has continued his connections with the community in Mali, even during a period when civil war prevented the student service delivery component. Fear initiated a program in Ireland, not included in the case-study chapters, that secured a Kettering Foundation grant to bring sev-eral community administrators to MSU for a two-week training program focused on identifying community needs and developing their own sustainable agenda. Program leaders should also reflect on the level of significance of the impact the projects have on the community, although this can be challenging to measure. Also, engaging students in meaningful ways with the community before and after the program can enhance the learning outcomes of the program and increase the sustainability of the partnership. In addition, students could be guided toward community engagement at home to help them make global–local connections.

Academics

CONNECTION TO HOME CURRICULUM

Some service-learning programs, including overseas activities, are situated in the realm of stu-dent volunteering or other outreach efforts and may not necessarily include academic credit. Fifty-two percent of respondents on the 2015 Campus Compact membership survey indicated that their institution designates community-based learning courses. As an institution's strategic focus on community engagement increases, it is likely that the connection for learning-abroad community-engagement programs to the institution's home curriculum may also increase.

INTERDISCIPLINARY FOCUS

Multiyear commitments to community engagement that include bringing participants from different disciplinary backgrounds can enrich the students' understanding of the complex factors that inform the community's needs and the university's ability to engage. The Peru program described in chapter 7 began with leaders from agriculture and engineering before the author of the chapter, with a social sciences background, assumed leadership. This broad range of disciplines increased the ability to support different projects and enriched the learning opportunities for participants.

ROLE OF FACULTY LEADER

The program leader most often provides the impetus for the guided reflection on the cultural experience and often stages cultural interactions and plays the mentoring role in cultural intervention. In some instances, the faculty members' expertise is primarily on the subject matter or the pedagogical delivery (e.g. chapters 3, 5, and 6). In other cases, the faculty members have developed deep connections to the communities (e.g. chapters 4, 7, 8, and 9). Depending on the nature of the planned engagement, faculty may prepare students beyond their language skills, especially focusing on knowledge of the history, economics, politics, social stratification, ethnic relationships, and other key features for the location of their work.

Community engagement can be approached in many ways, as illustrated through the case studies that follow in this volume. The authors bring their dedication to the value of international learning and illustrate their orientation, their thinking on their work with communities, and the program they designed to serve their goals. The framework oversimplifies the complexity of interaction among the different elements, as it is intended to provide guidance to inform future program design choices as program leaders and administrators reflect on desired learning outcomes for the students and the desired level of engagement with the community overseas. There are no right answers or value judgements in choosing one approach over another.

The following chapters relate eight different program cases from the perspective of the MSU program leaders who designed them. Chapters 1 and 10 provide a general preview of each chapter and a concluding analysis. They are arranged in a relative sequence toward the deeper engagement side of the continuum. However, this analysis is solely from the perspective of the authors of the present chapter. All program leaders have made program design choices they believed would optimize the primary learning goals of their program. In a large public university with a storied history of education abroad and possibly the nation's largest group of faculty program leaders, this framework was not developed with a normative intent. Rather, it is intended to help faculty and administrators evaluate program options germane to the potential power of community engagement abroad programming. Further research is needed to compare learning outcomes of students/volunteers, as well as impact and benefit to the community, along this range of programming components.

REFERENCES

Bonar, L., Buchanan, R., Fisher, I., & Wechsler, A. (1996). *Service-learning in the curriculum: A faculty guide to course development*. Salt Lake City: University Press.

Boyer, E. L. (1996). The scholarship of engagement. *Bulletin of the American Academy of Arts and Sciences, 49*(7), 18–33.

Bringle, R. G., & Hatcher, J. A. (1996). Implementing service learning in higher education. *Journal of Higher Education, 67*(2), 220–239.

Bringle, R. G., & Hatcher, J. A. (2011). International service learning. In R. G. Bringle, J. A. Hatcher, & S. G. Jones (Eds.), *International service learning: Conceptual frameworks and research* (pp. 3–28). Sterling, VA: Stylus.

Brotherton, P. (2002, April 25). Connecting the classroom and the community. *Black Issues in Higher Education, 19*, 20–24.

Campus Compact (2016). *Revitalizing our democracy: Building on our assets. 2016 Annual member survey. Executive summary*. Retrieved from https://kdpol43vw6z2dlw631ififc5-wpengine.netdna-ssl.com/wp-content/uploads/large/2017/03/campus_compact_executive_summary_2016_final3-2-1-2-1.pdf.

Carnegie Foundation for the Advancement of Teaching. (2014). *Community engagement elective classification*. Retrieved from http://classifications.carnegiefoundation.org/descriptions/community_engagement.php.

Center for Service Learning and Civic Engagement. (2014). *Outline history of the Michigan State University Center for Service-Learning and Civic Engagement*. Michigan State University. Retrieved from http://www.servicelearning.msu.edu/about/history.

Clayton, P. H., Bringle, R. G., & Hatcher, J. A. (2013). *Research on service learning: Conceptual frameworks and assessment: students and faculty*. Sterling, VA: Stylus.

Cucchiara, M. (2010). New Goals, Familiar Challenges? A Brief History of University-Run Schools. *Perspectives on Urban Education*. Retrieved from https://files.eric.ed.gov/fulltext/EJ894472.pdf.

DeWinter, U. J., & Rumbley, L. E. (2010). The diversification of education abroad across the curriculum. In W. H. Hoffa & S. C. DePaul (Eds.), *The history of study abroad: 1965–Present*. Carlisle, PA: Forum on Education Abroad.

Doberneck, D. M., Lally, M., & Chalou, C. (2015, June). *From host site to co-teacher/co-learner: Redefining roles in international experiential learning*. Paper presented at the Global Internship Conference, Dublin, Ireland.

Edwards, J., & Teekens, H. (2012). Leveraging technology and the international classroom for cross-cultural learning. In D. K. Deardorff, H. de Wit, J. D. Heyl, & T. Adams (Eds.), *The SAGE handbook of international higher education* (pp. 267–282). Los Angeles: Sage.

Ehrlich, T. (1996). Forward. In B. Jacoby & Associates (Eds.), *Service learning in higher education* (pp. xi–xvi). San Francisco: Jossey-Bass.

Engle, L., & Engle, J. (2003). Study abroad levels: Towards a classification of program types. *Frontiers: The Interdisciplinary Journal of Study Abroad, 9*: 1–20.

Enos, S., & Morton, K. (2003). Developing a theory and practice of campus-community partnerships. In B. Jacoby & Associates (Eds.), *Building partnerships for service-learning* (pp. 20–41). San Francisco: John Wiley & Sons.

Fitzgerald, H. E., & Simon, L. A. K. (2012). The world grant ideal and engagement scholarship. *Journal of*

Higher Education Outreach and Engagement, 16(3), 33–55.

Furco, A. (1996). Service learning: A balanced approach to experiential education. *Expanding Boundaries: Serving and Learning, 1,* 1–6.

Gray, M. J., Elizabeth, H. O., Fricker, R. D. Jr., & Geschwind, S. A. (2000, Mar). Assessing service-learning: Results from a survey of "Learn and Serve America, higher education." *Change, 32,* 30–39.

Grusky, S. (2000). International service learning: A critical guide from an impassioned advocate. *The American Behavioral Scientist, 43*(5), 858–867.

Hoffa, W. H. (2007). *A history of U.S. study abroad: Beginnings to 1965.* Carlisle, PA: Forum on Education Abroad.

Jacoby, B. (1996). *Service learning in higher education.* San Francisco: Jossey-Bass.

Kellogg Commission on the Future of State, Land-Grant Universities, National Association of State Universities and Land-Grant Colleges. (1999). *Returning to our roots: The engaged institution* (Vol. 3). National Association of State Universities and Land-Grant Colleges, Office of Public Affairs. Retrieved from http://www.aplu.org/library/returning-to-our-roots-the-engaged-institution/file.

Markus, G. B., Howard, J. P., & King, D. C. (1993). Integrating community service and classroom instruction enhances learning: Results from an experiment. *Educational evaluation and policy analysis, 15*(4), 410–419.

Olson, C., & Peacock, J. (2012). Globalism and interculturalism: Where global and local meet. In D. K. Deardorff, H. de Wit, J. D. Heyl, & T. Adams (Eds.), *The SAGE handbook of international higher education* (pp. 305–322). Los Angeles: Sage.

Potts, D. (2014). *Graduate perceptions of the early career value of international learning mobility: An exploratory study* (Doctoral dissertation). Michigan State University, East Lansing.

Potts, D., & Berquist, B. (2014). *Researching outcomes of international learning mobility: Taking the next steps.* (Research Digest 1). Retrieved from http://www.ieaa.org.au/iern/research-digests#1.

Simon, L. A. K. (2009). *Embracing the world grant ideal: Affirming the Morrill Act for a twenty-first century global society.* East Lansing: Michigan State University.

Stanton, T. K., Giles, D. E., Jr., & Cruz, N. A. (1999). *Service-learning: A movement's pioneers reflect on its origins, practice, and future.* San Francisco: Jossey-Bass.

Stoecker, R. (2016). *Liberating service learning and the rest of higher education civic engagement.* Philadelphia: Temple University Press.

Streitwieser, B., & Ogden, A. C. (Eds.). (2016, March). *International higher education's scholar-practitioners: Bridging research and practice.* Oxford: Symposium Books Ltd.

Thelin, J. R. (2011). *A history of American higher education* (2nd ed.). Baltimore: Johns Hopkins University.

Twombly, S., Salisbury, M., Tumanut, S., & Klute, P. (2012). *Study abroad in a new global century: Renewing the promise, refining the purpose.* (ASHE Higher Education Report, Issue 38, Number 4). San Francisco: Jossey-Bass.

Vande Berg, M., R. Michael Paige. R.M. & Hemming Lou, K. (Eds.) (2012). *Student learning abroad: what our students are learning, what they're not, and what we can do about it.* Sterling, VA: Stylus.

Ward, K., & Wolf-Wendel, L. (2000). Community-centered service learning. *American Behavioral Scientist, 43,* 767–780.

Weerts, D. J., & Sandmann, L. R. (2008, Fall). Building a two-way street: Challenges and opportunities for community engagement at research universities. *The Review of Higher Education, 32*(1), 73–106.

CHAPTER 3

Transforming Conventional Short-Term, Faculty-Led Study-Abroad Programs into Broader Platforms for Increased Community Engagement and Internationalization

Keri Dutkiewicz and Daniel Dutkiewicz

As a husband–wife academic team, we have co-led a short-term study-abroad program in India (the subject of this chapter), while Keri separately has led a study-abroad program in China and Mongolia and Dan separately has led programs in China and Japan. During this time, we encountered many real and imagined challenges to this kind of short-term program: Some claim that a month abroad is simply not enough time for students to develop a working cultural fluency. Medina-Lopez-Portillo's (2004) research comparing students in short-term with longer term study-abroad programs found that "students in the shorter program became more nationalistic than the students in the longer program, who returned with a more negative attitude toward the United States" (p. 189). Dwyer's 2004 study finds that even though there are significant benefits to a shorter term study-abroad program, students participating in a year-long program were more successful in every measurement category. This is not to say that shorter term programs (such as the two-week program described in the previous chapter) are irrelevant or ineffective. The research challenges us to consider not only the length of our programs but also the way we frame the issues. This chapter explores one option for sustaining a shorter in-country experience while simultaneously extending the learning contact hours in order to balance needs of all students while ensuring that program learning objectives are met.

Short-term, faculty-led study-abroad programs have seen increases in popularity as universities create more opportunities for students to participate in programs of varying duration (Hulstrand, 2006). Short-term (two to four weeks) programs have been found to result in similarly positive student learning outcomes compared to semester or year-long programs (Black & Duhon, 2005; Lewis & Niesenbaum, 2005; Peppas, 2005). However, as faculty leaders of short-term (three to four weeks) study-abroad programs we are aware that our program(s) could reinforce rather than challenge stereotypes, especially when well-intentioned "service projects" promote an unequal power relationship of privileged students "helping" disadvantaged members of the host community. In addition, short-term programs have been criticized for providing personal reflection time but little in-depth cultural understanding or adequate linguistic development when the goal of the program is second-language acquisition (Davidson, 2010; Day, 1987; Lumkes, Hallet, & Vallade, 2012). Academic colleagues may also critique a perceived lack of academic rigor in the overseas coursework, attributing the problem to "vacationing" students and part-time or visiting faculty. For example, Kline (1998) criticizes the relative lack of time spent in a classroom on "appropriate" academic work and asserts that course work in study abroad accounted for only 10 percent of student's time, and the course work was inappropriate for the situation (pp. 144, 157). Medina-Lopez-Partillo (2004) reinforces perceptions that short-term study-abroad programs are experienced as vacations: "Their comments and descriptions convey the impression that for them, study abroad provided a pleasant vacation in beautiful and historic Taxco; they had relatively little time to examine and reflect upon cultural, socio-economic and political issues. The opportunities they had for significant intercultural development were cut short" (p. 190). As a result, others assert that many study-abroad students (particularly women) are unprepared for cultural misunderstandings in conventional programs and may develop a resentment toward the host culture and a barrier to community engagement (Twombly, 1995).

While we agree that these concerns deserve attention, we question whether short-term, faculty-led study-abroad programs are inherently flawed. Opportunities exist within short-term overseas experiences to provide multiple opportunities for intercultural skill development, reflection, and academic rigor, with perhaps the exception of second-language acquisition (which is not our disciplinary expertise or the focus of our study-abroad program). Furthermore, we believe short-term study-abroad programs offer an important option to students who may not otherwise be able to participate in longer semester- or year-long international education experiences. For example, these shorter programs typically scheduled in the summer offer international opportunities to students who are not financially or personally able to live and study overseas for a more extended time frame, such as working professionals returning to school, young parents working to balance school and home, and those who simply cannot afford a semester without income. Other students may be frightened by spending such a long time away from home; can you imagine living overseas for a year if you have never been out of your state or on an airplane? Curricular issues also have an impact—if the study-abroad program interrupts a required sequence of courses and delays progress toward a degree, students may choose not to participate even though they understand the immense personal and long-term professional advantages of overseas study.

At the same time, we resist the institutional temptation to offer short-term programs as a "second-class" option for those students who are not able to participate in programs of longer duration; short-term programs are not inherently "less than" semester- or year-long programs offering a longer time overseas. Just as length of student time spent studying or increased instructor time spent lecturing does not necessarily translate into increased success on an exam, a longer time spent overseas may not necessarily equate to a more robust learning experience. The differentiation may more appropriately be attributed to the design of the learning activities of the study-abroad program. Length of overseas stay may be less important than the ways in which students are engaged before, during, and after their overseas experience.

If faculty members leading short-term study-abroad programs can design programs that extend the time spent actively engaging in the process of deepening cultural fluency, connect these engagement activities directly to students' work in their disciplines, and broaden conceptualizations of what constitutes academic credit-generating "seat time," this more expansive definition of faculty-led study abroad ceases to be defined as "short-term" and instead becomes an ongoing cycle of conversations, projects, and reflection that develop a community of practice comprised of students, faculty, community members, international partner organizations, and domestic partner organizations. We utilize the term "engagement ecology" to describe programs that achieve these goals and utilize a multimodal structure to support engagement. A multimodal structure is a blended learning environment intentionally crafted to support deep dialogue and engagement between and within the multiple communities of a study-abroad learning experience. Traditional class time, student-led community action, dialogue, personal reflection, and in-country experiences combine to help students deepen their understanding of their own cultural viewpoints and the ways these views shape interactions with others both locally and abroad, and to expand abilities to enter into genuine engagement with others.

Our India study-abroad program, Applied International Development and Community Engagement, offered through Michigan State University's College of Agriculture and Natural Resources, has been an experiment in extending the learning horizon or time frame to create this continuous cycle of student engagement with overseas partners, mentoring, and affiliated learning experiences (internships, student organizations, etc.). This program invites students and international alliance professionals to mutually identify and undertake a small- to medium-scale project aimed at addressing a so-called global "wicked problem" (i.e., a system of interacting complex problems like food insecurity). A problem-based, solution-focused approach deepens levels of internationalization by strengthening the intercultural problem-solving and communication skills that students need to address the daunting global challenges of the twenty-first century. Furthermore, by working collaboratively with students from different areas and with professionals in different fields, students deepen knowledge in many different areas—professional communications, fundraising, accounting, event planning, nutrition, nursing/rural public health, education, and so on.

To offer a metaphor and model, we envision this expanded view of short-term, faculty-led study abroad programs as an ecological learning system after work done by Brown (1999, 2001) in defining organizational and digital learning ecologies and by Hiram E. Fitzgerald (Fitzgerald & Simon, 2012: Fitzgerald & Zientek, 2015; Fitzgerald, Bruns, Sonka, Furco & Swanson, 2012) and others in community engagement.

Engagement Ecology Model for Study-Abroad Programs

An ecological model is a metaphor used to describe a networked, interconnected system with complex interdependencies, inputs, impacts, and results. Brown considers a learning ecology as a Web-mediated space where disparate views and multiple voices can come together in new ways, shaping powerful collaborations and innovations. According to Brown (2001), an ecology is "an active place where the virtual and the physical seamlessly and synergistically coexist" (p. 80). Here, as we apply this concept to a study-abroad program, we are expanding notions of "virtual" to encompass the ways communities and learning experiences stretch geographically and chronologically beyond national borders, specific class times, and even beyond the students and faculty members enrolled in a course. In so doing, we utilize the terms "learning ecology" and "knowledge ecology" to describe the ways an ecological model can be applied to higher education and specifically study-abroad programs focused on community engagement.

Brown's (2001) own explanation of the ways a learning network can broaden into a knowledge ecology helps make our choice of metaphor clearer. He explains:

> Learning networks resemble a virtual town, an open community in which each learner uses the network's resources as needed according to his or her learning styles, interests, and background . . . Learning networks can help transform the university into a learning organization and extend its reach across space. And they can serve as a springboard to an even more encompassing form, a broad *knowledge ecology* that reaches beyond the university's resources to draw on the strengths of the cultural institutions surrounding it (for example, libraries and museums) as well as on the equally important contributions of the region's corporations and government. Effectively linked, these resources would form an ecology that stimulates increasingly rich intellectual and educational opportunities. (p. 84)

Similarly, Fitzgerald and Zientek (2015), as proponents of effective community engagement, emphasize the importance of tapping continuously evolving cycles of knowledge interdependencies between individuals, organizations, and networks (that include but extend well beyond the university) in the promotion of innovation and system transformation. They explain:

> The relationship networks individuals and organizations create are influenced by socio-cultural norms and practices which in turn produce interconnected networks and increasingly complex systems of information exchange. To understand and to attempt to effect transformational change, therefore, require change agents to understand systems as interdependent and non-linear entities. (p. 27)

For both Brown and Fitzgerald, learning is not an isolated act, but part of a complex system that is quite literally built by the participants. For example, Brown writes in *Leader to Leader* (1999) that leaders, including, we would argue, faculty leaders of short-term study-abroad programs, "must build systems that support the interplay of social and intellectual capital. It is impossible to do that without the help of the users of the systems" (p. 34). So, first and foremost, a learning ecology creates space for the myriad voices essential to the study-abroad experience—including but not limited to students, community partners (both domestic and international), and faculty. In the language of community engagement, Fitzgerald, Allen, and Roberts (2010) remind us to liberate conceptions of community from narrow "place-bound" notions (also essential to any reimagined expanded short-term, faculty-led study-abroad program) and to focus instead on the idea of community as a social construction, engineered by dynamic networks of members regularly engaging in knowledge sharing and other collaborative endeavors. Operating under this shared mindset of mutual exchange (whether consciously or not)—as cocreators of a new knowledge ecology or network—seemingly diverse actors (in our case students and faculty members from Michigan State University [MSU] and staff members from a nongovernmental organization [NGO] in South India) perceived few if any barriers to working together at the outset and over the course of our study-abroad program.

Second, this engagement ecology is fundamentally a learning community—by highlighting the interdependent nature of the study-abroad experience, we place students within the community, not as external observers or tourists consuming an international experience. One goal of the study-abroad program is to shift students out of the more traditional observer/researcher mode and into the active participant and community member perspective. Fitzgerald, Allen, and Roberts (2010) assert that universities can most appropriately and effectively contribute to positive and sustainable community transformation by encouraging their students, staff, and faculty members to view themselves as full members of the communities in which they work and that only in this manner can universities position themselves as understanding and responsive partners to other members of the community. Students participating in community-engagement-focused study-abroad programs may also avoid the ill-fated trap of attempting to impose solutions from the outside (a process that typically reinforces rescuer/victim stereotypes and unequal power relations) by investing the time and effort necessary to create a newly imagined/formulated community in which areas of mutual concern emerge organically through intensive dialogue. Dialogue between participants, among and across communities, leverages the unique strengths of all members to support movement toward mutually derived solutions. We also want our students to gain both the explicit and tacit knowledge so important to successful navigation of the many communities in which they inhabit/operate. Tacit knowledge, the "mental models that all decision makers possess of 'how the world works'" (p. 20), needs to be sought out and brought to the surface to maximize impact and minimize unconscious bias and sustain meaningful, decision-focused dialogue.

We argue that study-abroad programs share Brown's (2001) commitment to becoming an "insider" rather than an outsider/observer. We are not teaching them solely how to function as part of an academic discipline or member of a professional community; instead, our program is dedicated to teaching them that they can learn to understand and function as part of a larger, more diverse international community than they perhaps ever imagined possible.

> People don't learn to become physicists by memorizing formulas; rather it's the implicit practices that matter most. Indeed, knowing only the explicit, mouthing the formulas, is exactly what gives an outsider away. Insiders know more. By coming to inhabit the relevant community, they get to know not just the "standard" answers, but the real questions, sensibilities, and aesthetics, and why they matter. (p. 82)

Brown refers to "naturally occurring knowledge assets" as those aspects of a community or organization that facilitate learning—they can be individuals, processes, cultural habits, technologies, and so on. Likewise, Fitzgerald et al. (2012) contend that effective approaches to community engagement must draw upon knowledge embedded within the community itself: "Undergirding this renewed approach to engagement is the understanding that not all new knowledge and expertise reside in the academy, and that both expertise and great learning opportunities in teaching and scholarship also reside in non-academic settings." (p. 10). As a tangible example in our study-abroad program, MSU students experience approaches to youth leadership development that foster and support opportunities for young people to assume greater levels of responsibility for action in families and communities that may not be available in the United States; as a result, our students are challenged to reconsider preconceived notions of the boundaries encompassing youth leadership.

The engagement ecology model we utilize consists of several key nodes connected by student and faculty professional/social networks. Thus, different components of our "program" engage like nodes or modules in a digital environment. Students come in and out of these varied activities, communities, and groups; not all students fully engage with all aspects of the study-abroad program, predeparture sessions, affiliated student organization, and ongoing work in related fields. Just like the Web uses a distributed intelligence model to leverage the small efforts or knowledge of the many, our program uses distributed intelligence to engage students in wiki-like activities where individual passions, strengths, and talents come together to form a well-rounded whole.

One example of the dynamic nature of the engagement ecology model is when students create new nodes. Students in our program desired to form a student organization dedicated to international development. This desire grew out of their experiences in the study-abroad program and their desire to offer greater financial support to one of the community organizations we partnered with in India. This student organization (SAID: Students Advancing International Development) helped expand the engagement ecology of the study-abroad program to include additional voices (students who were passionate about international development but who did not participate in the study-abroad program) and new learning opportunities (fundraising, event planning, etc.). These varied nodes come together to create a robust, longer term learning ecology with multiple types of engagement.

For example, during one phase of our on-site program in Coimbatore, India, students engage with a long-established community-based NGO based on Gandhian principles for a multiday practicum. This practicum cycles students through all of the partner organization's major project areas so they are aware of the projects and can begin to understand the complex interrelationships between these myriad elements of integrated development. Then students take responsibility for choosing the project to financially support. The ensuing debates and written work further increase awareness of project details, cost realities, and necessary trade-offs. When a project is selected, students have already participated in the hard, collaborative work of prioritizing and understanding needs, resources, and perspectives not only of their fellow students but also of community partners. In our experiences, through this collaborative dialogue process students may have shifted their understandings of international development work and their appreciation of the impact fundraising and community support have on project implementation. Their participation levels increase even more as they begin to develop communications and funding plans. When they return to campus in the United States and must educate others about the projects in order to gain individual, institutional, and financial support (i.e., increase awareness of the problem and solution inherent in their selected project), they again cycle through another level of responsibility.

No longer are they students "just" writing a paper—they are advocates, event planners, leaders of a student organization, mentors, and fundraisers. They participate in all aspects of the sociocultural–ethical ecology within which this type of international work and learning takes place. Just as natural ecologies and sustainable approaches to community engagement are not limited in time, this cycle of situated learning continues year after year, with students continuing to participate in the student organization several years after they actually enrolled and traveled as part of the formal study-abroad program. As these students continue their work with us, with each other, and with U.S. and international institutional partners, myths about self-capabilities and the range of opportunities available are debunked, overshadowed by the realities of their own impacts, struggles, successes, and failures.

Community partners in India benefited as well. In addition to students raising money for the programs, at a leadership level, our Indian partner NGO was able to leverage its experiences with the MSU program to refine marketing and fundraising communications targeting potential U.S. donors. It was able to clarify the "ask" and focus in on key pieces of information that would be perceived to be most relevant by U.S. donors. Deepening relationships, building trust, and understanding different culturally mediated communications expectations supported made these conversations about effective fundraising in the United States possible.

Awareness, responsibility, and participation are not independent—they are interwoven aspects of engaged learning. Much like the writing process is now understood not as a linear, simple process, we argue that successful development and implementation of a study-abroad engagement ecology is not a simple matter of linear "steps" that lead ever upward to perfectly polished, globally competent graduates.

To benefit from this ecological approach, student participants must be willing to reframe their understandings of their student role. Student responsibilities in the proposed reconceptualization of faculty-led short-term study-abroad programs revolve around Schattle's (2009) three essential characteristics of global citizenship:

1. Awareness—Clearly understand the program framework, including the responsibilities and opportunities offered by the extended learning horizon.
2. Responsibility—See themselves as the "owners" of the student organization, willing to negotiate differences, explore leadership structures, and identify/solve group dynamics issues as part of a dedicated team.
3. Participation—Have the schedule flexibility to participate in predeparture and postreturn meetings/sessions in addition to traditionally scheduled courses.

We build off Schattle's conceptualization to examine the relationship between cycles of awareness, responsibility, and participation (or action) as the process of transformative learning. O'Sullivan's (2003) description of transformative learning as a possible counter to market-driven consumer ethic directly echoes many of the goals we as faculty leaders have for our program. For example, he defines transformative learning as a deep shift that irrevocably alters "our understanding of ourselves and our self-locations; our relationships with other humans and with the natural world; our understanding of relations of power in interlocking structures of class, race and gender; our body awarenesses, our visions of alternative approaches to living; and our sense of possibilities for social justice and peace and personal joy" (O'Sullivan, 2003, p. 326). As faculty study-abroad leaders, we invest the significant time, energy, and personal funding required by our approach precisely because we have directly experienced the kinds of shifts O'Sullivan and Schattle describe. Many of us hope to offer our students the same opportunity to reconsider themselves, their communities, and their conceptualizations of possibility for both.

To start, increased awareness of self and others leads to faculty and student identification of opportunities for greater engagement with disciplinary content, local communities (both at home institution and abroad), and persistent, difficult questions of ethics and citizenship. Then, program-based initiatives that require faculty and students to take responsibility and directly experience the internal and external impact of responsible action build the right blend of humility, confidence, and skill needed to compete for and obtain access to increasingly more challenging opportunities. As a result of this process, both students and faculty members experience the personal and public transformations Freire (1970) calls consciousness raising (conscientization) and Mezirow (1991) refers to as perspective transformation.

By layering these concepts with Brown's understanding of the networked, systemic nature of learning and his concept of distributed intelligence, we were able to learn from early failures trying to integrate online instructional components. While our initial efforts to actually leverage Web-based technologies in support of course outcomes did not work well, due mainly to access challenges early on in India, this experience triggered our thinking about alternate methods for building an interconnected set of learning events that could interact much the same way that components of a robust online learning program come together to shape a whole greater than the sum of individual parts. If we were to run the program again today, these technology challenges would most likely not interfere.

To summarize, the engagement ecology model of short-term, faculty-led study-abroad programs outlined herein combines the networked structure defined by Brown's concept of the knowledge ecology and the approaches of community engagement proponents with the outcomes espoused by transformative educational theorists. The engagement ecology model we coevolved with students and community members in the United States and India is defined by three key features:

1. an extended learning horizon or time frame built on continuous and interrelated engagement with complex problems;
2. a network of relational and transactional-based institutional partnerships that persist beyond the faculty-led program;
3. long-term cycles of mentoring and collaborative activities intentionally shaped from the learning communities comprised of students, faculty, and other institutional/ professional partners.

While our program used a student organization in addition to a traditional faculty-led study-abroad program to facilitate these kinds of interactions, other methods may be equally if not more effective. Each of these three key attributes is further defined in the sections that follow.

Extending the Learning Horizon

The ecological model provides students and community members (both domestic and international)—irrespective of limited financial resources, curricular limitations, language challenges, or predilection to study abroad for shorter periods—continuous opportunities (predeparture, in-country, and postreturn) to engage in meaningful and personally transformative projects with local and international partners, where the risk of project failure is genuine and success in developing key intercultural problem-solving and communication skills is measured by meeting explicit project objectives and achieving tangible impacts. One of the most obvious differences between this approach and conventional short-term faculty-led programs is that our program extends the learning horizon to ten to eighteen months or longer. Within this model, the faculty-led study-abroad program shifts from a self-contained event to one component of a larger ecology of learning (Longo, 2007; Brown, 2001) that includes an international component.

This engagement ecology contains the following nodes:

- program orientation sessions
- predeparture coursework
- in-country learning events and coursework (approximately three to four weeks in India)
- student organization meetings and events
- professional internships and directed research opportunities
- continued ongoing relationships and collaborations with community partners in India

These nodes are not necessarily sequential; some students participated in the student organization for a significant amount of time prior to traveling to India. Furthermore, students participated in these different learning experiences in different ways and patterns, and for varying lengths of time. As they worked within these different learning opportunities or nodes, students practiced collaboration (imagine a group project that extends for three years) and continually resolved communications/group dynamics challenges, just as they will need to do in the professional world and as active community members and responsible, engaged citizens.

One of the unique aspects of this approach was the development of a student organization. As faculty leaders, we worked with students passionate about having a continued positive impact in India to help them found a student organization, Students Advancing International Development, or SAID. As described earlier, this organization is dedicated to building on the work begun in-country during the three- to four-week study-abroad program through fund-raising, identification of potential new solutions, recruiting new partners, engaging additional students, and so on. Dan acted as the group's faculty advisor. The community and framework of this organization supported both student orientation prior to their overseas experience and student reentry after time abroad. It also offered the opportunity for the types of continued engagement Hovey and Weinberg (2009) believe is essential to the long-term "learning, growth, and engagement" (p. 38).

In addition to supporting the foundation and continuance of this student organization at the request of the students themselves, we worked to extend the learning horizon by actively seeking opportunities for students (again at their bequest) to participate in more advanced internships and research projects that build on work begun with the study-abroad program. Examples include a research project on children's micronutrient deficiencies in Southern India and internship on early childhood educational interventions for vulnerable children in southern India.

Building and Nourishing Strong, Equitable Partnerships

Partners and the resources, challenges, and opportunities they provide, themselves comprise nodes in the knowledge ecology. The ecological model of combining multiple "nodes" of dialogue in a blended learning approach utilizes the short-term, summer study-abroad program to build and cement ongoing, sustainable alliances with professional international partners (e.g., local NGOs) by involving students directly in the advancement partners' work/mission. Strong partnerships are required in order to provide continued opportunities for student engagement beyond the study-abroad component (internships and research projects), per the preceding section. These partners also provide genuine opportunities for meaningful development work carried out through the student organization, SAID. In addition, these partners provide opportunities for academic service-learning projects that are not imposed on a host but codesigned with overseas partners.

There are numerous benefits to establishing the kind of trusting, collaborative partnerships we have been privileged to enjoy with our colleagues in India. Rather than a one-time donation, resources accumulate over time through monetary donations made over multiple years. Development of tacit and explicit knowledge about partners and programs reduces on-boarding time for new students and minimizes partner resources required (i.e., when you work together for longer periods of time, you can work more efficiently and not require as many resources in order to learn enough to help and thereby make a more immediate impact).

As with most faculty-led programs, these partnerships are closely tied to faculty leaders for the program. It is our goal to shift these partnerships to institutional partnerships that persist beyond an individual faculty-led program. This type of institutional partnership can compensate for sudden shifts in faculty leadership and can help ensure that the collaboration continues even as jobs and professional priorities shift over time.

As many of our colleagues in this collection have expressed, these partnerships must be equitable. As faculty leaders, we have the responsibility to establish mutual respect, professionalism, and collaboration between students, our institution, and our international partner(s). At a practical level, a durable partnership must be one in which both sides benefit. Brustein (2009) explains that "viable and sustainable partnerships typically evolve from collaborations where both partners believe that they are benefitting from the relationship." To support this type of empowered partnership, we work closely with new students and partners to facilitate the development of "Terms of Reference" between student group and international partners. This common language is crucial to maintaining an effective long-term professional relationship. It takes time and conscious attention to build shared vocabulary and understanding. By enabling student participation in these early conversations as much as possible, students, partners, and faculty leaders deepen understandings that partnerships are consciously created; they don't just happen.

As part of these conversations, we also actively talk through ways to leverage unique strengths of each partner, including faculty leaders, students, and our U.S. institution. Dividing project and program responsibilities based on strengths collectively enables the alliance to accomplish an important goal that each partner could not accomplish separately (e.g., the student group raises money for the project within the United States, and the international partner implements the project at home). It also facilitates skills in realistic self-assessment in students and helps build a sense of community where everyone (students, faculty, and partners) is seen as a complex blend of strengths, talents, and areas that need continued development. Some of these strengths may be functions of the larger community, such as relative economic privilege, and others may be unique to the individual (written communication, salesmanship, or accounting skills). The ongoing nature of these partnerships gives ample opportunity to develop mutual trust and respect when the faculty leader actively works toward what Hovey and Weinberg (2009) refer to as a "commitment to reciprocity" (p. 38). We worked with students to view their relative economic privilege as opportunity for other kinds of growth, as opposed to pity-based rationale for "helping" those with fewer resources.

Recently, we have begun expanding our knowledge ecology across additional U.S. partners, traveling with a group of mid-level managers and professionals from state government, agriculture, and education to study leadership in India. By collaborating with the Great Lakes Leadership Academy, we expanded community engagement opportunities in order to connect community members in our local area with other communities overseas.

The Engagement Ecology Model Requires Continuous Communication, Mentoring, and Collaboration

A network does not exist without communication. Brown's concept of a knowledge ecology and effective community engagement according to Fitzgerald and others depends upon communications between and across multiple nodes of a system. So, too, does our engagement ecology for study abroad depend upon the communication between local and international stakeholders, partners, students, and faculty. These layers of collaboration and the extended learning horizon work together to create and nourish ongoing mentoring opportunities within the community of students and between students and international partners/faculty. For example, experienced students mentor students new to SAID and to learning about India or international development; by teaching they reinforce their own learning. Additional types of mentoring that occur include:

- New students bring new ideas that may challenge status quo of the group—force realistic consideration of alternatives (SWOT analysis exercise).
- Students engage in postprogram internships with partner institutions.
- Program alumni continue to participate in fundraising events even after graduation.
- Students experience phases of collaboration (group and individual development over time) and must resolve communications/group dynamics challenges.

One especially impactful aspect of this collaboration and mentoring is around intercultural communication. Our program and affiliated student organization are designed to intentionally allow students to directly experience success by meeting objectives and achieving impacts and failure by not meeting objectives and failing to deliver desired impacts. As such, when students experience tangible success, they are able to share this victory with others. In talking it through, they mutually reinforce their confidence in the validity of their emerging intercultural competencies.

Failure, on the other hand, provides an opportunity to reflect and make the adjustments necessary to achieve desired results at a later time. Specifically, students engage in the following types of communications:

- conducting background research to better understand the nature of the problem the alliance is seeking to address and communicating the details accurately to a variety of domestic constituents (including potential donors)
- identifying key incentives motivating the student group and international partner to put forth their best possible good faith efforts
- working to accurately understand and communicate the international partner's capacity and limitations when making public claims about project objectives and impacts
- building cooperative alliances with domestic stakeholders and other parties interested in advancing the project by identifying and aligning key incentives
- conducting/managing awareness-raising events and fundraising campaigns to meet the objectives and achieve the desired impacts of the project
- coordinating with international partner to implement details of the project

Students, like all of us, struggle during stressful times to take responsibility and not blame others for shortcomings. One unintended outcome of the engagement ecology model is that the long-term friendships that evolve support increased directness in communication; students argue, debate, possibly withdraw (then ideally decide to reengage), and then come to a decision. Emotions do tend to run high, but then we can talk about the experience and collectively reflect on effective strategies for managing conflict. Furthermore, students are given the opportunity and responsibility to communicate directly with individual and institutional donors/supporters to share good and bad news. With coaching and practice, they learn to formulate effective, professional messages even around difficult topics.

Benefits of the Engagement Ecology Model

In summary, the engagement ecology model provides students and community members—irrespective of limited financial resources, curricular limitations, language challenges, or predilection to study abroad for shorter periods—continuous opportunities to engage in meaningful and personally transformative international projects with local partners, where the risk of project failure is genuine and where success in developing key intercultural problem-solving and communication skills is measured by meeting explicit project objectives and achieving tangible impacts. Students/faculty members/international partners become an integrated, international learning community or ecology of learning (Longo, 2007) in order to enter into effective community engagement practices. In so doing, this enables the formation of an interdependent team of students from different academic areas and professionals working in varied fields. For this team to succeed, a diversity of skills sets and knowledge is needed; community participants learn from each other's strengths and academic expertise. They also confront inevitable conflict and practice effective strategies for communicating through conflict that will serve them well in the workplace.

The brief case study that follows gives specific examples to clarify the ecological approach and validate these claims.

Embracing Engagement Ecology

Applied International Development and Community Engagement started unremarkably enough in 2008 with the twin objective of introducing students to (1) a set of best practices in sustainable, capacity-building international development work in India and (2) the complex interplay between the social and cultural forces in India—including India's linguistic, ethnic, religious, caste, class, and geographical diversity—shaping/informing these best practices. Participants traveled throughout northern and southern India for approximately three weeks to experience firsthand the country's stunning diversity and to spend meaningful time at local NGOs dedicated to strengthening current (or building new) capacity for the benefit of vulnerable children, their families, and communities. Despite a few logistical hiccups, the first-year program unfolded, more or less, as originally envisioned, but something unexpected happened along the way that would launch the program on an entirely new trajectory during a half-day familiarization visit to a local NGO based in Coimbatore, Tamil Nadu, India, dedicated to realizing the Gandhian ideal of improving conditions for the most disadvantaged segments of Indian society. The students, without exception, remarked on the exceptional nature of our partner NGO and strongly recommended that the program spend more time at their main campus the next summer (in 2009). The students expressed a sense of awe when witnessing the impressive rapport and high levels of trust that our Indian partner NGO had clearly established with diverse members in the local community during its first twenty years of operation, and the high degree of receptivity that the organization demonstrated to working with the students from the outset (i.e., the leadership and staff validated the students' aspirations in international development and embraced them as professional equals). Although we did not know it at the time, the students and staff at the NGO had already coselected each other as long-term collaborators, and the formation of a new learning ecology thereby had entered its embryonic stage.

In 2009 we wisely followed the advice of our students and devoted three full days of the program to on-site collaborations with this same NGO, with the aim of deepening levels of community engagement and internationalization. Such an opportunity presented itself when the leadership of the organization offered to convene a three-day practicum on integrated development for the students. The NGO leadership team proposed beginning each morning session of the practicum with a seminar to establish the basic contexts necessary for the students to participate in highly interactive, community-based field visits that comprised each afternoon session. For example, students in one of the morning sessions received a briefing on the challenges that children aged three to five living below the poverty line in southern India typically experience, including nutritional deficiencies and uneven access to early childhood education services. This session prepared them for the afternoon field visit to a special school founded by the same NGO to bridge these gaps in nutrition and education. In this afternoon session, students directly interacted with the children, parents, and teachers to evaluate for themselves the effectiveness of this type of intervention. Needless to say, this was a powerful experience for the students due to the high stakes involved: If not for the careful health monitoring and nutritional supplementation pro-vided at these schools, the young students there likely would suffer from nutritional deficiencies and related cognitive impairments that would permanently limit their academic achievement. Although the high stakes involved, no doubt, captured the attention of our students, they still remained virtual outsiders to the process—no matter the level of their intellectual understand-ing of the development-related issues and interventions at hand, and no matter the degree of empathy or affection they developed for the students, teachers, parents, and members of the wider local community.

Our challenge as the faculty leaders of the program was to transcend this insider–outsider divide by providing our students a stake in our Indian partner's work and by extension in the local communities' well-being. We attempted to do so by requiring the students to (1) rotate through our partner's major programs, (2) develop a rubric based on the principles of sustainable, capacity-building development for assessing the impacts of each program, and (3) recommend and actually make a targeted donation to one of our Indian NGO partner's programs based on the empirical findings of this assessment at the conclusion of the three-day practicum. We intention-ally established the level of the small donation to meet the following two key conditions: It had to be sufficient to make a significant difference in the lives of a small group of vulnerable children served by the NGO, but, mirroring everyday budget realties in international development work, it had to require the students to make hard choices. In other words, the students could fund a small handful of educational scholarships for children, a few hundred childhood vaccinations against potentially fatal diseases, or nutritional supplementation to dozens of vulnerable children, but the students could not do it all (and thereby assume the role of privileged saviors swooping in from the outside with all the answers).

This exercise changed the terms of engagement between the students and all actors in India. The students became more purposeful, intentional, probative, consultative, and humble in their approach to learning about international development and its India-specific societal and cultural contexts. Now that they were part of the larger system, now that their decisions and actions would yield tangible and significant consequences, the students wanted to collect and examine every available data point for their analysis (e.g., what is a better investment in a child's future—a vac-cination or a scholarship?). They asked more relevant questions (sometimes profoundly simple questions; other times, appropriately complex, multifaceted questions), checked their assumptions with greater rigor, and attempted to understand the development issues from a greater diversity of perspectives, including those from the leadership and staff at the NGO, Indian government officials, business leaders, health professionals, and educators allied with the NGO, as well as a wide array of other community collaborators who shape, inform, and benefit from the NGO's programs. Our students raised interesting questions and made thoughtful observations, while our colleagues and friends in India did the same. As a result, our mutual respect and understandings of each other and the development contexts of India grew as we collectively moved in the direc-tion of shared responsibility and action. In short, we were evolving into a community of practice.

In fact, the students strongly expressed their desire at the end of the visit in 2009 to "stay connected" to the work of our partner NGO, particularly the projects aimed at improving condi-tions for vulnerable children and their families subsisting below the poverty line. The notion of partnering on a vaccination project to protect eight thousand vulnerable children against measles, mumps, and rubella (MMR) was first raised, and the students exhibited a remarkable enthusiasm for the effort. This discussion in India—with the students present as full partners determining the nature and direction of the project in collaboration with the staff at our partner NGO—in hindsight probably was the most critical factor in the eventual success of the project because the students owned the project from its inception. Motivation was not an issue after this point because the project was not foisted upon them; they helped to invent it. This early and full participation explains, we believe, the willingness of the group to devote countless of hours of volunteer time over the next year (2010) to make the project happen.

Upon their return to campus, the students formed SAID. SAID members researched the high prevalence of measles and measles-related deaths among children in India (an emotionally charged subject among SAID members and supporters since this potentially fatal disease is easily and inexpensively prevented). SAID and our Indian NGO partner rationally divided the work according to the competencies and capacities of each organization: The NGO oversaw administration of the vaccination program, while SAID raised approximately $20,000 to vaccinate thousands of children (providing community immunity to a much greater number). In addition, the NGO worked to extend the alliance in India to include a local hospital and government-sponsored Child Development Centers (to better conduct the vaccination clinics and to make certain that the most vulnerable children could be reached). For its part, SAID developed complex awareness and fundraising campaigns executed over the entire 2009–2010 academic year, including the following components:

- creating project brochures, handbills, and flyers
- creating and delivering project presentations to potential donors
- organizing pledge-based fundraisers for marathon runners
- building public–private partnership between SAID/MSU and Lansing, Michigan-based corporate sponsors
- soliciting donations from the Model United Nations
- soliciting private foundations and corporate donations
- tapping family and personal networks for donations
- holding a Grand Gala with silent auction at the end of the academic year

Interestingly, the formation of SAID as an extension of key learning activities initiated during the study-abroad program actually resulted in an expansion of the learning horizon for the study-abroad program. In other words, the study-abroad program, rather than being defined as an educational end in itself, became reimagined as one node on a long continuum of mutually reinforcing activities that support the development of vital intercultural communication and problem-solving competencies in students. In addition, the productive interplay between SAID and the Indian NGO on the macro level nourishes and sustains a multifaceted collaboration that draws on the unique strengths of both organizations in order to achieve tangible results in the context of international development; the interplay among and between individuals with SAID and our partner NGO allows each organization to create multiple opportunities in the respective organization for individuals to move in and out of this evolving learning ecology according to availability, interest, and competency. In this manner, students can build international competencies whether they actually participate in the study-abroad program or not. As long as members of each organization proceed in accordance with the principles of shared responsibility and action in executing the objectives of the MMR program, the learning ecology remains strong. For example, SAID functioned in 2009 as a springboard for recruiting to the 2010 program because students who invested in the MMR project wished to visit the Indian NGO coordinating the project the following summer to witness firsthand the impacts of the project on public health. In addition, students who participated in the 2010 program reenergized SAID because it was their turn in the queue to propose a new project in consultation/collaboration with the Indian NGO.

Specifically, the 2010 program offered students an opportunity to complete a five-day practicum on integrated rural development. This practicum included rotations through our partner NGO's major programs with a dual mandate: develop an assessment rubric to make small targeted donations, while searching for a major project that could be jointly developed between SAID and the NGO. Through dialogue, SAID members in India and our partner NGO decided to focus on a joint project to increase food security for thousands of families living below the poverty line in Coimbatore, India. This food security project is a true capacity-building enterprise: It employs women to meet the food security needs of their communities. After the decision was made to focus on this project, SAID conducted awareness-raising and fundraising campaigns for the food security project on campus and beyond throughout the academic year.

To raise funds, students created project flyers, handbill, and a website—meeting the tough challenge of succinctly and persuasively explaining the merits of their collaborative project. SAID continued the public–private fundraiser with a local corporation and even formed a team of runners who participated in a half or full marathon for pledges. They also envisioned and coordinated all aspects of a major fundraiser event held at the conclusion of the academic year.

In 2011 the program was canceled due to underenrollment, but after learning about the close ties forged between SAID and our Indian NGO partner, the Great Lakes Leadership Academy selected southern India as the destination for its international leadership experience in February 2012. By bringing this group of approximately twenty-five midcareer, emerging leaders from Michigan to visit our Indian NGO partner for five days of leadership study (i.e., investigating the role of servant leadership), this study abroad expands and deepens levels of community engagement by directly involving community members from Michigan in issues/challenges commonly experienced by leaders in both southern India and Michigan.

As of the publication of this volume, the program at Michigan State has formally ended (after the 2013 program) but the relationships continue. Student participants have continued relationships with each other and with faculty leaders.

Conclusion

The proposed revisioning of short-term, faculty-led study-abroad programs into engagement ecologies that persist across time and space challenges us to conceive of new roles for faculty leaders, students, and educational institutions. Brustein (2009) describes the systemic approach institutions must embrace to build global competency in students; one key "pillar" in his model is support and incentives for faculty participation in designing and leading short-term study-abroad programs (p. 255). According to Brustein, faculty reward and tenure should include teaching abroad (p. 258). The engagement ecology model does not happen all at once—it grows over time. Faculty members require institutional support to build and maintain these generative, innovative, but extremely time-consuming programs. However, at many institutions, the system rewards are not in place to enable this type of work.

In our own experiences, our efforts to expand the learning horizon were not met with reward. As a visiting adjunct instructor and academic specialist, we did not have the benefits of tenure or a department chair to offer institutional support. Instead, we were largely on our own, facing administrative challenges when our new approach did not align with the standard model of short-term, faculty-led study abroad at our institution. We also faced significant challenges when our program was evaluated by individuals who had never personally traveled to India and who may have based their perceptions of program safety on limited sources of information. Even scheduling predeparture classroom sessions was initially challenging. We had embraced a new model and perspective, but struggled to effectively share and gain support for this new model.

To effectively implement this vision, three key shifts are required.

- Reframe faculty role to one of colearner.
- Develop institutional flexibility to embrace alternative learning delivery methods and structures.
- Encourage student reconceptualization of what it means to participate in study abroad.

First, the faculty leader must reframe his or her role definition to enable increased participation in a longer horizon of learning events and must embrace his or her own opportunities for learning and personal growth. The faculty member must be willing to position self as a colearner with partners and students. To effectively work within an engagement ecology, faculty members must reconstruct their role away from "manager" of the experience to facilitator of community-based conversations. Brown (1999) explains, "Just as no one manages the Internet, no one can manage a knowledge ecology. But we can understand the working principles of our communities, adapt our roles to be more effective, and improve the tools that support creativity" (p. 36). Faculty members must also develop a communications strategy to build institutional support for their new model. This support may not come easily if your faculty-led programs are "owned" by university units outside your disciplinary work or department. In fact, while larger universities with established study-abroad programming offer many advantages, flexibility in program structure may be more easily tolerated at smaller, more nimble organizations where faculty members have greater control over their own programs.

Second, the home institution must be willing/able to flex processes to accommodate unique vision for a short-term study-abroad program that is part of a larger framework of learning opportunities and university academic and nonacademic activities. While standardized, scalable processes for managing study-abroad programs are essential, the constraints (in terms of both faculty time required and perceived lack of support for innovation of this kind) connected to institutional processes can be the biggest barrier preventing faculty members from launching this kind of extended learning event. Institutions that are aware of the demands this kind of long-term, multicomponent learning event places on faculty will be better able to support and maintain faculty success in this expansive role.

To support and enable this model of faculty-led study abroad, institutions could

- Recognize the value of an extended learning horizon and offer support for room scheduling and nontraditional structure of class contact hours. Online learning can be used to alleviate some of the pressures on room space if needed.
- Explore opportunity to grant credit throughout the academic year to students engaging in program activities.
- Support faculty activities through stipends, teaching release, or credit affiliated with program—faculty members may not have time to engage in the year-long activities unless the institution explicitly supports it.
- Value efforts to expand student engagement in international service-based activities— decisions around promotions, recognition, and so on must demonstrate that the institution supports the faculty efforts and time involved with these kinds of programs.
- Support fundraising efforts by providing training on university fundraising processes and on accounting best practices, and by offering event space at free/reduced cost to the student organization.
- Offer program budgets that disperse tuition-based funding back to the faculty member for use to extend and expand student engagement (i.e., multiple trips to host country needed to solidify relationships).
- Engage appropriately and respectfully to extend collaborative partnerships beyond the scope of the faculty-led program. Many times, the institutional relationships formed through these programs can flourish into larger opportunities. However, university leadership should respect the faculty member's role as key contact and trusted colleague with international partners. If the "deep partnerships" described by Gillespie et al. (2009) are to persist, the faculty member cannot be replaced by other more senior administrators once the institution recognizes the potential of larger scale collaborations.

Finally, students must be supported in redefining what it means to participate in a study-abroad program. From the first recruiting sessions, to the postprogram reflections, to the continuing student group meetings, the importance of the process itself must be explained to students. Ultimately, students are required to take responsibility for their own learning and continued active engagement with the program activities. This level of engagement results in an international experience that engages students in the kind of civic agency described by Hovey and Weinberg (2009) as a community-based ecology of learning. The model we espouse agrees with Hovey and Weinberg's statement that "learning intercultural awareness and understanding of the global community is critical for the mission of higher education to prepare capable and engaged citizens" (p. 35).

Students are asked to take responsibility not only for their learning, but for the success or failure of the international project they collaboratively select as the program focus (Schattle, 2009).

Through all these shifts, the faculty leader initiating a study-abroad model that extends across time and space into an engagement ecology must put in the work up front to educate colleagues and administrators about the rationale and learning goals behind this approach. As mentioned earlier, we believe we succeeded with helping students flourish within our international engagement ecology surrounding applied international development in India, but failed when it came to gaining the institutional awareness of and support for our approach.

Further work is needed around the assessment of these longer term programs—how do students change academically over a twelve- to eighteen-month horizon? How do their values and perspectives change? What types of assessment practices would be most effective in evaluating program success? How should success or failure (or relative rates thereof) of the on-site service-based projects be evaluated? Does the engagement ecology approach serve students who do not participate in extensive program-related activities taking place after the international component?

James Skelly's "Fostering Engagement" (2009) expresses hope that effective study-abroad initiatives will "address the serious systemic problems that we face as humans living on this planet. This cannot be done by simply going about our ordinary routines" (p. 31). According to David Watson (2007), civic and community engagement falls victim to the self-referential power of precedence and administrative processes that become an end in themselves. Taking risks, innovating new approaches, and possibly failing are important attributes of faculty leaders of short-term study-abroad programs. Of course, these failures and risks should not be at the expense of student safety or ethics. However, we cannot forget the importance of innovation to effective teaching, including study abroad. By extending the learning horizon around study-abroad programs, by deepening faculty and student connections to each other and to partners in host countries, and by allowing students to experience both successes and failures, faculty-led study-abroad programs can make a difference, as the student successes from graduates from this program indicate.

Institutions that increasingly work to commodify overseas education may find these kinds of innovations problematic in terms of budget, credits awarded, faculty compensation, and other areas. However, if a common focus on student learning and engagement can be reached, faculty leaders and institutional offices of study abroad can collaborate to build flexible cultures and processes that encourage and support international experiences embedded within a multiyear, student- and community partner-based engagement ecology.

REFERENCES

Black, H. T., & Duhon, D. L. (2005). Assessing the impact of business study abroad programs on cultural awareness and personal development. *Journal of Education for Business, 81*(3), 140–144.

Brown, J. S. (1999). Sustaining the ecology of knowledge. *Leader to Leader, 12,* 31–36.

Brown, J. S. (2001). Learning in the digital age. In M. Devlin, R. Larson, & J. Meyerson (Eds.), *The Internet & the university: Forum 2001* (pp. 65–91). Published as a joint project of the Forum for the Future of Higher Education and EDUCAUSE.

Brustein, W. (2009). It takes an entire institution: A blueprint for the global university. In R. Levin (Ed.),

The handbook of practice and research in study abroad: Higher education and the quest for global citizenship (pp. 249–265). New York: Routledge.

Davidson, D. (2010). Study abroad: When, how long, and with what results? New data from the Russian front. *Foreign Language Annals, 43*(1), 6–26.

Day, J. (1987). Student motivation, academic validity, and the summer language program abroad: An editorial. *The Modern Language Journal, 71*(3), 261–266.

Dwyer, M. (2004). More is better: The impact of study abroad program duration. *Frontiers: The Interdisciplinary Journal of Study Abroad, 10*, 151–164.

Fitzgerald, H. E., Allen, A., & Roberts, P. (2010). Campus-community partnerships: Perspectives on engaged research. In H. E. Fitzgerald, C. Burack, & S. Siefer (Eds.), *Handbook on engaged scholarship: Contemporary landscapes, future directions. Community-campus partnerships* (Vol. 2, pp. 5–28). East Lansing: Michigan State University Press.

Fitzgerald, H. E., Bruns, K., Sonka, S. T., Furco, A., & Swanson, L. (2012). The centrality of engagement in higher education. *Journal of Higher Education, Outreach and Engagement, 16*, 7–28.

Fitzgerald, H. E., & Simon, L. A. K. (2012). The world grant ideal and engagement scholarship. *Journal of Higher Education, Outreach and Engagement, 16*(3), 33–55.

Fitzgerald, H. E., & Zientek, R. (2015). Learning cities, system changes and community engagement scholarship. *New Directions for Adult and Continuing Education, 145*(Spring), 21–33.

Freire, P. (1970). *Pedagogy of the oppressed.* New York: Herder and Herder.

Gillespie, S., Becker, J. A., Billings, B., Bogolanou, S., Davis, C., Haniff, F., Kajee, A., Keenan, T., Koposov, N., Kupe, T., & Moakhov, V. (2009). Creating deep partnerships with institutions abroad: Bard College as global citizen. In R. Levin (Ed.), *The handbook of practice and research in study abroad: Higher education and the quest for global citizenship* (pp. 445–465). New York: Routledge.

Hovey, R., & Weinberg, A. (2009). Global learning and the making of citizen diplomats. In R. Levin (Ed.), *The handbook of practice and research in study abroad: Higher education and the quest for global citizenship* (pp. 33–48). New York: Routledge.

Hulstrand, F. (2006, May–June). Education abroad on the fast track. *International Educator*, pp. 46–56.

Kline, R. (1998). Literacy and language learning in a study abroad context. *Frontiers: The Interdisciplinary Journal of Study Abroad, 4*, 139–165.

Lewis, T. L., & Niesenbaum, R. A. (2005). The benefits of short-term study abroad. *The Chronicle of Higher Education, 51*(39), B20.

Longo, N. V. (2007). *Why community matters: Connecting education with civic life.* Albany, NY: SUNY Press.

Lumkes, J., Hallet, S., & Vallade, L. (2012). Hearing versus experiencing: The impact of a short-term study abroad experience in China on students perceptions regarding globalization and cultural awareness. *International Journal of Intercultural Relations, 36*(1), 151–159.

Medina-Lopez-Portillo, A. (2004). Intercultural learning assessment: The link between program duration and the development of intercultural sensitivity. *Frontiers: The Interdisciplinary Journal of Study Abroad, 10*, 179–200.

Mezirow, J. (1991). *Transformative dimensions of adult learning.* San Francisco: Jossey-Bass.

O'Sullivan, E. (2003). Bringing a perspective of transformative learning to globalized consumption. *International Journal of Consumer Studies, 27*(4), 326–330.

Peppas, S. C. (2005). Business study abroad tours for non-traditional students: An outcomes assessment. *Frontiers: The Interdisciplinary Journal of Study Abroad, 11*, 143–163.

Schattle, H. (2009). Global citizenship in theory and practice. In R. Levin (Ed.), *The handbook of practice and research in study abroad: Higher education and the quest for global citizenship* (pp. 3–20). New York: Routledge.

Skelly, J. (2009). Fostering engagement: The role of international education in the development of global civic society. In R. Levin (Ed.), *The handbook of practice and research in study abroad: Higher education and the quest for global citizenship* (pp. 21–32). New York: Routledge.

Twombly, S. (1995). Piropos and friendships: Gender and culture clash in study abroad. *Frontiers: The Interdisciplinary Journal of Study Abroad, 1*, 1–27.

Watson, D. (2007). *Managing civic and community engagement.* London: Open University Press.

CHAPTER 4

Experiential Learning and Study-Abroad Programs: A Partnership between Michigan State University and TU Dortmund University

Zenia Kotval, Christiane Ziegler-Hennings, and Anne Budinger

The urban and regional planning profession demands the training of practical planners who have some experience with community development, citizen participation modules, and conflict resolution skills. Curricular community outreach provides students with needed exposure to practical applications of textbook lessons and exposure to group dynamics, community clients, and complex problems. The recognized need for practical training in any planning curriculum is most often addressed through community outreach-based courses, such as planning studios, practicum projects, and study-abroad programs, and in lectures that are woven into seminar courses.

The basic structure of all these classes typically supports teams of students working with particular communities on specific planning-related activities. These outreach courses, however, pose some of the greatest teaching and learning challenges in the entire curriculum (Dalton, 1986; Vakil, Marans, & Feldt, 1990; Wiewel & Lieber, 1998). Even though the need for experiential learning is accepted and understood, practice-based courses often lack the same prestige and distinction in academia as theory-based courses and need constant justification (Kotval, 2004).

In recent years, there has been a significant focus placed on service-based learning as a form of training students in the urban and regional planning field. The increased interest in outreach and service-based learning, within the planning profession, has been well documented by scholarly articles in mainstream professional journals. The *Journal of Planning Education and Research* highlighted the importance of this topic when a special issue was published geared solely to community outreach partnerships (JPER Special Issue, 1998). Angotti, Doble, and Horrigan (2011) reflect on the need for service-based learning in addition to traditional theory-based learning. Scholarly work (Johnston, 2014; Wiek, Xiong, Brundiers, & van der Leeuw, 2014) has shown that a blended approach to teaching urban and regional planning education that includes both theory and service-based learning gives students a well-rounded education, grounded in both the philosophy and process of the planning discipline.

Scholarship and Practice

According to Boyer (1990), scholarship in American higher education may be traced through three distinct yet overlapping phases. In the seventeenth century, colleges were focused on building personal character and teaching civic and religious leadership skills. Faculty were mostly theologians and were valued for their religious commitment, rather than scholarly ability.

By the mid-nineteenth century an evolution in the educational paradigm was taking place and was represented by universities focusing on the needs of a growing nation. The 1862 Morrill Act established land-grant colleges and enhanced the role of state universities in teaching skills for practical applications. Many land-grant colleges focused heavily on subjects such as agricultural sciences, forestry, engineering, education, and other disciplines and fields. This allowed universities to formally devote their resources to moral and intellectual development and focus on service in their mission. By the late 1800s the focus of education for many universities was practical utility (Cockett, 2014).

The third phase introduced a renewed emphasis on basic research in American higher education based on the Humboltian research university concept that was adopted by Johns Hopkins, the University of Chicago, and Harvard University, among others (Goodchild & Wechsler, 1997). This research mission spread to all research institutions and was further advanced by the development of the National Science Foundation (NSF) in 1950. With grants and funds available from the NSF, institutions could require professors to continue to research and publish as tenure requirements.

Equating research and publication with scholarship may deter junior faculty members from participating in community-based problems of contemporary society, ironically at a time when societal concerns are more varied and complex than ever before (Wiewel & Lieber, 1998). Our universities must become reengaged in the social issues that are prevalent in society and focus on teaching and the application of knowledge, not just its discovery for the sake of publishing.

This disconnect between scholarship (as defined by research publications and grants) and practical applications of knowledge is detrimental to students who will ultimately practice the profession of urban planning. Schön's (1983) seminal work, *The Reflective Practitioner,* highlights the nature of reflective practice and its constraints. According to Schön, the divergence of research and practice exacerbates the dichotomy of scholarship and practice through their assessment of planning theorists, by aligning theorists into two camps. The first group advocates planning as a rational, structured process and that knowledge of specific urban regimes lead to action (technical rationality) (Feldman, 1997; Lauria, 1996). The second group sees planning as a pragmatic, incremental or communicative model wherein situations are confusing and it is impossible to start out with a fixed goal and plan the intermediate strategies to reach the goal (Healy, Foote & Hay, 2000; Hoch, 1997; Innes, 1995).

In planning education, however, the rational planning model still dominates, despite the growing recognition that planning practice rarely reflects that model (Hoch, 1997; Baum 1996). Often, recent graduates from planning programs will reflect on the disconnect between what they learned in classes and what they are doing in practice in the planning profession. Alternative planning theories such as "disjointed incrementalism" (Braybrooke & Lindblom, 1970) seem more appropriate to planning practice. Planning processes are oriented toward building relationships, taking advantage of strategic opportunities, and remaining fluid (Wiewel & Lieber, 1998).

With theoretical shortcomings in technical rationality and disjointed incrementalism, service-based learning is considered a worthwhile pedagogical strategy that connects students with communities, with the goal of integrating theoretical learning and practical experience. It exposes students to the complexities and uncertainties of practical situations that cannot be duplicated in traditional lecture courses, and it enhances academic learning and civic engagement by involving students in community service activities (Kotval, 2004; Roakes & Norris-Tirrell, 2000).

The ability to work with community members to develop a plan that suits the needs of an entire community requires the "meshing" of academic knowledge and practical skills. Experiential learning teaches students at a higher integrative and creative level and can be a humbling experience (Johnston, 2014; Kotval, 2004; Wiek et al., 2014).

Moreover, given the diversity of student skills and knowledge, these courses can be difficult to structure. There can be an educational disconnect for some students when reality doesn't mirror theoretical constructs. Many students may discover that they have difficulty relating to citizens from diverse backgrounds with different, often conflicting, desires—as in most communities.

Experiential Learning in an International Cooperative Framework

Experiential learning challenges are magnified when service learning is applied to study-abroad courses or an international audience. In these settings, students have to deal with cultural differences, academic nuances, and distance learning. Despite these challenges, Michigan State University (MSU) is one of the top U.S. universities when it comes to commitment and participation in international programs. The following section presents a case study of one such international cooperation program that is focused on experiential learning and service-based activities, designed to enhance students' theoretical understanding of planning.

Partnership Between Michigan State University and TU Dortmund University

Since 1984, faculty and students of the Urban and Regional Planning Program at Michigan State University and the School of Spatial Planning at TU Dortmund University have been engaged in a study-abroad partnership in Michigan and Germany. The partnership has included short-term student group exchanges with both universities taking turns hosting and traveling to the other country, every other year. The short-term visits usually offer students the opportunities to have presentations by professors and meet key community members and officials. Some students and faculty members choose to do longer term stays on fellowships funded by the Heinrich Hertz Foundation and the Fulbright Foundation.

In 1990, the first service-learning student project took place at MSU, when German planning students attended a workshop about improving the industrial city of Flint, by reusing abandoned industrial sites and brownfields. In 1995, official academic exchange papers were signed by both universities for cooperation between the Urban and Regional Planning Program at MSU and the Fakultät Raumplanung, Universität Dortmund. From this date on, an official exchange of professors and students has taken place, supported by the two faculties and the academic exchange offices, at MSU and TU Dortmund.

Between the years 1995 and 2016, the partnership matured and grew. Over that period, it became clear that it was relatively easy to bring German students to MSU to study for one semester and for them to attend planning lectures, due to their good knowledge of the English language. Having MSU students attend the TU Dortmund for a full semester was more difficult. Lectures are predominantly given in German and are therefore not suitable for the typical American planning student. Even American students who have a basic knowledge of conversational German found it difficult to read and speak in academic terms, at the university level. For them, professional trips in a student group, supervised by an American and German teacher, have been more effective. Despite these challenges, between 2005 and 2016, about 15 teachers and roughly 120 students have taken part in this exchange.

Ongoing program evaluation and maintaining an open dialogue have been integral to improving the exchange program, and to finding a structure to bring the highest value and benefit for the involved partners. Based on experiences from the program and the exchange of ideas, a structure was developed that fulfilled the demands of effective learning of the students and the acceptable effort of the teachers. The structure rotates annually, with the American planners visiting TU Dortmund one year and the German planning group visiting East Lansing the following year. Having worked well for both partners, in 2012 this particular model of cooperation won the college-level award for best long-term international partnership.

During the last ten years, five German student groups visited the United States and five American groups went to Germany (about 120 students). The structure of the student study trips consists of a joint workshop between MSU and DUT, and a field trip to different cities and interesting planning projects. In addition, MSU and DUT faculty members have become involved in their own exchanges by teaching as guest instructors for one or two semesters, or by collaborating on papers and projects with each other—some receiving publication.

Over time, a supporting structure between the two colleges has matured into a strong partnership. Several documents of understanding have been signed by the deans and university administrations. On each side, representatives for the cooperation have been appointed. Professors from DUT have been appointed as adjunct professors in the Urban and Regional Planning Program at MSU.

Choosing Partners and Building a Successful Program

Implementing and maintaining a successful international exchange program depends on choosing interested partners and very motivated colleagues carefully. Due to the combination of structured long-term planning and the need for short-term flexibility, the communication between the individuals involved must be efficient. Faith and trust in each other's capabilities are also important requirements. Getting along with each other easily, short paths of communication, and fast clarification are only possible if a good relationship exists between the partners.

Beside the demand of social skills, different professional backgrounds are necessary. Spatial planning and urban development are interdisciplinary tasks and therefore demand varied experiences in different fields, such as urban design, landscape architecture or planning, and urban economic development. On the basis of these different professions, interesting topics for research and teaching can be developed, including an ongoing exchange of ideas, between the disciplines.

As the partnership between the two universities continues to grow, there are broad possibili-ties for scholarly research and for continuing to make the student projects an impactful part of the student experience. With a decades-old working partnership, the underlying structure is well implemented and most obstacles have been easily overcome. The faculty members who have been involved in the partnership have often been involved for more than ten years, providing for a stable framework.

In addition to a solid cooperation structure, the partnership has relied on the commitment and diligence of the faculty involved. The program would not be successful without the tireless work of faculty members at each university, as well as support from their departments, universities, and sponsors. Specifically, student study trips are rather expensive and require financial aid. As a result, several foundations exist, as well as academic support programs at the university level. In addition to the support of the universities, the faculty members also make a personal com-mitment to the success of the partnership, often inviting individuals to stay in their homes for short-term exchanges. This is another example of how the long partnership has been beneficial for solving problems and why it continues to evolve over time.

Over the life of this long partnership, organizers have identified several preconditions for the success of this and programs like it. These include

- a clear responsibility of certain persons for the program,
- leaders of the exchange having longer contracts,
- the program being well accepted by the academic units,
- feedback from the students, and
- an annual visit of colleagues, desirable to keep the contact with the partner university.

Dimensions of the Study-Abroad Program

The study-abroad program, which has existed in this way since 2003, is a yearly trip, with alter-nating hosting. One year the Dortmund students travel to MSU; the other year the MSU students come to Dortmund.

German—TU Dortmund

For the German students, participation in the biennial trip to Germany by the MSU is impactful. They can improve their knowledge of international planning problems and practice their use of English. Students are expected to be engaged with the work and participate fully in the pre-sentations, which are in English. This is part of a two-semester studio class, which is one of the required courses in the spatial planning curriculum at DUT. For the first semester of the studio class while still at DUT, German students prepare the content of the workshop taking place in the United States at MSU, the topic of which has to be discussed with the MSU teachers every year. However, even when the Dortmund students are not traveling to MSU, they host the MSU students and work with them in Dortmund within the one-week workshop and additional trips.

The semester starts in October every year and with the decision for the studio class, the students have the option to take part in the international study program with MSU. Preparing for two semesters, they end up with a planning guideline or idea for an area in the Ruhr Area, which they present to the MSU students when they visit them.

Over the years, it has turned out that September is the best month to visit MSU and work with the Urban Planning students. That means that the DUT students are traveling after they finish their studio class. The starting point for the DUT spatial planning students is Chicago. They spend a week visiting successful brownfield redevelopment projects and meeting with officials from different organizations dealing with abandoned sites. A fixed point every second year is the Chicago Center for Green Technology and the Chicago Brownfield Initiative. After getting in touch with the U.S. planning system during the studio class and in Chicago, the German students start a "hands-on" week in East Lansing, Michigan, at MSU.

In mixed German–American groups, with peers from Urban Planning and Landscape Architecture, students work in four-day charrettes on a specific site in or around Lansing/East Lansing. The groups of students are supported by the supervisors of DUT and MSU and get input from different experts and officials from the county and the city in which the students are working. At the end of the charrette, a jury consisting of members of the DUT and MSU supervising team and the city officials reviews the contributions of each group. After a presentation by each group, the jury ranks the different designs.

Study-Abroad Program at Michigan State

The Urban and Regional Planning program at Michigan State University strongly encourages all undergraduate and graduate students to enroll in one or two international learning experiences during their degree programs. It offers two study-abroad programs, every other year, in Europe and Asia. Leaders of the Urban and Regional Planning program view these experiences as an important means for integrating classroom work and pragmatic planning in actual community situations. As a teaching vehicle, the study-abroad programs help students to increase their knowledge and confidence, while providing a needed service to communities. Experiential learning provides a vehicle for substantive learning and the integration of techniques with theory, resulting in graduates who are better able to apply theory to practice, and thus more reflective planners.

Planning and Pretrip Strategies

Undertaking an international trip with students has to be carefully planned and organized and does not work without the enormous engagement of the supervising faculty members. The first study-abroad trips to the United States were at the end of the German winter semester, which meant that students spent the last weeks of spring term in America. This was not working for a joint workshop with MSU and DUT students, because the MSU students could not spend excessive amounts of time to work one week only for one class. Going to DUT proved to be more flexible, because the course plan is not as strict as it is at MSU. Because the study-abroad classes take place in the break between spring and fall term, the MSU students go to Europe and Germany after their spring term in May. Thus, the joint student workshop takes place in summer, and they have the whole winter semester to get prepared for the workshop and field trips.

The overall theme, which is a guideline for the two-semester studio class of the DUT students and main topic of the field trips in the United States and Germany, has to be of interest in both states. Michigan and North Rhine Westphalia, where DUT is located, have long industrial histories and are currently dealing with structural changes and abandoned former industrial sites. Consequently, brownfields are a challenge in both states and a field of common interest to students and professors at both universities. The themes of the studio classes and the workshops in East Lansing and Dortmund change each year, but they usually involve some aspect of brownfields. Different perspectives that have been studied include brownfields at the waterfront and empty sites as a potential open space that can increase the value of surrounding real estate and quarters.

Finding adequate community partners in different municipalities who are interested in brownfield revitalization is not always easy. However, the long-lasting cooperation between DUT and MSU has made it possible to build strong relationships with different organizations and actors willing to be contacted every other year to work with the partnership again. In addition to established contacts, the partnership continues to add new contacts to the list of people with whom we do our field trips. Chosen partners always have a strong relation to the topic or charrette area of the year, such as the owner of the site or people working with special organizations like the Trust for Public Land with its Center for Park Excellence.

Experiential Learning

One of the focuses of this chapter is to share the challenges and successes of structuring and teaching an experiential learning course in the urban planning curriculum. The discussion relates to the fundamental objectives of fieldwork: firsthand experiences, dynamics of small-group learning, and value of transferable skills. It aims to provide insight for others teaching similar courses in planning and allied disciplines.

Recommendations Based on Challenges and Opportunities

The following recommendations are for improving and strengthening the practicum course experience based on experiences gained from teaching the course for several years and from the experience of others teaching similar courses.

Understand and Articulate the Importance of Experiential Learning and the Study-Abroad Program Clearly

Although a majority of planning educators strive to create good practicing planners, few of us articulate the purpose of our courses in our syllabi. Planning affects all aspects of a society—economic, social, political, and cultural. Yet in many educational institutions the focus is on the importance of theoretical work over practical experience. Students realize that, too often, greater emphasis is given to theory and not practice. In fact, some professional programs deemphasize the importance of practice by offering additional academic courses in lieu of fieldwork. In contrast, forty years ago, the core of planning was practice. The curriculum allowed the student to gain perspective from the eyes of various direct, active players in urban and regional development (Vakil et al., 1990), and workshop (as it was frequently called) was the fundamental part of planning curricula. Practice-oriented courses enhanced planning theory, communication, and mediation skills, which were better taught in an applied sense than by conventional lecture and seminar formats (Dalton, 1986).

Study-abroad programs can be an exercise in self-confidence, team building, conflict resolution, understanding of multicultural concepts in planning and development, and, above all, a forum for the practical application of planning theory. Study-abroad programs can give students hands-on experience in the field of planning and development. Furthermore, interaction with community organizations that serve as clients facilitates the integration of public service into the classroom (Alonso, 1986). Ideally, this form of cooperative learning serves as a learning tool by building communication skills and connecting planning theory with planning practice. The importance of these learned skills for an effective planner are outlined in the Planning Accreditation Board (PAB) requirement for accredited planning programs.

Furthermore, students entering a planning program come from a wide variety of disciplines, such as geography, anthropology, economics, architecture, civil engineering, natural sciences, and sociology. Students may not necessarily have any prior formal training or practice in dealing with planning problems. Moreover, those who are from the arts, social sciences, and even natural sciences are typically more familiar with "description" than "prescription." They have likely had few opportunities to collect information, analyze data, and make recommendations for a specific action. They need to learn that one never has all the information required, that local values are important, and that "all politics are local." Experiential learning is intended to help students build on their past experiences, apply new knowledge, and gain confidence to make meaningful decisions.

Structure the Course and Its Relationship to the Entire Curriculum Such That It Reflects Its Unique Characteristics

Some university programs organize study-abroad programs that last an entire semester. Some professional programs require all students to engage in international experience and have endowments to support the students that take part in these experiences. The international program is clearly defined and articulated in the curriculum, such that all students understands that they will be expected to participate. The planning program at MSU does not mandate that every student participate in an international experience; however, opportunities to participate in one or two study-abroad opportunities are always available, strongly encouraged, and financially supported. This makes a huge difference in the participation rate for the programs.

Foster Strong Client Relationships to Ensure Good Community Projects and Effective Working Partnerships

In addition to the organizational partnerships important for international exchanges, it is also critical to find projects that lend themselves to the short-term brainstorming of ideas and presentation of themes and design alternatives. In this way, the students are engaging directly with people in the community who are in need of some specific project for their city. Engaging directly with community members allows the projects to be more practical and useful to the actors involved. The client receives a tangible product produced by the students with guidance, and the students gain working knowledge of planning, working with international teammates, presenting ideas and concepts using graphic arts, and working directly in their community.

Encourage Healthy Group Dynamics and Foster Transferable Skills

One of the cornerstones of experiential learning is the ideal of cooperative peer learning in a small-group setting. The potential for teamwork, deep learning through closer interaction between students and teachers (Gibbs, 1992; Higgit, 1997), and greater student responsibility and accountability for constructing knowledge (Black, 1994) are seen as critical elements of active learning.

Furthermore, opportunities to combine discipline-specific subject skills with practical, transferable skills are seen as an integral part of experiential learning. Subject skills are not necessarily the same ones used in a variety of career-oriented situations, such as skills in teamwork, communication, self-management, self-motivation, leadership, social interaction, and personal development. "These skills are just not taught by conventional note-taking and reading. Instead, they must be developed through experiential learning: guidance and demonstration reinforced by practice" (Haigh & Kilmartin, 1999, p. 205).

Given the potential and opportunities presented by small-group learning, it is imperative that groups be structured with care. Learning will only occur when the group functions in a cohesive and efficient manner. When the positive interdependence needed to link group members is absent, the team will falter and the learning experience, as well as the project, will be compromised.

Managing group dynamics poses many challenges, ranging from the size and composition of the group to expectations and grading. Devoting time to teaching communications skills and the importance of teamwork is critical. Students often have difficulty working in groups, managing and scheduling time, and taking responsibility or being accountable to peers. Effective groups are based on five basic principles. These are interdependence, face-to-face interaction, individual accountability, teamwork and social skills, and group processing (Johnson, Johnson, & Smith, 1991).

Encourage Greater Faculty Involvement to Seamlessly Link Theoretical and Practical Instruction

Often, professors do not see involvement in practice-based courses as providing extrinsic rewards in terms of merit salary and promotions. More weight is given to research publications than to outreach activities in merit considerations. As such, in several programs, fieldwork is delegated to a practicing planner who may not hold a university appointment.

The rationale for hiring professional planners for these courses is typically quite sound. Professionals know how to plan in a realistic way. There are, however, potentially unfortunate impacts of utilizing professionals in this way. A course taught by a guest, not a professor, could alter the perceptions and expectations of the importance of the course in the minds of students. Further, it unnecessarily separates theoretical knowledge (that taught by professors) from the practical training (taught by practitioners). This is particularly worrisome for those of us who believe the link between theory and practice is essential. One way to overcome these concerns is to team-teach such offerings. Complementary skills of faculty and practitioners could create a good dynamic in class.

Nonetheless, it is essential that regular faculty become involved in the practicum experience. By so doing, they are able to stay in touch with planning practice, are able to test their ideas, and are able to demonstrate the importance of the course in the curriculum. They need not be the instructors of record or the "studio masters." They can offer learning modules, provide pinpointed practical lectures, or even serve as guest critics. Students often have a difficult time linking theory and coursework to practical problems encountered in the field. They are not experienced researchers and need guidance in fieldwork objectives, social interaction, and dealing with multiple publics (Fuller, Rowlinson, & Bevan, 2000). Lectures by different faculty members that focus on various aspects students might encounter in the field, such as ethical dilemmas and dealing with disadvantaged groups, along with subject-specific content and study of analytical techniques, can be advantageous. In all cases, it is important to ensure that there are seamless connections between nonstudio and studio instructors and courses.

Evaluating the Process and Results

As an overall keynote about running such a successful exchange program over such a long period of time, one can simply say, "Engagement is it all!" Engagement is a key element in two different ways. First, the enormous engagement of advisors and teachers who organize the trip and workshop is essential. Second, the huge engagement from students who host other students from the partner university, do the workshop in a foreign language (for the German students), work in mixed groups with individuals from different planning backgrounds, and produce one common design is essential for the student experience.

Without the continuous engagement of the responsible teachers of both participating schools, the MSU Urban and Regional Planning Program and the TU Dortmund School of Spatial Planning, this exchange program would not be what it is now: an annual collaboration between two partnering planning schools with an intensive exchange of knowledge between teachers and students.

It takes time to create a good working program, which is also very dependent on the specific cooperation partners. In the case of MSU and DUT, it was important, even necessary, to appoint colleagues who are obligated to the program and feel responsible for it over years. When it began in the 1980s, one could get the impression of a more private initiative, not recognized by colleagues. In Germany, with an increasing focus on international relations, the program became more appreciated, and more teachers and students became interested.

It is a good approach to create a common subject for the workshops, to ensure a continuous interest on both sides. The theoretical background information on this topic can be used over and over again. An established program can more easily acquire funding for the study trips, as the project doesn't have to be explained repeatedly. However, it is also an experience that the program has to pass through different phases and that the financial and social surrounding varies. Thus, flexibility is highly demanded.

As a result of all the effort, these cooperation projects have resulted in benefits for professors and students. Having an international experience in one's curriculum vitae is an advantage on the job market. Students with a study-abroad semester might find their first employment easier.

Leaders of other academic programs considering building an exchange with an international partner are advised to take a multiyear approach and plan to develop the program over time, possibly several years. They should also find the right partners within each university and each community where the exchanges will take place. Once the partners are identified, it is vital to have engagement from both sides of the exchange. A project such as this cannot be done successfully with only one side working on it. Lastly, it must attract students interested in working across countries and spending time abroad. A successful study-abroad partnership focused on experiential learning can be difficult to organize and maintain, but the benefit is enormous and these cooperation projects guarantee a very interesting work.

Conclusion

It is evident that service-based learning, which involves students working in communities with the goal of integrating theoretical or textbook learning, is a worthwhile pedagogical strategy. It exposes students to the complexities and uncertainties in practice situations that cannot be duplicated in traditional lecture courses, and it enhances academic learning by involving students in community service activities.

The ability to work with community members in developing a plan that suits the needs of a community requires the meshing of academic knowledge with social skills during practicum. Practicum fosters a higher level of integration and creativity. However, given the diversity of student skills and knowledge, these courses can be difficult to structure. Students can become confused when reality does not mirror theoretical constructs and have a difficult time dealing with real people from diverse backgrounds with different, often conflicting, needs.

Experiential learning is an essential part of planning and should remain in the curriculum of degree-granting programs. Practicum courses and practice-oriented study-abroad programs can be valuable teaching vehicles that help students increase their knowledge and confidence through the provision of a needed service to communities. Experience shows that these courses provide a mechanism for substantive learning and the integration of techniques with theory. The result is graduates who are better planners. Students learn valuable lessons through cooperative learning and assist community organizations in the process. Experience gained and skills learned in practice-oriented work provide students with valuable tools when dealing with actual planning problems. If we understand the present and historic perceptions of practice-based courses in our curriculum, and consciously work to educate our peers and students on the importance of these courses, their structures, and implications, we could promote their status and adoption in professional programs. Furthermore, if we understand theories of cooperative learning, service-based learning, and group dynamics, we can better teach the courses and ensure that they are valuable learning experiences, and that we are helping our students become reflective practitioners as they move forward with their careers.

REFERENCES

Angotti, T., Doble, C., Harrigan, P. (Eds.) (2011). *Service-learning in design and planning: Educating at the boundaries.* New York: New Village Press.

Alonso, W. (1986). The unplanned paths of planning schools. *The Public Interest, 82,* 58–71.

Baum, H. S. (1996). Practicing planning theory in a political world. In S. Mandelbaum, L. Mazza, & R. Burchell (Eds.), *Explorations in planning theory* (pp. 365–382). New York: Routledge.

Black, K. A. (1994). What to do when you stop lecturing: Become a guide and a resource. In S. Kadel & J. A. Keehner (Eds.), *Collaborative learning: A sourcebook for higher education, Vol. II* (pp. 140–144). University Park, PA: National Center on Postsecondary Teaching, Learning and Assessment.

Boyer, E. L. (1990). *Scholarship revisited.* Princeton, NJ: Carnegie Foundation for the Advancement of Teaching.

Braybrooke, D., & Lindblom, C. (1970). *A strategy of decision: Policy as a social process.* New York: Free Press.

Cockett, N. (2014). Responsibilities of being the land grant institution for the State of Utah. *Journal of Developments in Sustainable Agriculture, 9*(1), 1–7.

Dalton, L. (1986). Why the rational paradigm persists—The resistance of professional education and practice to alternative forms of planning. *Journal of Planning Education and Research, 5,* 147–153.

Feldman, A. (1997). Varieties of wisdom in the practice of teachers. *Teaching and Teacher Education, 13*(7), 757–773.

Fuller, I., Rawlinson, S., & Bevan, R. (2000). Evaluation of student learning experiences in physical geography fieldwork: Paddling or pedagogy? *Journal of Geography in Higher Education, 24*(2), 199–215.

Gibbs, G. (1992). *Improving the quality of student learning.* Bristol: Technical and Education Services.

Goodchild, H., & Wechsler, L. (Eds.). (1997). *The reader on the history of higher Education* (2nd ed.). Needham Heights, MA: Simon & Schuster.

Haigh, M., & Kilmartin, M. (1999). Student perceptions of development of personal transferable skills. *Journal of Geography in Higher Education, 23*(2), 195–206.

Healy, M., Foote, K., & Hay, I. (2000). International perspectives on learning and teaching geography in higher education. *Journal of Geography in Higher Education, 24*(3), 217–218.

Higgit, M. (1997). Addressing the new agenda for fieldwork in higher education. *Journal of Geography in Higher Education, 21*(30), 391–398.

Hoch, C. J. (1997). Planning theorists taking an interpretive turn need not travel on the political economy highway. *Planning Theory, 17,* 13–64.

Innes, J. E. (1995). Planning theory's emerging paradigm: Communicative action and interactive practice.

Journal of Planning Education and Research, 14(3), 183–189.

Johnson, D. W., Johnson, R., & Smith, K. A. (1991). *Active learning: Cooperation in the college classroom.* Edina, MN: Interaction Book Company.

Johnston, A. (2014). A pedagogy for interdisciplinary research and collaboration in planning and environmental design. *Journal of Planning Education and Research, 35*(1), 86–92.

JPER Special Issue. (1998). *Journal of Planning Education and Research, 17*(4).

Kotval, Z. (2004). Teaching experiential learning in the Urban Planning curriculum. *Journal of Geography in Higher Education, 27*(3), 297–308.

Lauria, M. (Ed.). (1996). *Reconstructing urban regime theory: Regulating urban politics in a global economy.* New York: Sage.

Roakes, S. L., & Norris-Tirrell, D. (2000). Community service learning in planning education: A framework for course development. *Journal of Planning Education and Research, 20*(1), 100–110.

Schön, D. (1983). *The reflective practitioner.* New York: Basic Books.

Vakil, A., Marans, R. W., & Feldt, A. (1990). Integrative planning workshops: The Michigan experience. *Journal of Planning Education and Research, 10*(1), 61–69.

Wiek, A., Xiong, A., Brundiers, K., & van der Leeuw, S. (2014). Integrating problem- and project-based learning into sustainability programs. *International Journal of Sustainability in Higher Education, 15*(4), 431–449.

Wiewel, W., & Lieber, M. (1998). Goal achievement, relationship building, and incrementalism: The challenges of university-community partnership. *Journal of Planning Education and Research, 17*(4), 192–306.

Learning Outcomes of Short-Term Global Health Electives

Christina Dokter and Gary Willyerd

Medical schools are increasingly creating international opportunities for their medical students, and more than half of medical schools reportedly provide international elective rotations for students (McKinley, Williams, Norcini, & Anderson, 2008). With three medical colleges, Michigan State University (MSU) encourages civic engagement for its medical students in the form of international elective rotations. MSU defines engagement and service learning within the framework set out by Thomas Ehrlich (2000, p. vi), who said, "Civic engagement means to make a difference in the civic life of our communities and developing the combination of knowledge, skills, values, and motivation to make that difference. It means promoting the quality of life in a community, through both political and nonpolitical processes."

Likewise, the Michigan State University College of Osteopathic Medicine (MSUCOM) short-term study abroad aims to provide medical service to the underserved in developing nations as a form of engaged study abroad. Students work alongside residents and physicians by giving physical exams to people in communities who have no access to medical care. The trip intends to promote cross-cultural understanding, and at the same time, as students engage with underserved patients, to provide opportunities for the students to examine their own outlook as future physicians. As students engage in these communities, they perform research about the host environment, such as by promoting public health issues.

These international medical service trips exemplify the university's "Boldness by Design" initiative, in which students engage in activities that help create sustainable and resilient communities in underserved areas of the world. The students involved in the planning aspect engage with lead faculty as well as community leaders overseas. During the semester, students also receive language training and other information about the host country, including information about the culture and the environment of the host area. Thus, Boldness by Design elements are fully engaged. The service abroad results in community-based partnerships with host cities that benefit both parties. Community voice and expertise are recognized and respected as students provide valuable information about the host country's health environment through public health research. Students also visit host hospitals and local academic institutions and learn why the medical service to the underserved is important. They also learn that they are often the only source of health check that the locals access over the year.

MSUCOM's short-term study-abroad medical mission program began in 2009, when doctors and residents teamed up with a handful of students for a ten-day mission service to Antigua, Guatemala. Their aim was to serve the economically disadvantaged in Antigua's surrounding areas. Such trips eventually included the mountainous regions of Peru, and by 2011 about thirty students attended, and research became a regular component of the program. In 2013, the program expanded to include tribal people living along the Amazon River.

This study is based on a one-credit-hour course housed in the College of Osteopathic Medicine. Students may sign up for more credits, depending on the amount of involvement in the planning stage (which takes place over the duration of a year), although the trip abroad lasts not more than two weeks. The students, along with residents and physicians, travel from place to place, setting up makeshift tents in the middle of the mountain community, sometimes rotating in a building furnished by the Rotary Club, and at other times visiting local hospitals and dental clinics. Under the supervision of physicians, students provide primary medical care, furnish supplies (such as medicines, blankets, and toothbrushes), and conduct health research.

Despite such apparent benefits, qualitative studies on the nature of the students' experiences are largely missing (Battat et al., 2010). While idealism and improved clinical performance have been cited as outcomes (McKinley, Williams, Norcini, & Anderson, 2008), the nature of student learning, ethical considerations (Crump, 2008), longitudinal patterns, and the structure and essence of the international experience should be studied in order to assess such programs' success (Thompson, Huntington, Hunt, Pinsky, & Brodie, 2003). From there, we can begin to coalesce policies, processes, and practices that should become elements of successful programs.

To this end, this study joins the bourgeoning literature evaluating medical students' engagement in overseas experiences, outcomes, and longitudinal patterns. The study aims to take a phenomenological approach to studying the student participants of global health electives in terms of their scope and scale of professional development and unpack the learning outcomes, if any, as a result of their participation.

Background and Significance

Recent focus on this burgeoning literature, calling for more research on study-abroad medical service trips and global health electives in developing countries, targets the issue in several ways. Several studies address these programs as vehicles through which students expand their vision and enhance their commitment to mitigating medical access disparities, seemingly enlarging the students' vision for primary care and their willingness to attend to the underserved (Battat et al., 2010; Gupta, Wells, Horwitz, Bia, & Barry, 1999; Ramsey, Jaq, Gjerde, & Rothenberg, 2004; Smith & Weaver, 2006; Thompson et al., 2003).

A number of studies document overseas electives, noting learning outcomes and competencies. Some of the learning outcomes include better knowledge of the global burden of disease (Federico et al., 2006), travel medicine, global health systems, immigrant health (Houpt, Pearson,

& Hall, 2007), intercultural communications, and openness to cultural differences (Battat et al., 2010; Grudzen & Legome, 2007). Federico et al. (2006) also noted that such experiences form new relationships with overseas institutions. Thompson et al. (2003) conducted a literature review and concluded that participants came back knowing more about tropical diseases, communicating across cultures, and systems-based practice. These authors also pointed out studies that show students gain problem-solving and clinical skills in their learning outcomes.

McAllister et al. (2006) studied intercultural learning of students who undertook fieldwork in Indonesia and Vietnam. Through the lens of critical incidents, they studied students' international experiences and their sense-making. They explored coping strategies and intercultural communication patterns and noted the importance of reflective exercises among the students. Wasson (2006) pointed out that these international experiences promote preexisting cultural competence and also tend to raise awareness to new levels. If nothing else, participants recognize the need to understand cultural differences. She concluded that "giving medical students and residents access to cultural competence through international experiences prepares them personally and professionally for the important task of successfully communicating with and caring for multicultural communities. Extending this concept to interpersonal competence would prepare them to successfully communicate with and care for all of their patients" (p. 829).

Most of the studies just described also present findings that show that intercultural experiences tend to foster transformative learning, which has profound influences on the development of one's self-identity and formation. Some studies, for example, show that students develop idealism, humanism, and interest in serving the underserved (Thompson et al., 2003). These abstract concepts are difficult to document, but many educators and medical associations urge more studies on learning outcomes and experiences of students so that a uniform set of global health training objectives can be developed for all schools (Bateman, Baker, Hoornenborg, & Ericsson, 2001; Battat et al., 2010; Crump, 2008; Houpt, Pearson, & Hall, 2007; Smith & Weaver, 2006).

Others question the absence of ethical guidelines and note that many students may be ill-prepared for the types of skills and procedures needed to treat patients. Skeptics say that students may actually be doing more harm than good by not partnering up with the local leadership (Ackerman, 2010; Crump, 2008; Mosepele, Lyon, & Dine, 2010; Philpott, Houghton, & Luke, 2010). Others warn of the need to prepare for unforeseen safety and security issues (Steiner, Carlough, Dent, Peate, & Morgan, 2010).

However, as indicated above, the bulk of the research suggests that service engagement activities in host communities enable students to understand the indigenous culture in ways that books and classroom learning cannot. Furthermore, MSUCOM delved into methods of community engagement with careful planning of the short-term study-abroad course. The Berquist and Milano adaptation in chapter 2 of the landmark Engle and Engle typology (2003) of study-abroad programs provides a framework for explaining the type of study abroad offered to medical undergraduate students at MSUCOM.

Table 1 shows that this program meets all criteria for planning a mid-level engagement program with the exception that the duration is short-term and the type of housing was not with locals. Students take Spanish lessons before the trip for at least a semester to familiarize themselves with medical Spanish terminology. There is guided interaction in which students visit hospitals,

Table 1. Analysis of MSUCOM Program for Levels of Service Provided

	LEVEL 1	LEVEL 2	LEVEL 3	MSUCOM MEDICAL STUDY
Program components	low	mid	high	
Length of service activity	1–4 weeks	5–8 weeks	>8 weeks	Low
Entry target-language competence	None	Intermediate	Proficiency	None to intermediate
Language used in course work and/or service work	English	English and host language	Host language	English/Spanish
Types of student housing	Hotel or guesthouse	With local students	Homestay	Hotel or guesthouse
Provisions for guided/ structured cultural interaction	Only as part of service interaction	Combination	Cultural interaction organized in addition to service	Combination of service interaction and some cultural interaction with community
Guided reflection on cultural experience	Student initiative	Weekly facilitated reflection	Min. 3x/week individual or group guided reflection	Weekly facilitated reflection meeting; daily journaling
Role of faculty	No leader or simple coordination	Facilitator with some expertise in development and/or culture of region	Owner of community relationship, facilitator with expertise in development and culture of region	Facilitator with years of experience; overseas students who organize and lead the trip
Level of self-determination by the community for service undertaken	Minimal	Negotiated	Initiated by community	Negotiated and planned between both community and the school
Sustainability of community relationship/partnership	One-time projects	Multiyear commitment but only during project work	Sustained long-term commitment, including communication with community outside service delivery	Usually multiyear, but only during project week

meet with mayors, and engage in cultural activities planned by the host institutions. Students keep a daily reflective journal and participate in a weekly debriefing session with the faculty guide. These journals have provided data for this research. Faculty members have visited the host site multiple times prior to bringing students to the site and have multiple years of expertise from prior trips to the area. Both faculty members and students have, prior to the trip, arranged meetings and collaborations with local doctors, dentists, Rotary Clubs, and community officials. Many students engage in multiyear attendance of the same activity, although the duration is always short-term. This short-term nature of the trips is due in part because of the nature of the medical school schedule and workload.

Theoretical Construct

Mezirow (2000) defines transformative learning in terms of one's ability to identify problems in one's values and beliefs and critically examine them against newly gained information and experiences. The role of self-reflection (Schön, 1983) has become one of the central tenets of identity development. Reflection aids the process of contextual human life-span development (Sigelman, 1999) and the process of transformative learning (Mezirow, 1990, 1991, 2000). Since identity formation is contextually dependent, the process of becoming critically aware of one's own and others' assumptions and expectations plays a key role in making an interpretation that leads to identity development and change.

Thus, for this study, students kept reflective journals during their trip abroad. After the trip, they answered key questions about their experience, their feelings, and their learning progress. The journals became part of the data collection, as well as a requirement for the course. From reading student journals, from observation of behavior, and through various other instruments, we hope to match the learning outcomes that students discuss posttrip with the ideas behind transformative learning. These learning outcomes are based on the core competencies that all medical students need to achieve: (1) medical knowledge, (2) patient care, (3) professionalism, (4) practice-based learning, (5) communication skills, (6) systems-based practice, and for MSUCOM, (7) osteopathic principles and practice.

Methodology

The Michigan State University College of Osteopathic Medicine (MSUCOM) has been offering medical service electives for more than a decade through the partnering hospitals of its Statewide Campus System (SCS). For each trip to Guatemala or Peru, the program also collaborates with the host institutions' nongovernmental organizations (NGOs) in the developing country, such as the Rotary Club, native physicians, and/or the local hospitals.

Working with MSU's Office of Study Abroad and Institute of International Health to orient students and take appropriate safeguards, preparations for the trip are complex but well planned. Students must complete a set of predeparture requirements such as personal essays and interviews, extensive planning, and a language class. These activities are designed to provide leadership opportunities and instill a sense of commitment. Students are involved in spearheading physician recruitment, fundraising, and planning, which forces them to learn more about travel medicine and security issues. Students also raise funds for their own support and to buy supplies and medications for the underserved in the developing country. Preparation begins a year in advance of the trip and includes recruiting a required ratio of students to physicians (3:1) so that a medical team is well staffed to deal with the challenges of serving in primary care situations overseas.

Despite the well-conceived preparations, the learning outcomes that result from these trips have remained unclear, and a thorough evaluation of each trip has been needed to inform program improvement. We knew from other studies that study-abroad service missions tend to generate self-awareness in their participants and that this is the first step toward transformation. These elements are difficult to quantify and can only be determined by a qualitative study using a narrative framework. For these reasons, we undertook a largely qualitative study exploring the phenomenon of a study-abroad medical service.

As such, semistructured interviews, reflective journals, and observations of critical incidents

were recorded, coded, and reported based on salient examples pertinent to the core competencies of medical students. The interview questions and survey questions are included in the
appendices.

Data were collected for Guatemala and Peru medical service missions from 2009 through the
summer of 2012. There were fifty-eight students who participated in the study, which included
reflective journals and observation by physicians, critical incident focus groups, and survey
research. A subset of thirty-five students was interviewed pre- and posttrip. In the future, we
expect to expand this study to follow students over time for longitudinal analysis.

Research Questions

- How do students make sense of their attendance of the global medical service pretrip?
  What motivates them to go?
- What does critical thinking look like as they reflect on their experiences?
- What learning outcomes (of the Core Competencies of medical students) can be
  unpacked during and after the trip?
- Do students show signs that transformative learning took place?
- What are some critical incidents that can inform us about this experience?
- What are some longitudinal patterns of change that arise?

Instruments

Students wrote daily reflective journal entries and answered key questions before and after the
trip by engaging in semistructured interviews. They answered the following questions:

- What were your main activities for the day?
- What experiences stood out for you?
- How did these experiences affect you and your feelings toward your profession?

The data also included attending and participating faculty's evaluations of the students. Analysis
of these documents depended on the kinds of incidents students encounter. Additionally, as part
of a possible longitudinal study, the students were asked to take a survey pre- and posttrip about
their background and their abilities in each of the core competencies, They also took a pretest
and posttest designed to examine their knowledge about tropical diseases. About halfway into
the trip, a focus group of students (the same students who were interviewed) participated in
mid-trip debriefings in which they pointed out critical incidents.

The Setting

In Guatemala, students, residents, and physicians base their medical service in Antigua and
take bus rides to rural areas of Chimaltenango. These trips are organized in conjunction with
DOCARE International, and physicians from around the country join the group. Several areas of

Guatemala are classified as "extremely poor" by the United Nations Development Programme (UNDP) Human Development Index (2002).

Huamachuco, Peru, is a small town in the northern Andes Mountains with a population of approximately 42,590. Most of the inhabitants live in isolated areas of the mountainous terrain. The area depends heavily on open-pit mining and contains a socioeconomically disadvantaged population. Their average per capita income is $4.73/day or $141.90/month, and the area is considered one of the twenty poorest within Peru. Public health issues abound in terms of accessibility and in terms of environmental and educational needs related to the general well-being of the inhabitants.

In 2013, the program expanded to include visits to tribal groups living along the Amazon River. Under the supervision of physicians, students provided primary medical care, furnished supplies (such as medicines, blankets, and toothbrushes), and conducted health research.

Results

There are three categories of students who participated in these service trips. First, there are students who seem dedicated to serving the underserved as a calling. These students have been on trips similar to the medical service-learning trip we examined. They regularly participate in national meetings related to such service-learning opportunities, and often have a religious or moral sense of dedication. They are described by peers as totally dedicated, admirable, and sacrificing because even when they become ill, they try to participate in the daily activities of seeing patients. These students tend to come back from the service trip and say they want to go again.

Sally (not her real name), a second-year student who participated in a service elective to Peru in 2011, typifies students of this category—which seems to be the majority of the first-year or second-year students who participate. Sally has been to Honduras with Global Medical Brigade and also went to Haiti over spring break. She says her mother modeled Christian principles, and she has become really dedicated to global health. Sally would like to lead these trips and help plan them. She put a lot of effort into the trip, including practice-based learning of making flash cards of medical Spanish and taking practice exams for diseases. After the trip to Peru, she remembers a woman whose husband had died and who had no money for food but had medical bills. Sally expected people to be poorer and less developed than she found them in Huamachuco. She found that the trip was disorganized and that she had to exercise patience, but she felt that she developed in all the core competencies of the medical profession during the trip.

Second, there are students who are curious about the trip because other students have spread the word about its positive effects, such as increase in medical knowledge; opportunities to meet other physicians, thus opening doors for residency; opportunities to serve the underserved; and experience to enrich their résumés. These students tend to say either they will go again or they will never go again. Dan (not his real name), who has traveled all over but never to an underdeveloped country, exemplifies such a person. He felt fortunate to be living in the United States and felt bad for the poor people who live in Peru. He was afraid of doing clinicals, but after the trip reported feeling more confident in his skills. Dan partnered with a first-year resident and learned a lot. He remarked on how warm and welcoming the Peruvians were and mentioned how the local mayor came out with school bands performing as well. Dan plans to continue going on service trips, but feels that his lack of Spanish is a problem. He wants to improve more of his clinical skills. In retrospect, he thinks about how he might change his attitude toward those who look different from him. In his words, "There are thoughts that I have if a patient is not well dressed . . . doesn't have good hygiene. It's hard to not come up with negative thoughts."

Third, there are students who have never been outside the country and want to experience this as a travel opportunity but have a passing interest in helping the underserved. These students are described by others as being late to events, going off to sightsee rather than doing service, and not being dedicated to the cause. These students did not participate in the interview-based study and are only known to us through critiques from their peers. There are just a handful of these types of students in all the years combined.

Literature shows that a student's background, prior knowledge, and a host of other factors affect learning outcomes. While we cannot say with certainty that the categories just described affect different learning outcomes, the degree of learning is affected by motivation. If a student goes off to sightseeing rather than participating in patient care, obviously he or she will attain less of the competencies. Moreover, if a student has never traveled outside the country, he or she may be more motivated by the opportunity to travel than by the opportunity to provide patient care (as seemed to be the case with one interviewee).

Critical Thinking as Reflection on Their Experience

According to Paul and Elder (2008), those who engage in critical thinking "attempt to live rationally, reasonably, empathically." They tend to question what they see, formulate problems, interpret information, and come up with conclusions while "testing them against relevant criteria and standards." Students show evidence of this through emotional empathy and critical judgment of others.

Two themes emerged repeatedly in the data. First, students became aware of how fortunate we are in the United States to have access to care by going to the emergency room even if we do not have insurance. Second, students became emotional. Sometimes they realized that the pain was too much to bear. They turned inward and became aware of their attitudes, and of what they could or could not handle.

For example, Kim spoke about how it was difficult for her to deal with babies who have torn clothes and missing shoes. She decided she would not go into pediatrics because she could not deal with knowing how much children suffer.

Other students spoke about desperate patients who will likely never receive treatment for their severe illnesses because they do not have the means to pay for care. The students remembered the conditions of their patients and spoke of them with feeling, sometimes with tears welling up in their eyes.

For example, Jeff, who has been on these trips multiple times, spoke of "a guy who came in with a bandaged foot that had been infected due to lack of care. The stench was terrible, but we could not do anything for him . . . my heart goes out to him," he said. "It just broke my heart" is a common phrase heard from students.

As students spoke about this they seemed to remember vivid images of encounters that evoked painful emotion. Posttrip, there may be a need to help students process emotions and deal with a sense of hopelessness. A follow-up about such emotions, such as "how do you think this might relate to patients back home?" or "how will you process this experience so that something positive can be gained?," might be good to foster discussion.

Students seemed to have high standards upon which they judged their own and others' behavior—especially physicians who mentor them on the clinical skills. Most students have a sense of moral purpose for what they are doing, so they scrutinized others' behavior based on this standard. Students pointed out physicians who lack bedside manners or had little regard for women's privacy. They also pointed out how they themselves found it difficult to overcome prejudices if a patient behaved a certain way or had poor hygiene habits. There seems to be a heightened awareness of one's own and others' commitment to helping the less fortunate. This was most apparent by the way students described others' commitment. A prime example is students who came back from the 2011 Peru trip. Apparently conflict arose when some media people filmed the trip. There were verbal arguments between students who accused certain students of being less committed to the patients but more focused on gaining attention from the media.

Learning Outcomes Unpacked During and After the Trip

We used the core competencies set forth by the American Osteopathic Association to categorize the students' learning outcomes. We list here the seven core competencies and then explain our observation of student learning outcomes in each category.

1. Medical Knowledge

Students must demonstrate understanding of established and evolving medical knowledge. This includes psychomotor skills as well as basic medical knowledge. Under supervision, students are expected to meet the required knowledge base that is appropriate for their level of training and be able to apply knowledge to clinical problems.

Students have opportunities to learn to diagnose many symptoms. Students commonly learn to perform a pelvic exam, assist in surgery by tying knots, and participate in diagnosing symptoms such as renal failure, ventricular gallop, gastrointestinal (GI) irritation, diastolic hypertension, and vaginal bacteriosis. They also work in pharmacy and become adept at writing prescriptions.

Journals show that students have logged many hours with patients presenting assorted symptoms. The following are examples of comments that show that students had ample opportunity to practice patient care and clinical skills:

> With the help of Gary Willyerd from Michigan, Aashish Dadarwala from New York, and Mary Jo Vopel from Michigan, I learned about and observed patients with the following conditions: parasitic infections, gastrointestinal issues, GERD, anemia, nutritional disorders and malnutrition, joint problems, acute and chronic somatic dysfunction, neurological disorders, neuropathy, obesity, hypertension, diabetes mellitus, metabolic syndrome, heart abnormalities, circulation abnormalities, tachycardia,

bone fractures, bone tumors, respiratory infections, skin infections, urinary tract infections, polyne-phritis, genital.

I performed rotations in Surgery, Dentistry, Psychiatry, Oncology, Emergency and Internal Medi-cine in both Carhuaz and Lima.

I scrubbed-in and was first-assist on a hernia repair surgery. I assisted by retracting as well as completing a suture during closing.

I can now very accurately measure blood pressure with all the practice we got in internal medicine. I learned to properly diagnose chronic allergies based on patient history and orthoscopic exam.

I have become much more confident in filling prescriptions. When a specific drug or dose was not available, I was able to substitute for a different drug of the same class.

2. Patient Care

Students must demonstrate the ability to effectively treat patients by taking a basic clinical exam (obtain a medical history and perform a complete physical exam) and recording their findings.

Here are quotes from students who described their partner's performance or remarked on their own performance in their journal or during their interview:

Stephanie spoke to and comforted a young patient experiencing nightmares due to family trauma.

I have greatly enhanced ability to take a good history. This includes my ability to ask my patients the necessary questions to either support or eliminate a differential. Such was the case when a mother brought in her daughter for grinding her teeth. Knowing the unsanitary conditions of the area, I asked about the daughter's BM which led to a diagnosis of pinworms.

I improved SOAP note writing skills, as I documented each of the patients we saw when shadowing (in Lima with Infectious Disease), to give to my partner so that he could understand the cases following patient interviews.

I learned how to keep information organized and separated so that I may document the information correctly and efficiently. As well as being able to interview a patient while pursuing one diagnosis, I learned to keep other key history or symptom information handy. I also learned helpful ways of patient redirection during a patient history interview in order to remain on task and on time.

The patients were different from English-speaking American patients students were used to back home, so to understand these Spanish-speaking patients, the students really had to listen and take careful note of history and physicals. One journal entry exemplifies what other students have expressed as well:

I remember our first patient. He was a young man with persistent headaches. Fortunately, I am fluent in Spanish so it helped us tremendously in obtaining the best history possible. Throughout the day, I also realized that our patients really had so much history to give. I mean, in addition to their physical-related sign and symptoms history, the other history is their occupation, environment, social and cultural components which were also important in determining their diagnosis.

3. Communication Skills

Under supervision, students must begin to demonstrate interpersonal and communication skills and abilities to team with patients, their patients' families, and professional associates. Although most students are not fluent in Spanish, they learn a lot about communication skills by increasing their observation skills of nonverbal communication. For example:

Due to my lack of Spanish experience, I had to rely on my observation and interpretation of the non-verbal communication of patients. My skills in this area greatly improved during this trip. I am now able to obtain a patient history even in the most convoluted of cases.

A peer review comment commended efforts of another student:

She entered the trip with no Spanish background but gave her best effort using people, dictionaries, and notes to communicate with the patients and was able to communicate with patients to a much better degree by the end of the trip.

Chuck was able to take a solid history of chief complaint without assistance. He came to Peru with no Spanish-speaking ability but took every opportunity to learn terminology and improve his communication with patients. Chuck consistently took the time to be certain he was understood and that he too had the accurate information.

Although I do not speak Spanish, with the help of aids and dictionaries, I always explained to my patients how and when to take their medications. After which I had them repeat the directions back to me. I did not let anyone leave with medications if I felt he/she did not completely understand how and when to take them.

The same student also said:

Since my lack of Spanish-speaking abilities created such a profound language barrier, I greatly utilized the osteopathic power of touch and non-verbal communication with all patients in order to make them as comfortable as possible.

One Spanish-speaking fourth-year student said:

Although my partner did not yet speak any Spanish while we were on the surgery evaluations rotation, I taught him several phrases and how to decipher the potential answers so he could participate in gathering patient histories.

4. Professionalism

Students must demonstrate a commitment to carrying out professional responsibilities, adhering to ethical principles, and being sensitive to a diverse patient population. Students should be able to demonstrate consideration and respect with peers, personnel, and patients—and take responsibility for patient care appropriate for his/her level of training.

Students seemed keenly aware of physicians who modeled good patient care, work ethic, and ability. More often than not, students mentioned outstanding physicians, but there also seemed to be a few physicians who, everyone noted, did not meet expectations (as mentioned by all students interviewed during one particular trip).

Students often commended other students for sacrificing from their own pockets to help a patient:

> Nisha proved to be a very committed, empathetic healthcare provider for her patients. She took her patients' concerns to heart more than most and even purchased a two-month supply of medications for one of her patients with heart disease who could not afford the medications she needed.

A male clerkship student learned about culture while in Peru:

> I developed an understanding of culture regarding food, attire, and lifestyle, and incorporated that knowledge into identifying potential etiologies for clinical problems and prescribing a plan. For example:
>
> - Finding out that a woman's shoulder pain was simply due to her job selling items at the market, where she always carries a basket in one hand and reaches with the other.
> - Prescribed a plan for her to switch arms every day, change her posture, and apply ice to affected area.
>
> I improved heavily in cross-cultural competency within the medical setting, which facilitated implementation of DPR skills and efficient information gathering.

5. Practice-Based Learning

Students must stay motivated to meet clinical, reading, and other learning commitments. They must be prompt, show motivation to carry out assignments, and come prepared. Under supervision, students are expected to demonstrate a commitment to ongoing professional development and to learn independently—which also includes the ability to read and integrate evidence-based medicine into patient care.

Students talked about going the extra mile to learn Spanish, but little was mentioned about looking up information or independently researching diseases or the cultures of Peru or Guatemala. Nisha, for example, created vocabulary lists to help those students with limited Spanish language fluency and held optional meetings for students to come together and practice speaking Spanish. However, these trips eventually added a research component, such that students involved in research conducted evidence-based literature reviews and studied their topic area in order to form hypotheses and submit their studies to the institutional review board for approval.

In addition to clinical knowledge and skills development, students are increasing their research capacity. A faculty member began leading research with students when she discovered, during her visit in 2009, that local open-pit mining practices and the occupational status of the parents may mean that children carry higher than normal lead levels in their blood. Therefore, in 2010, she and a team of students collected and sampled blood levels as part of a research study. Although the levels were not as high as initially suspected, they were found to be in the high range of normal and within the cautionary level range listed by the Centers for Disease Control and Prevention. Therefore, as part of this project, there will be ongoing research about women and children's health. Additionally, her team will be mapping children's growth and development because of suspicions that many children are malnourished. Presently, there is no known record of children's development in this region. By sampling heights, weights, and head, arm, and waist circumferences, the team predicts it will find relatively developmentally delayed children in Huamachuco, on of Peru's rural areas.

6. Systems-Based Practice

Students must begin to demonstrate an awareness of and responsiveness to the larger context and the ability to effectively call on system resources.

After seeing the living conditions of their patients, students often said that they had been taking things for granted back home. These factors were heightened as they conducted research and found environmental factors detrimental to patient health. Students compared and contrasted their home culture with the host culture—often leading them to show compassion toward the underserved. People in these developing countries tend to show more gratitude than those who are back home, several students said: They hug and kiss us in appreciation of the few things we did.

> The poor in this country do not get medical care because they lack access to transportation; and although healthcare is free, medication is not covered, so even if the patient sees a doctor, they cannot receive palliative care.

> [I am] deeply moved by the extent to which people in Peru flat out lack resources that we take for granted in the US. A good example is the group of patients at Loayza and the special cases that Dr. Herford was able to help in Lima. [I] observed the poverty and lack of resources that people live with daily. In doing so, I gained a deepened appreciation for what I have in America to help treat patients.

In addition to remarking about resource differences, students felt that they were, for the most part, working well as a team. One student described it as organized chaos:

> It seemed a wonderfully chaotic organized system. Everybody moving rapidly from room to room, everybody working together, and soon enough things were getting organized, and everybody seemed to double check everything. We all came together in about two hours or so, I think it was a great start for the week to come.

A male clerkship student seemed to have developed a sense of teamwork when he commented:

> I have become extremely comfortable asking both attending physicians and colleagues for help, second opinions as well as being able to admit when I did not know the answer to a clinical problem.

7. Osteopathic Principles and Practice

The student demonstrates the application of osteopathic principles, and appropriately includes osteopathic treatment in patient evaluation and management, including neuromusculoskeletal findings.

A fourth-year clerkship student described the following:

> I performed soft tissue OMT on the cervical paravertebral muscles of a patient presenting with a tension headache and depression. Used stretching and distraction techniques on the patient's occipital region to release tension. Also performed medical massage therapy on patient's face and head for tension release. Patient claimed that headache went away.

Another male student said, "I applied muscle-energy and myofascial techniques to treat back-muscle tonicity and provide some immediate relief to patient." It is important to note, in terms of the pre- and posttrip surveys and exams, that we were not able to gather valid data. Upon return from the trips, students seldom wished to reenter the learning management system to follow through on the posttest. If they did, it did not seem like they tried seriously to enter valid data. There were too few numbers of possibly valid data worthwhile to calculate.

Transformative Learning Signs

If transformative learning is defined by one's ability to identify problems in one's values and beliefs and critically examine them against newly gained information and experiences (Mezirow, 2000), then three types of transformative learning that seem salient and common among the groups occurred. First is reflection on one's response to the patient and then concluding with one's own shortcoming. This is often in response to a patient who elicited an emotion one could not handle well.

A clerkship student who took a leadership role in planning the trip observed: "I examined a child with autism and severe bruxism. I really valued this experience, as I learned that I am not cut out for working with special-needs children." Several other students questioned how they react to patients who have less income or poor hygiene.

Second, students seem to think about commitment to the patient population in idealistic ways. At one point the Rotary Club allowed wealthier, Rotary-affiliated people to be brought in for treatment. Students said this was not right and that they were there to help the poor people and not those who already have the means to find health care. Such reflective thinking shows that students believe their initial motivation for attending these trips was purely for helping the poor. When people come dressed better than expected, students learn that their idealism need to become transformed to reality—that in the end, delivering care involves care for all types of people.

Third, through the process of picking apart the behaviors of those who are committed and those not committed, beliefs are solidified in either direction. Students therefore choose to go again; a few choose never to participate again. One student said it was too much of a time commitment and too much work. Some students faced the reality that their commitment was not as strong as initially believed and learned transformatively that their true selves prefer the comforts of home.

Critical Incidents About This Experience

During the interviews, it was clear that depending upon the amount of prior knowledge that students had before the trip, their perspective transformation differed remarkably. For example, one student described the bus ride up the edge of the mountain as if it were a death ordeal. After listening to his description, I (Dokter) thought it was a very old, tattered bus. Another student also described the bus ride as harrowing, but the bus was not so bad. The last interview was with a student who had been on service mission trips to developing countries since high school—she said it was a very nice, luxury bus.

The same can be said about student complaints that nothing was organized. Student after student remarked that they had to wait and wait and that no one knew when anything was going to happen. The last student said, "Oh, it's the culture . . . that's how they are with time. They have a different sense of time, they don't keep to a schedule; life seems to be more important than worrying about time. Things eventually all work out. Other students don't understand that it's a cultural thing!"

Common Transformative Change Observed in Students

Longitudinal patterns of change have to do with student appreciation for all that we have in the United States. Students begin to question the differences between the haves and have-nots. Students also attend more trips, creating a pattern of attending two or three such trips. For example, a leader will rise out of the group and will continue to go on medical service trips, each time taking on more responsibility.

In terms of our original question about whether such trips tend to produce future primary care physicians, most attendees were already committed to primary care initially. Those who were not tended to stay with their chosen area of specialization. Indeed, out of thirty-five interviewees, only one said he was undecided before the medical service trip, but after the trip, he thought he would indeed go into primary care.

Conclusion

Most study-abroad programs are coordinated and led by faculty members. Over the years, our program has evolved to include student leadership and coordination. Not only do students plan and coordinate the trip, they also raise thousands of dollars for medical aid and participate in research. They have learned team, lifelong learning, leadership, and fundraising skills. Through research about the community they service, they have learned about systems-based practice and public health. The latter are skills and outcome elements that few study-abroad or medical missions trips tend to produce.

Through the process of evaluating, we found that we were engaged in action research (Lewin,

1946). That is, our evaluation led us to improve the program progressively as we continued to research. We want to share that other schools can benefit from evaluating programs because their evaluation will perpetuate improvement of the program.

Throughout the years, our program has evolved to include all of the core competencies discussed earlier partly because we set out to evaluate the program based on those core competencies. The first year we added research, and then we added osteopathic manipulation, followed thereafter by visits to hospitals and medical schools to learn about the host country's medical system. As our program broadened, media attention and sponsorship grew. Our students gained national attention for their research results.

We conclude that when students see the contrast in lives between the rural poor overseas and the lives we lead here in the United States, the majority of participants have a transformative experience in which their emotional self is touched by their patient care experiences.

APPENDIX 1. Medical student perceptions of short-term medical service study-abroad experiences

Interview Protocol

BEFORE STUDY ABROAD: IDENTITY STATUS INTERVIEW

1. Tell me a little about your overseas experiences:
   a. What kinds of international experiences have you had before this planned trip?
      i. Travel to other countries?
      ii. Study of a foreign language?
      iii. Roommates with students from other countries?
      iv. Have members of your immediate family traveled to or lived in different countries? Who?
5. What interested you in or attracted you to this experience?
6. What are some of your expectations and goals you have for this study abroad experience?
   a. What do you hope to learn from this experience?
   b. How do you see this experience relating to your goals for graduate education? Your career goals?
   c. What sorts of activities or experiences do you hope to have while in _____?
7. What about this experience concerns you at the moment?
   a. What are some of your fears and anxieties for this medical service program?
8. At this point in time, how do you see yourself relative to people who live in _____?
   a. In what ways are you similar?
   b. In what ways are you different?

CONCLUSION OF INTERVIEW

9. Is there anything else about your upcoming experience that you would like to tell me that I haven't asked you about?
10. Thank you for your time and agreeing to talk with me.

APPENDIX 2. Medical student perceptions of short-term medical service study-abroad experiences

Interview Protocol

AFTER STUDY ABROAD

1. Can you describe for me your overall impressions of the experiences that you had in _____?
   a. What surprised you about your experiences in _____?
   b. What stands out for you in these various experiences? What makes it stand out?
   c. Before going you described some of your hopes, goals, and expectations for the trip [Review these with the interviewee].
      i. What aspects of these hopes, goals, and expectations were realized by your experiences?
      ii. What aspects of these hopes, goals, and expectations were not realized by your experiences? What was it about the experience that you did not realize these goals or hopes?
3. Can you describe some of the visits or activities in which you engaged while you were there?
   a. What medical sites did you visit?
      i. Who was with you on these visits?
      ii. What do you remember about these practices sites?
   b. What other sites in _____ did you visit besides the practice sites?
      i. Briefly describe what you felt or thought while visiting these other sites.
   c. How much time did you spend with the _____n patients and/or staff while you were there—formally or informally?
      i. What was the nature of your interactions and relationships with the _____n patients, physicians and staff, or some of the _____n hosts?
2. Can you describe a few incidents during your visit that seem particularly meaningful or important to you? [These could be experiences that you felt were either positive or negative for you.]
   a. Describe the incident for me.
      i. What was the context?
      ii. Who were you with?
      iii. What was happening?
      iv. What were you thinking or feeling while in that particular experience?
   b. What made that particular experience memorable or particularly significant for you? [Encourage them to be as specific as they can.]
5. What would you describe as the key or major outcomes of this experience for you?
   a. What have you taken from this trip that will make a difference or change in your personal or professional life?
   b. What did you learn most about?

      i. What aspects of the experience do you think contributed to that learning?

    c. What would you have liked to learn more about?

    d. In what ways would you like to see the experience be different?

      i. What would you like to do differently?

2. What did you learn about yourself through this experience?

    a. What about the experience has influenced you to see things differently?

    b. In what ways did you come to see yourself differently?

      i. If you see yourself differently, what aspects of the medical service experience do you attribute to these changes?

    c. What interactions did you have during your week(s) abroad that helped you understand or think more deeply about _____n or American culture?

      i. What effect did this interaction had on how you view yourself?

2. Is there anything else about your experience that I have not asked you about that you would like to tell me about?

3. Thank you for your time and agreeing to talk with me about your experiences in this short-term medical service experience.

ACKNOWLEDGMENTS

We acknowledge Resa Nassiri, Norma Baptista, and Craig Reed for their effort in helping to make this study successful.

REFERENCES

Ackerman, L. K. (2010). The ethics of short-term international health electives in developing countries. *Annals of Behavioral Science and Medical Education, 16*(2), 40–43.

Bateman, C., Baker, T., Hoornenborg, E., & Ericsson, U. (2001). Bringing global issues to medical teaching. *The Lancet, 358*(9292), 1539–1542.

Battat, R., Seidman, G., Chadi, N., Chanda, M., Nehme, J., Hulme, J., & Brewer, T. (2010). Global health competencies and approaches in medical education: A literature review. *BMC Medical Education, 10*(1), 94.

Crump, J. J. (2008). Ethical considerations for short-term experiences by trainees in global health. *Journal of American Medical Association, 300*(12), 1456–1458.

Ehrlich, T. (Ed). (2000). *Civic responsibility and higher education.* Westport, CT: Oryx Press.

Engle L., & Engle, J. (2003). Study abroad levels: Towards a classification of program types. *Frontiers: The Interdisciplinary Journal of Study Abroad, 9,* 1–20.

Federico, S., Zachar, P., Oravec, C., Mandler, T., Goldson, E., Brown, J. (2006). A successful international child health elective. *Archives of Pediatric Adolescent Medicine, 160,* 191–196.

Grudzen, C. R., & Legome, E. (2007). Loss of international medical experiences: Knowledge, attitudes and skills at risk. *BMC Medical Education, 7*(1), 47. 10.1186/1472-6920-7-47.

Gupta, A., Wells, C., Horwitz, R., Bia, F., & Barry M. (1999). The international health program: The fifteen-year experience with Yale University's Internal Medicine Residency Program. *American Journal of*

Tropical Medicine, 61(6), 1019–1023.

Houpt, E., Pearson, R., & Hall, T. (2007). Three domains of competency in global health education: Recommendations for all medical students. *Academic Medicine, 82,* 222–225. 10.1097/ACM.0b013e3180305c10.

Lewin, K. (1946). Action research and minority problems. *Journal of Social Issues, 2*(4), 34–46.

McAllister, L., Whiteford, G., Whiteford, G., Hill, B., Thomas, N., & Fitzgerald, M. (2006). Reflection in intercultural learning: examining the international experience through a critical incident approach. *Reflective Practice, 7*(3), 367–381.

McKinley, D., Williams, S., Norcini, J., & Anderson, B. (2008). RIME: Proceedings of the Forty-Seventh Annual Conference November 2–November 5, 2008. *Academic Medicine, 83*(10) Supplement: S53–S57.

Mezirow, J. (1990). Toward transformative learning and emancipatory education. In J. Mezirow (Ed.), *Fostering critical reflection in adulthood: A guide to transformative and emancipatory learning* (pp. 354–375). San Francisco: Jossey-Bass.

Mezirow, J. (1991). *Transformative dimensions of adult learning.* San Francisco: Jossey-Bass.

Mezirow, J. (2000). *Learning as transformation: Critical perspectives on a theory in progress.* San Francisco: Jossey-Bass.

Mosepele, M., Lyon, S., & Dine, J. (2010). Commentary: Mutually beneficial global health electives. *Virtual Mentor, American Medical Association Journal of Ethics, 12*(3), 159–166.

Paul, R., & Elder, L. (2008) *The miniature guide to critical thinking concepts and tools.* The Critical Thinking Community. Retrieved from http://www.criticalthinking.org/pages/defining-critical-thinking/766.

Philpott, J. F., Houghton, K., & Luke, A. (2010). Physical activity recommendations for children with specific chronic health conditions. *Clinical Journal of Sports Medicine, 3,* 167–172.

Ramsey, A. H., Haq, C., Gjerde, C. L., & Rothenberg, D. (2004). Career influence of an international health experience during medical school. *Family Medicine, 36,* 412–416.

Schön, D. (1983). *The reflective practitioner. How professionals think in action.* London: Temple Smith.

Sigelman, C. (1999). *Life-span human development,* 3rd edition. Independence, KY: Brooks/Cole.

Smith, J. K., & Weaver, D. B. (2006). Capturing medical students' idealism. *Annals of Family Medicine, 4*(suppl. 1), S32–37.

Steiner, B. D., Carlough, M., Dent, G., Peate, R., & Morgan, D. R. (2010). International crises and global health electives: Lessons for faculty and institutions. *Academic Medicine, 85*(10), 1560–1563.

Thompson, M. J., Huntington, M. K., Hunt, D. D., Pinsky, L. E., & Brodie, J. J. (2003). Educational effects of international health electives on U.S. and Canadian medical students and residents: A literature review. *Academic Medicine, 78,* 342–347.

Wasson, L. T. (2006). Do international experiences develop cultural sensitivity and desire for multicultural practice among medical students and residents? *Virtual Mentor, American Medical Association Journal of Ethics, 8,* 826–830.

CHAPTER 6

Leadership in Medicine for the Underserved: Making It Real

Rae Schnuth and Cheryl Celestin

> Of all the forms of inequality, injustice in health-
> care is the most shocking and inhumane.
> —Dr. Martin Luther King Jr.

The need for competent and culturally sensitive physicians to serve diverse populations in underserved communities has been well documented and is becoming more critical as the demographics of the United States change and the practice of medicine becomes more global (Bazargan, Lindstrom, Dakak, Ani, Wolf, & Edelstein, 2006; Goldstein & Bearman, 2011). It is the responsibility of medical schools to prepare future physicians to meet the challenges of an increasingly diverse patient population, with dominant emphasis on active engagement with societal constructs that contribute to the health of communities. To operationalize the skills, attitudes, and behaviors necessary to impact those who are marginalized, medical students must effectively collaborate with their peers, as well as engaging with community members. The literature has suggested that community-based experiences can increase the likelihood medical students will develop positive and enduring attitudes about their professional responsibilities in the communities where they practice (Turner & Farquhar, 2008).

To encourage medical schools to enhance their community engagement activities, the Liaison Committee on Medical Education (LCME), the accrediting agency of MD degree programs in the United States and Canada, has developed standards directing organizational and curricular structure. It specifies that an institution that offers a medical education program should make available sufficient opportunities for medical students to participate in service-learning activities and should encourage and support medical student participation. The national Community Campus Partnership for Health (CCPH) group defines service learning as a structured learning experience that combines community service with preparation and reflection. Medical students engaged in service-learning provide community service in response to community-identified concerns and learn about the context in which service is provided, the connection between their service and their academic coursework, and their roles as citizens and professionals. (CCPH, 1998, n.p.)

To accomplish the integration of service learning, it is recommended that medical schools develop collaborations with relevant communities or partnerships. In addition, the LCME stresses the necessity for medical schools to develop programs or partnerships aimed at broadening diversity among qualified applicants for medical school admission.

Consistent with prior studies, the Health Resources and Services Administration, an agency of the U.S. Department of Health and Human services, has projected that the demand for primary care physicians will grow more rapidly than the physician supply, resulting in a projected shortage of approximately 20,400 full-time equivalent (FTE) physicians by 2020. The decline in primary care physician availability is anticipated to accelerate due to decreased production and accelerated attrition of primary care physicians nationwide. While this decline is multifactorial, it cannot be minimized in the responsibility held by medical schools to meet the demand for quality health care (U.S. Department of Health and Human Services, 2013). According to the Robert Wood Johnson Foundation (Goodell, Dower, & O'Neil, 2011), the aging of American society, social issues, and health care insurance laws will increase the demand for primary care physicians by 20 percent in the coming years. One major reason for the shortage of primary care physicians is that medical students opt to pursue specialized careers, a decision driven by indebtedness, personal choice, and the structure of health care. In fact, one study of thousands of medical students showed that the appeal of primary care in internal medicine declined by about 25 percent from 1990 to 2007 (Schwartz, Durning, Linzer, & Hauer, 2011). Recent studies suggest that medical students change their preference of specialty depending on a variety of factors, including demographics, medical school experience, the health care environment, identity development, and the choice process (Bennett & Phillips, 2010; Schnuth, Vasilenko, Mavis, & Marshall, 2003).

More than twenty million people in the United States live in areas that have a shortage of physicians available to meet their basic health care needs. This lack of access to quality health care for many people, particularly those living in rural and urban underserved communities, is a serious health care problem. Health care delivery in rural and urban communities poses many unique challenges, and students must be aware of these challenges when studying and practicing medicine. In response to the physician shortage, medical schools have adopted a selective medical school admission policy to enhance a primary care choice in underserved communities. Although some students initially recruited do eventually practice in underserved communities, many do not. While medical schools recruit physicians in training for underserved areas, most do not have a curriculum that supports this mission. Unfortunately, medical students are discouraged in both subtle and overt ways from entering the primary care specialties that serve underserved communities (Young, 1990).

In the past, health care delivery systems have failed to recognize and address the beliefs and lifestyles of vulnerable rural and urban communities that are underserved. If their unique perspectives are overlooked in health care delivery, the result will be health care programs that are inaccessible or unacceptable to rural and urban communities (Coulehan & Williams, 2001). By understanding the general differences in which these communities perceive health, medical students can maximize the delivery of adequate and efficient care to people of rural and urban underserved communities. Through organized activities of community engagement with reflective emphasis, students may develop a set of skills, attitudes, and behaviors that encourage them to embark on successful and rewarding careers in caring for the underserved (Turner & Farquhar, 2008).

In order for community engagement to be thoroughly incorporated in a medical school culture, it must be embedded in components of the college structure, including the following: the statement of mission and program outcomes; appointment, tenure, and promotion guidelines; research and community-engaged scholarship; recognition of faculty and/or students for engagement; admission criteria; and sources of funding (Goldstein & Bearman, 2011).

To address this concern, the Michigan State University (MSU) College of Human Medicine (CHM) established the Leadership in Medicine for the Underserved (LMU) certificate program in 2004 to prepare a cohort of physicians who possess, in addition to core competencies for the medical degree, a special set of knowledge, skills, and attitudes to address the needs of medically underserved and vulnerable populations of the United States and abroad. This program is rooted in the mission statement of the college and university, and academic, administrative, and faculty support demonstrate commitment to its success. By emphasizing the responsibility of medical education to develop physicians who will care for the whole of society, CHM developed this experiential learning program, which focuses on providing care for underserved populations, working to improve health care delivery for these patients, understanding the public health system, learning how to advocate for change, and contributing to the community through service and research. An overarching theme of the curriculum is to understand how poverty, social justice, and health status impact the populations served and the choices physicians make in providing care to meet these needs. Whether the patient is an uninsured mother in Flint, Michigan, or in Las Delicias, El Salvador, the CHM asserts that a physician needs to be able to examine and understand how the determinants of health and the health care system interact, and how health status is impacted by poverty, access to care, neighborhood conditions, safety, and income inequality, and the role of advocacy for social justice to eliminate health disparities and bring about more equity.

According to Ho, Chen, and Hirsh (2012), the purpose of the LMU program curriculum is to:

1. Provide experiences to medical students to help them care for underserved/vulnerable populations with sensitivity and expertise, while helping communities address public health needs affecting the level of wellness of individuals and groups.
2. Appreciate the impact of direct care delivery, epidemiologic research, social justice, and health education on health status, as well as health policy implications.
3. Encourage medical students to select career choices in the area of primary care.

Most importantly, the LMU program attempts to address the real issues of underserved care by providing students with unifying experiences of human engagement as they develop their commitment to this population (Ho, Chen, & Hirsh, 2012). By immersing students in communities with cultures unfamiliar to them during a two-year commitment, our intention is to engage students in developing empathy for the human condition and suffering to increase sensitivity and skill in working with people from diverse cultures in the United States and abroad. Such transformative experiences of immersion may contribute to the students identifying the importance of engagement and connectedness with patients as critical attributes when selecting disciplines and residency programs for their future careers. Cultural competency is woven into the curriculum, and strengthening culturally sensitive behaviors through active engagement is paramount. Consideration of the significance of social context as a determinant of health, and connecting to the suffering of individuals in their communities, influence the commitment of students to choose to serve underserved populations.

Applying the Berquist and Milano adaptation of Engle and Engle's (2003) framework (see chapter 2) to our program development provides a structure of program design that blends the purposes of the program and incorporates components that drive efficacy of service work and structured cultural interaction, while utilizing reflection as a means of student and faculty growth. These components consistently promote community perspective and involvement in the community relationship/partnership by informing faculty members in developing and evaluating program design choices. The LMU program strongly emphasizes sustainability in selecting study-abroad sites as well as local sites when developing programming and allocating resources. Students are encouraged to routinely evaluate sustainability of programming in terms of meeting the needs of the present population, without compromising the ability of future generations to meet their own needs. The purpose of emphasizing sustainability is to foster trust between the program and the community so ongoing growth and development through intervention can be facilitated. We prize cultivating relationships and ongoing collaboration in providing service and intervention that inform student learning. It is critical that the program benefits the community as well as the students. Rather than a one-shot and short-term experience mostly for the benefit of students, this ongoing and reciprocal collaboration drives the majority of programming for LMU. LMU program leaders believe that by modeling the importance of sustainability as the students see the program unfold, they will be less likely to contribute to the "fly in, fly out" model of Western medical mission work frequently embraced by those desiring to share skills; however, that does little to change the circumstances contributing to targeted health concerns.

Selection

The selection of a cohort of students begins with the college admissions process, as students apply to medical school and determine their interest in learning about and caring for the underserved. Although we have experimented with various admissions points to the LMU program across the first two years of medical school, our current practice is to admit students at matriculation so that they may target experiences during the preclinical years for opportunities to learn from underserved and vulnerable populations. In addition, this timing provides the college with a means to recruit students with the promise of admittance to this two-year clinical experience certificate program.

At the time of application to medical school, students are informed about the LMU program through written materials such as brochures and websites. Potential candidates are advised that completing the program meets the college requirement for service-learning hours; it also prepares them for future service to various underserved populations and vulnerable groups. It is emphasized that in addition to meeting the regular medical education requirements for the medical degree, students are required to participate in various components comprising the LMU curriculum and that failure to complete components will result in lack of certificate completion. Those who remain interested in the program after this review complete an application comprised of the following four essay questions that are submitted as part of their secondary application to the college:

1. Why are you interested in the Leadership in Medicine for the Underserved Program? Be specific.
2. How have your experiences prepared you for the challenges of a medical practice in an underserved area?
3. A requirement of this program is that the student will have achieved low intermediate Spanish proficiency by the time they reach their third year of medical school. Explain your current Spanish proficiency and/or plan for meeting this requirement.
4. What are the advantages of using a public health approach to maximize individual and population health status?

These essays as well as the American Medical College Application Service (AMCAS) application are reviewed by the LMU Selection Committee, and students are ranked according to specified criteria for acceptance into the program. Personal interviews may be used as part of the selection process, and students must evidence a low intermediate level of Spanish by the time they begin the program in their third year to remain competitive. An alternate list is created as a means of ensuring a full complement to the program. Students are notified of their acceptance by mail and then continue with the process of accepting their admittance to the college as well as to the LMU program.

Program Design for Urban, Rural, and International Engagement

Once students enter the LMU program they focus on the following learning objectives throughout the third and fourth years of medical school:

- identify and understand the relationship between health conditions and poverty;
- know the conditions that illustrate disparities in health status and health care;
- recognize barriers to access for health care;
- work effectively with immigrants and refugees in the community;
- communicate successfully with individuals of all social classes, educational levels, and cultural backgrounds;
- define primary, secondary, and tertiary prevention and how each relates to socioeconomic factors in health care outcomes;

- collaborate with other professionals (e.g., social workers, dieticians, public health professionals) to promote the welfare of people in underserved settings or who are members of vulnerable groups.

These objectives are addressed by means of three main components of the LMU program, occurring in the third and fourth years of the medical school curriculum:

1. Urban—inpatient and ambulatory care in shortage designated facilities for pediatrics, internal medicine, surgery, family medicine psychiatry, and obstetrics/gynecology (OB/GYN) clerkships. The students participate in residents' clinics comprised of a high percentage of underserved/vulnerable patients as well as other shortage-designated clinical sites.
2. Rural—During the family medicine clerkship students are assigned with family medicine preceptors for three weeks of the eight-week rotation in medically underserved rural areas (this component has been developed subsequently into its own certificate program in the college).
3. International—an organized/faculty supervised experience in the third and fourth years of the curriculum (with recent curricular redesign, these two electives are taken in the fourth year) in a developing country for experience in clinical activities, public health programming and evaluation, and cultural immersion.

In addition to creating clinical experiences in the required rotations in the urban, rural, and international arenas, the LMU program is woven around the required medical school curriculum in various ways. Strategies involving student participation include the following: orientation to the program; community exploration geographically and socioculturally via an audio tour completed in groups of students highlighting community sectors, resources, neighborhoods, health care settings, and cultural and social factors influencing the community; community agency linkages completed by site visits and/or panel discussions; coordination of a community resources website; contribution to a community medical education newsletter; Spanish for conversation and providing basic health care; reflective activities including journaling and small-group discussions; research projects; speaker and didactic sessions; and development and implementation of public health/health education projects based on community assessment. Primary care mentorship and curricular experiences with respect to social issues, community engagement, cultural skills, medical humanities (including ethics of local and international program development), and alternative/complementary medicine are emphasized to enhance the likelihood of students developing a primary care interest.

Didactics and small-group learning sessions are utilized in the first half of the program to provide a foundation from which the students will build as they work within the community, as well as to facilitate group building and process among the students and faculty. Examples of sessions building community awareness and leadership skills include but are not limited to the following areas for the most recent students:

- Exploration of Flint community/public health statistics and orientation to other assessment data within the community for comparative analyses between communities within the state, nationally, and internationally.
- Review of federal, state, and local government agencies responsible for public health findings and statistics (U.S. Department of Health and Human Services, Michigan Department of Human Services, Michigan County Departments of Community Health).
- Discussion of poverty and its associated sequelae. In one experience, students are provided with local assistance criteria and then are divided into family groups. Based on the assistance monies available to their unit, they must travel with local transportation to a location (convenience store, grocery, gas station, market) to buy groceries to feed the unit for the day, being mindful of cost and nutrition; they must also purchase a prescription for a common antibiotic. Students then debrief about their experience in accessing nutritional foods, working within a specified monetary limit, and managing their family unit within the time and transportation system involved, reflecting on challenges and feelings related to the experience. We have partnered with our local MSU Extension office to provide a meal using available ingredients within a calculated assistance budget that were both nutritional and appealing.
- Incorporate community assessment for a selected community, wherein students develop a survey to elicit client and staff perspectives on needed services related to health. Students then conduct the surveys, collect and analyze data, develop and implement programming, and evaluate the programming. Examples of programming have included information and presentations on healthy lifestyles, managing hypertension, what is diabetes, healthy eating, first aid, hygiene in challenging situations, resources available in the community for health care, general safety practices, sex education, physical exam screenings for sports participation, blood pressure screenings, and glucose testing.
- Participate in group leadership activities such as conflict resolution, group dynamics, critical thinking in decision making, and organizational management.
- Organize equipment/supplies for the international clinical experience, where students solicit donations and work with international partners to determine supplies for sustainable activities at the selected sites. This involves students researching common problems of the international sites, systematically networking with donors, procuring supplies and equipment, communicating with ministries of health for securing admittance of supplies through Customs, developing manifests for transport, delivering supplies and equipment to the sites, and distributing the supplies.

In addition to these structured experiential and didactic activities, which are accomplished from 12 p.m. to 3 p.m. on Wednesday afternoons through the third year, students are also required to complete four hours of volunteer service activity in the community for a total of eighty-eight hours across the third and fourth years. This is self-directed learning based on students' specific interests and may be accomplished with individuals exploring agencies or based on long-term relationships developed in the community. Examples of agencies and activities are listed below.

Students log their activities electronically into a database that contributes to a community re-sources document available to local practitioners for referral purposes and to future students for site selection, as follows:

- homeless services: soup kitchen, YWCA domestic violence shelter, Carriage Town Homeless Shelter
- health care centers: Planned Parenthood, free health clinics, refugee health center, Wellness AIDS, Odyssey House (substance abuse)
- community services: community cleanups, Reach Out and Read, faith-based screening programs, city planning commission, anti-smoking campaigns, low-income child sports physicals, Salem Lutheran Church Bottled Water Distribution Site, CASA, Boys and Girls Club of Greater Flint
- professional organizations: Flint Pediatric Public Health Initiative, Safe Space (MSU CHM organization), Genesee County Medical Society

During the second half of the third year, students lead the Wednesday afternoon sessions to ad-dress their group and individual interests in the community, and continue with the programming initiated in the first half of the year. These sessions are conducted based on student decision making as to the best strategy for learning. Strategies include using speakers, visiting community sites, online programming, journal club format, and small-group discussions. Examples of areas developed by students are listed in table 1.

International Engagement Through Immersion

During the fourth year of medical school, students in the LMU program complete two electives in caring for the underserved. The majority choose to participate in a structured learning envi-ronment in an international setting. We have partnered with various organizations in the past not only to structure the direct experiences but also to provide in-country support. Our recent partner is the Foundation for the Medical Relief of Children (FIMRC) based in Philadelphia, PA. It has clinics located globally to provide health care services for the underserved in developing countries using a sustainability model that allows us continuity to build from our past efforts each year that we return with the LMU students.

The intent of these two electives that occur in January/February of the fourth year is to im-merse LMU medical students in diverse and unfamiliar cultures in order to broaden their cultural perspectives and advance their ability to communicate effectively with the increasingly diverse patient populations with whom they will work in the United States and abroad. Almost all health care professionals now treat patients whose cultural, religious, and political backgrounds are dif-ferent from their own. To provide effective care, it is essential that they understand the differences in health care beliefs, practices, and expectations. In addition to preparing students for experi-ences overseas, these international health courses serve as a valuable means of transferring skills learned in the previous year to a new setting. Areas of focus include the study of community and public health in a developing country, primary care management, health care for the underserved,

Table 1. Medical Student-Directed Sessions

TOPIC	LEARNING STRATEGY
Lesbian, gay, bisexual, and transgendered groups and their health needs	Preclass readings, class discussion, case studies
Homelessness	Site visits, health education program presentation
Maternal and infant health	Participate in water crisis health education programs in community and schools
Needle exchange programs	Site visit and participation in exchange program
Community planning meetings	Attend community and city planning for revitalization
Environmental hazards	Attend local and regional meetings discussing water crisis
Food deserts	Work with public health researcher using qualitative and spatial analysis to address disparities in social determinants of health
Violence in the community	Experiential group activity, discussion with law enforcement and violence prevention/protection homes
Spanish to engage groups	Migrant health care, Latino populations in the medical setting, visit to migrant center

epidemiology, and infectious and tropical diseases. As students learn about and participate in prevention and other intervention strategies abroad, they will be able to transfer this learning back to the United States in a variety of ways (e.g., containing the spread of dangerous infectious diseases, incorporating effectiveness of strategies employed in national health programs, culturally sensitive practice, and appreciation for alternative/complementary medical/health practices and their outcomes). International study experiences allow students to diagnose and treat diseases that are rare in the United States but recently on the rise (e.g., malaria, dengue, cholera, Zika, and tuberculosis). Also, United States students may gain familiarity with diagnosing and treating diseases that have progressed to advanced stages not often seen in the United States.

Working in developing countries with limited resources can provide important lessons for working in similar situations in the United States, although the problem in the United States is more likely related to resource allocation, rather than lack of resources. Physicians may be able to utilize similar strategies in these situations using minimal resources to expand health care coverage to as many people as possible. Learning to work in environments with limited access to diagnostic and therapeutic resources calls for greater reliance on students' primary clinical skills and ingenuity regarding treatment options. Students are prepared with enhanced and more efficient strategies for medical practice upon return to the United States.

Prior to departure for the international setting, students have one week of orientation that complements ongoing lectures, readings, and activities of the past year related to this experience. Areas addressed in orientation include, but are not limited to, the following: ethics of international development; safety and travel abroad; syllabi for the two elective courses; specific country readings; and discussion regarding politics, health care delivery, safety, and cultural comparisons in and between countries. For the international component, students are responsible for the complete travel cost and work through the MSU Office of Study Abroad. Students fly to their designated sites, where they are met by staff members from the sponsoring foundation and taken to host families/living sites where they reside for the next seven weeks, comprising the two elective courses. Students are under the direct supervision of the FIMRC foundation faculty and staff members, as well as at least one MSU CHM faculty member who oversees the students' experience in the international setting. Since students are sent to multiple countries based on the total number participating, current activities of the host site, preparation and interest of the student, and faculty resources, priority setting is necessary months in advance of the trip to ensure adequate collaboration statewide and in-country. In addition to participation in primary care clinics and public health efforts, students share in didactic and small-group sessions on a weekly basis, and contribute in reflective activities to maximize the learning within this environment. A portfolio is used to collect such reflections for processing with faculty members and other students in forums that include coursework back in Michigan. In addition, students may select to share elements of their learning at national and international health meetings.

One of the experiences revered by the students is the opportunity to work with community health workers. Students greatly appreciate the ongoing relationship that the workers have within the community. The impact that they observe of this role in the delivery of health care and the ease with which the workers embrace the students and provide an opening into the community dynamics form a seminal learning event for the students. Although at home they have understood the importance of co-opting local community leaders in strategies to improve health within a community, the experience of observing the dynamics as community health workers engage with the locals and leaders proves to be transformative for the students. The pictures in figure 1 are of students in Africa and Nicaragua.

The students implement faculty-approved public health/health education project(s) during their international experience. These projects may have been initiated while stateside through ongoing communications with the international site and/or may be the result of onsite awareness of areas requiring intervention. As an example of a preplanned effort, students were asked to develop a program on first aid for a rural Nicaraguan community due to the distance required to reach health care management. Students developed the curriculum and lesson plans, created audiovisual aids using posters and digital media, and constructed a mannequin using empty two-liter bottles for lungs and other locally available materials (duct tape, plastic pipes, etc.) to simulate cardiopulmonary resuscitation (CPR) equipment, so that participants could experience the action of compressions and respirations.

Students then conducted multiweek sessions with the designated community responders and were evaluated, and where necessary they remediated skills, culminating in a graduation and public acknowledgment of their abilities. An example of an emergent health project occurred during an outbreak of dengue fever while students were in-country. Students who were associated with a clinic became part of a governmental outreach to notify, educate, and prevent the spread of the disease. After preparing their materials and having the water treatment in hand, students were transported as far as possible by ox cart into the mountains and walked from house to house (approximately thirteen miles) spreading the word and engaging with the people. Students identified additional potential cases, provided education to the families, and treated standing water. Students had the opportunity to participate in and evaluate their public health/health education projects and prepare recommendation for project follow-up.

Students have ample opportunity to compare the health system (private, governmental, mission) and delivery settings within the developing country and understand the impact of

FIGURES 1A and B. Students in-country engaging with local community.

cultural factors, politics, and economic conditions on the health of the people. Students work in the outpatient setting maximizing public health strategies, and in limited inpatient settings to gain a stronger appreciation of similarities and differences in health systems and disease management. An opportunity to work with indigenous populations may comprise part of the clinical component. An example of the importance of student exposure to systems different from the United States frequently occurs approximately halfway through the experience. After being involved in community campaigns and experiencing delivery of care in local and regional community clinics, as well as at the FIMRC clinic, students begin to realize that there is much to be learned from countryside delivery of health care under government organization, which is reflected in a question common to each student group upon seeing the effectiveness of this kind of public health delivery: "Why don't we do this at home?" This recognition allows a different kind of exploration of responses to fix health care in the United States than is sometimes possible.

Students experience mixed feelings as they contemplate returning to the United States. Most are eager to return home, yet having bonded with people in their new setting, their sense of loss and even of abandonment when they return to their stateside reality is palpable. As they continue to process in their written reflections upon their return, many find that their known reality has been altered forever by their immersion in the culture of another people, and through experiences that reveal a common and shared humanity.

Evaluation

Evaluation is an important component of developing a program responsive to the needs of the medical students and the community. We evaluate in various ways.

EVALUATION OF STUDENTS

Reflection is a critical aspect of helping students internalize the impact of their experiences and determine their growth in the LMU program. Students are required to submit weekly reflective journals using an electronic format. These journals are reviewed by the program director. Students are encouraged to share unique segments in small-group discussions based on their comfort level. The program director meets quarterly to discuss program specifics and any outstanding journal notations in order to enhance student development.

The following is an example of a student reflection while participating in the international rotation in Peru:

There's a natural conflict inherent to medical training that often goes unspoken. On the one hand, patients typically receive the best care (and least harm) when treated by the most experienced and seasoned clinicians. On the other hand, it's impossible to create seasoned clinicians without having novices gain experience treating real patients. Medical education has created certain ways in which novices can gain experience without putting patients at risk: case-based book learning, a well-regimented hierarchy of supervision for trainees, and high-fidelity simulations, to name a few. Nevertheless, we have yet to figure how to completely protect patients from the learning curve of trainees and other less-experienced doctors. It's a puzzling and tremendously challenging Catch-22 in medical education.

I've reflected on this much during my training at home, and have continued to do so now in a Global Health context. In the US, I work hard to maintain a subtle balance in my training: on the one hand, proactively challenging myself to take on new responsibilities, while on the other hand, knowing when something is so far beyond my level of expertise that it would ultimately compromise patient care. Of course, much of the decisions about what is or is not appropriate for a medical student of a certain level of training to do comes from medical educators. Some of these boundaries are designed directly into medical school curriculums, but in my experience much of the decision behind "do I feel comfortable with medical student X doing patient care task Y" falls on the individual level of trust built between a student and a preceptor. If the student shows they are well-read, comfortable, professional, and capable, then they get to take on patient care responsibilities possibly above the level of some peers. If they exhibit a critical lack of knowledge, poor clinical skills, unprofessional behavior, immaturity, or significant discomfort with basic patient care tasks, then they stay working on the basic patient care tasks and possibly get closer supervision to boot. For me, I've consistently felt that I learn the most when I'm challenged with the most amount of patient care responsibility, within reason.

Abroad in the Global Health context, however, things are a bit different. Not since my first clerkship a year and a half ago have I so often been a simple observer rather than an active participant in patient care and medical decision making. However this is the spot I often find myself now in the emergency departments here in Peru. I am still learning a lot, but not in the same hands-on taking care of my own patients sort of way I've become accustomed to. I've thought about it a lot, and I'm not certain that pushing for more than this would be appropriate, for a couple of reasons. First, the patient care resources here are both vastly different and generally less abundant than in the U.S. For this reason, applying my knowledge and experience of American medicine to medical decision-making in Peruvian patients will, while for the most part OK, create at times an unacceptably high risk of making serious errors due to a lack of understanding of Peru's medical resources. Secondly, while I speak Spanish well enough to get by in the majority of both conversational and medical interactions, I am still far from the level of a native speaker. As such, taking histories without supervision and presenting patients to non-English speakers does have a risk that subtle but critical details will be lost in translation.

So what has this meant for my learning here in Peru? For the time here to be a valuable addition to my clinical training, I needed to be challenged in a way similar to domestic clerkships that test my clinical skills and clinical knowledge. Despite taking a far more conservative than normal approach to clinical training here in Peru, I still think these learning goals have satisfactorily been met. On the one hand, a large part of my interest in doing a Global Health experience was the possibility to greatly improve my clinical communication abilities with Spanish-speaking patients. This certainly has been the case, as working directly alongside doctors and patients who don't speak a word of English has forced me to get better very quickly. Additionally, I've learned a lot from analyzing both the direct medical decision-making as well as the greater healthcare system as a whole in Peru and comparing it to what I know at home. Both the similarities and differences are illuminating, and I think I'm gaining some great perspective with every comparison of what seems to work and what doesn't. And finally, it's been interesting to see many presentations of diseases that are rare but important in the US, like TB or stomach cancer. So, though I might not be putting in central lines or evaluating multiple critical patients on my own before staffing them with a preceptor, I feel that the clinical experience has been well worth it and a strong addition to my final year before residency.

Other instruments are used to assess student outcomes in the program, specifically the Health Professional's Attitude for the Homeless Inventory (HPATHI), which assesses the impact of educational experiences that involve working directly with the homeless on the attitudes, interest, and confidence of medical students and other health care professionals. Preliminary results indicate that medical students' intention to continue to work with the homeless is maintained or increases as a result of participating in the LMU program. This result is encouraging when considering that students without exposure to a structured program of experiential learning often decrease in their desire to care for vulnerable groups, the longer they are in a medical school curriculum.

Peer evaluation is used to provide insight regarding contribution to group activities as a pre and post measurement of participating in the international rotation.

The LMU program Evaluation tool addressing program components, elective course evaluation at the completion of the underserved electives in the fourth year, community intervention evaluations, and reflection journals comprise the major components evaluation of the program. In addition, MATCH USMLE results for residency selection indicating frequency of primary care as a career choice are used as program goal outcome measures.

Program Outcomes

As stated earlier, the motivation for creating the LMU program was to increase the numbers of students entering primary care and to create a cohort of skilled practitioners who find their passion in serving the underserved.

INCREASING INTEREST IN PRIMARY CARE

The LMU program exposes medical students to the dynamic opportunities present within primary care practice and specialty practice while focusing on the needs of the underserved. Various studies indicate that interest in primary care declines as students advance further in their medical education and training. However, two curricular experiences in medical schools, family practice clerkships and community/social involvement around health issues, seem highly correlated with increases in the numbers of students choosing primary care (Bland, Meurer, & Maldonda, 1995; Coulehan & Williams, 2001).

Thus, there are windows of opportunity to assess the widening gap between medical students who choose highly specialized career paths, and those who opt to become primary care practitioners. Consequently, examining the role of curricular clinical experiences and training with respect to social issues, community engagement, cultural skills, medical humanities, and complementary medicine may reveal a relationship with primary care interest in medical students and subsequently provide a means of addressing the needs of the underserved.

Research on the "choice" process of medical students has provided various contexts for analysis. For instance, medical students who choose a particular specialty are strongly influenced by the culture and faculty composition of the institutions they attend (Bland et al., 1995). A study on the influence of role models on specialty choice was strongly associated with medical students' choice of clinical field for residency training (Wright, Wong, & Newill, 1997). It seems that one of the most influential factors of medical student choice of primary care careers is the existence of faculty role models (Martini, Barzansky, Xu, & Fields, 1994). Based on this concept, first-year medical students interested in primary care were paired with primary care mentors in a recent study; this relationship resulted in significant increases of students matching into primary care, compared to the overall discipline-specific match rate (Indyk et al., 2011).

From the evidence gathered on interest in primary care, immersion in a community culture and observing a model of primary care practice characterize the main parameters that could increase medical student interest in primary care careers. However, there is significant difficulty in getting students to participate in optional service-learning experiences (Ahmed, Beck, Maurana, & Newton, 2004) that provide such opportunities. Medical school, a particularly rigorous course of study, is itself equivalent to a full-time job (Buckner, Ndjakani, Banks, & Blumenthal, 2010). One interesting approach to get medical students involved revolves around the organization of free health clinics, often, potentially run by medical students as an informal type of service learning, as compared to course-based service learning. Indeed, such community-based learning may play a formative role in the perception of students who only later enter formal clerkships (Stoddard & Risma, 2011). Free clinics provide care to the uninsured, to the working poor, and to many others who have fallen out of the conventional health care system (Gertz, Frank, & Blixen, 2011). Community-learning initiatives, such as free clinics, undoubtedly can play a role in shaping student interest toward a primary care career. In addition, experience gained through involvement with a "free" or "community" health clinic exposes medical students to the various ways they can become agents of social change in their communities and institutions. There is need for more research in the realm of gauging the efficacy of participation in free-health/community-based clinics during medical school and the eventual selection of a specialty.

PASSION TO WORK WITH THE UNDERSERVED

In the midst of a primary care shortage, we want to engage medical students' interest in pursuing a career in primary care and care for vulnerable populations by providing them with experiences in settings where providers enjoy their work and by partnering with the community to contribute to its health and well-being.

Throughout the program, students are encouraged to work in multidisciplinary groups to gain an understanding and appreciation of the strengths of each member as an individual and of their specific disciplines (public health, nursing, med tech, community health workers, etc.). Students are also supported through adult learning principles to engage in partnerships throughout the community. The leadership opportunities provided through service learning and outreach help to ground the medical students in feeling they are prepared and able to interface effectively with the public in the community (Long et al., 2011).

Connectedness through human engagement impacts the quality of experience students report and the likelihood of selecting careers in primary care or incorporating career paths with emphasis on care of the underserved. Provision of immersion and engagement learning advance the development of future physicians to be better able to meet the needs of diverse individuals, families, and communities in the United States and around the world.

REFERENCES

Ahmed, S. M., Beck, B., Maurana C. A., & Newton, G. (2004). Overcoming barriers to effective community-based participatory research in US medical schools. *Education for Health (Abingdon)*, *17*(2), 141–151.

Bazargan, M., Lindstrom, R. W., Dakak, A., Ani, C., Wolf, K. E., & Edelstein, R. A. (2006). Impact of desire to working in underserved communities on selection of specialty among fourth year medical students. *Journal of the National Medical Association*, *98*(9), 1460–1465.

Bennet, K. L., & Phillips, J. P. (2010). Finding, recruiting, and sustaining the future primary care physician workforce: A new theoretical model of specialty choice process. *Academic Medicine*, *85*(10 suppl.), 81–88.

Bland, C. J., Meurer, L. N., & Maldonda, G. (1995). Determinants of primary care specialty choice: A non-statistical meta-analysis of the literature. *Academic Medicine, 70*(7), 520–541.

Buckner, A. V., Ndjakani, Y. D., Banks, B., & Blumenthal, D. S. (2010). Using service-learning to teach community health: The Morehouse School of Medicine Community Health course. *Academic Medicine, 85*(10), 1645–1651.

Campus Community Partnership for Health (CCPH). (1998). Service-learning. Retrieved from https://ccph.memberclicks.net/service-learning.

Coulehan, J., & Williams, P. C. (2001). Vanquishing virtue: The impact of medical education. *Academic Medicine, 76*(6), 598–605.

Engle, L., & Engle, J. (2003). Study abroad levels: Towards a classification of program types. *Frontiers: The Interdisciplinary Journal of Study Abroad, 9*, 1–20.

Gertz, A. M., Frank, S., & Blixen, C. E. (2011). A survey of patients and providers at free clinics across the United States. *Journal of Community Health, 36*(1), 83–93.

Goldstein, A. O., & Bearman, R. S. (2011). Community engagement in US and Canadian medical schools. *Advances in Medical Education and Practice, 2*, 46–49.

Goodell, S., Dower, C., & O'Neil, E. (2011). Primary care workforce in the United States. Robert Wood Johnson Foundation. The Synthesis Project. Policy Brief 22.

Ho, M. J., Chen, W. S., & Hirsh, D. (2012). On being there. *Academic Medicine, 87*(7), 931–932.

Indyk, D., Deen, D., Fornari, A., Santos, M. T., Lu, W. H., & Rucker, L. (2011). The influence of longitudinal mentoring on medical students' selection of primary care residences. *BCM Medical Education, 11*, 27. Retrieved from https://www.ncbi.nlm.nih.gov/pmc/articles/PMC3128853.

Long, J., Lee, R., Federico, S., Battaglia, C., Wong, S., & Earnest, M. (2011). Developing leadership and advocacy skills in medical students through service-learning. *Journal of Public Health Management and Practice, 17*, 369–372.

Martini, C. J. M., Barzansky, B., Xu, G., & Fields, S. K. (1994). Medical school and student characteristics that influence choosing a generalist career. *Journal of the American Medical Association, 272*(9), 661–668.

Schnuth, R., Vasilenko, P., Mavis, B., & Marshall, J. (2003). What influences medical students to pursue careers in obstetrics and gynecology? *American Journal of Obstetrics and Gynecology, 189*(3), 639–664.

Schwartz, M. D., Durning, S., Linzer, M., & Hauer, K. E. (2011). Changes in medical students' views of internal medicine careers from 1990 to 2007. *Archives of Internal Medicine, 171*(8), 744–749.

Stoddard, H. A., & Risma, J. M. (2011). Relationship of participation in an optional student-run clinic to medical school grades. *Teaching and Learning in Medicine, 23*(1), 42–45.

Turner, J. L., & Farquhar, L. (2008). One medical school's effort to ready the workforce for the future: preparing medical students to care for populations who are publicly insured. *Academic Medicine, 83*(7), 632–638.

U.S. Department of Health and Human Services, Health Resources and Services Administration. (2013). National Center for Health Workforce analysis. Projecting the supply and demand for primary care practitioners through 2020. Rockville, MD: U.S. Department of Health and Human Services.

Wright, S., Wong, A., & Newill, C. (1997). The impact of role models on medical students. *Journal of General Internal Medicine, 12*(1), 53–56.

Young, P. (1990). Residency training for rural primary care. *Academic Medicine, 65*(12), S25–S27.

Community Engagement as Collaborative Inquiry

Rene Rosenbaum

I left Huamachuco, Peru, thinking that I was leaving things in good shape. The eight students in the Michigan State University (MSU) Office of Study Abroad program staying behind were deeply immersed in their community engagement outreach projects. As part of bringing closure to their participatory action research activities in less than three weeks' time, they each had to deliver a PowerPoint presentation, in Spanish, to the nongovernmental organization (NGO) or other local entity where they were conducting their community service and research. After four weeks in Huamachuco, students had fallen into a daily routine and felt at home with their host families and the people and city of Huamachuco. They knew where to go and who to seek in the event of an emergency. They saw each other nearly every day and engaged in structured student group activities and reflections at least twice a week. Two of the students had appeared on local television and two others had been on live radio. The evening before my departure, the students and I were invited to a farewell dinner arranged by our local contact and coordinator, Luis Canaval Chavez, who we fondly called Lucho. He is a former city council member and retired state employee who helped form the Rotary Club of Huamachuco, of which he has been its only president. At the invitation of a local restaurateur and fellow Rotarian, the students and I gathered at his restaurant with other local Rotarians for dinner, followed by gifts and karaoke. My farewell celebration turned into a welcome reception for my faculty colleague from the university who had arrived earlier in the week to take my place in Huamachuco with the students for the remaining two weeks of the program.

Increasingly referred to as "the Peru Community Engagement Study Abroad Program," or simply "the Peru Program," the "Community Engagement and Interdisciplinary Study of Global Issues in the Peruvian Andes Program" at MSU is a summer-long, multicollege-sponsored study-abroad program. First implemented in Huamachuco in 2009, the program was the result of the collaborative efforts of two MSU professors, Irv Widders in horticulture and Brian Thompson in mechanical engineering, and an MSU alumni who belonged to Rotary International, the Lansing–DeWitt Sunrise Rotary Club. Members of the Lansing–DeWitt club had founded the

Huamachuco Rotary Club, and the club had functioned for many years as a community economic development organization for Huamachuco. Over the years, it had been the sponsor of many community engagement activities to help the poor in Huamachuco, where eighty-five percent of residents live in poverty, as defined by World Bank. Initially, the Lansing–DeWitt and the Huamachuco Rotary Clubs provided these activities, but subsequently they grew to include regular visits by international teams associated with Surgical Eye Expeditions and Volunteer Optometrists of Service to Humanity (Brown & Mondol, 2010). As president of the Huamachuco Rotary Club, Lucho had been the local leader of those efforts, so that when Dr. Widders worked through the MSU administration to establish the Peru study-abroad program, the Huamachuco Rotary Club and Lucho were instrumental in making things happen. They were also a critical link in facilitating medical student practicums offered in Huamachuco by the MSU College of Osteopathic Medicine beginning around the same time (see chapter 5 by Dokter & Willyerd).

October 2012 marked a little more than a year's time since I had taken over the Peru program. Upon assuming leadership, I made my academic department in the College of Agriculture and Natural Resources, the program's new academic home. A formal understanding about academic credits was reached between my college and the two other colleges sponsoring the program, the College of Social Science and the College of Arts and Letters. At the suggestion of Widders, who had invited me to take leadership of the program, in November 2011, I took a week-long planning trip to Peru to meet our partners in Cusco and in Huamachuco, where I met Lucho and renewed MSU relationships with community leaders and organizations. Despite the uncertainty associated with the continuation of the program in 2012, and delays in marketing its availability that spring, we were able to recruit eight students for the summer program that year.

The purpose of this essay is twofold. One is to describe the MSU Peru program in terms of its elements and as a university–community partnership and intervention that uses community engagement pedagogy to achieve student learning outcomes and grassroots development. The other is to bring a faculty perspective to the community engagement work I conducted as program leader when reinstating the study-abroad program in Huamachuco. To guide my analysis and interpretation of my work, I rely on the framework articulated by Fear and colleagues in their book *Coming to Critical Engagement: An Autoethnographic Exploration* (Fear, Rosaen, Bawden, & Foster-Fishman, 2006), and in their journal articles on the same topic (Fear, Rosaen, Foster-Fishman, & Bawden, 2001; Fear, Bawden, Rosaen, & Foster-Fishman, 2002; Fear & Sandmann, 2001–2002). Fear, Rosaen, Foster-Fishman, and Bawden (2001) see the "engagement interface framework of engaged learning" as a unifying frame of reference for scholarly work on engagement that can help both "older hands" (p. 29) and newcomers learn important lessons by sharing experiences about their work in the interface. The framework interprets engagement as "new scholarship" that represents a methodological stance in favor of "collaborative forms of action inquiry," and an alternative to the historically dominant paradigm where control of the engagement process tends to reside with the university and its prevailing "reformist agenda to fix what is wrong" (Fear et al., 2006, p. 62).

Using the engagement interface framework to analyze the Peru study-abroad program, my work as faculty program leader provides the opportunity to review and reflect on the program and the work I did in the name of community engagement as collaborative inquiry. The framework provides the standard of practice and offers the capacity to assess my work as program leader in all aspects of reinstating the Peru program. One goal of this evaluative exercise is to inform my understanding of the actions I took as program leader in the context of something other than in terms of the university dominant technologically rational worldview, where control of the engagement discourse is largely in the hands of university administrators and experts (Fear et al., 2006, p. 55). In addition to the personal benefits gained from reflecting on my work as collective inquiry, the insights generated from the analysis elucidate not only a way to study community engagement in the context of study-abroad programs, but also a way to study the broader academic field of community engagement by institutions of higher education.

University Community Engagement as Pedagogy

In 2002, the Committee on Engagement of the Committee on Institutional Cooperation (CIC) of the Big Ten Universities was tasked to define engagement and identify a set of benchmarks member institutions can use in demonstrating their goals and values as engaged universities. The CIC Committee on Engagement's report (2005) developed the following definition of engagement:

> Engagement is the partnership of university knowledge and resources with those of the public and private sectors to enrich scholarship, research, and creative activity; enhance curriculum, teaching and learning; prepare educated, engaged citizens; strengthen democratic values and civic responsibility; learning; prepare educated, engaged citizens; strengthen democratic values and civic responsibility; address critical societal issues; and contribute to the public good. (p. 2)

The field of engagement in higher education has continued to evolve. There are now at least fifteen journals in the field and most of them focus on community-based research and community-based participatory research approaches to engagement (Fitzgerald, 2016). There have also been changes in what we call activities to enhance "curriculum, teaching, and learning" and "democratic values, civic responsibility, and preparing 'engaged citizens.'" The preferred term to use historically has been service learning. At MSU, faculty activities and scholarly obligations in supervising or directing civic or community service performed by students in conjunction with an academic course or program, in either a domestic or international location, are categorized as experiential/service learning (Church, Zimmerman, Bargerstock, & Kenny, 2003). According to the National Service Learning Clearinghouse, service learning is "a teaching and learning strategy that integrates meaningful community service with instruction and reflection to enrich the learning experience, teach civic responsibility, and strengthen communities" (Bandy, 2012a).

The term "service" in service learning, however, has received criticism from some; an array of other terms, also with their detractors, have become common, such as community-based teaching or learning, civic education, civic engagement, and public scholarship. Increasingly the term "community engagement" appears the privileged concept to refer to these pedagogies (Bandy, 2012b). Faculty members at the Center for Teaching at Vanderbilt University define the term as "a form of experiential education where learning occurs through a cycle of action and reflection as students . . . seek to achieve real objectives for the community and deeper understanding and skills for themselves. In the process, students link personal and social development with academic and cognitive development . . . experience enhanced understanding; understanding leads to more effective action." Typically, community engagement in a classroom takes the form of an outreach project designed between faculty, students, and community partners to address both student learning and community action goals (Bandy, 2012b).

According to Bawden (2001), community engagement reflects the growing recognition that there is more to learning than is provided through reason alone—that much of what we learn is derived from the interpretation of our own experiences. Similarly to Schön's concept of "reflection in action" (Schön, 1983), in the community engagement type of learning system, learning occurs through a cycle of action and reflection as students seek to achieve real objectives for the community and deeper understanding and skills for themselves. This reflexive process serves to provide a link between the community engagement experience and a host of learning outcomes, in particular critical thinking skills (Bandy, 2012a).

Not all recognized experiential/service-learning activity is classified the same at MSU. Academic service learning, for example, is the type of faculty experiential service-learning activity that involves community engagement education for course credit. Other forms of faculty experiential learning also recognized at MSU include career-oriented practicums or internships, or student voluntary community service if faculty members are involved (Michigan State University, University Outreach and Engagement, 2012).

Community engagement pedagogies linked to academic service learning that combine learning goals and community service with community in ways that enhance both student growth and the common good have grown in popularity because of their benefits to both students and the community. Grounded in the ideas of Paulo Freire (1970) and John Dewey (1919), these learning strategies are increasingly being integrated into study-abroad programs, which are themselves growing in popularity and becoming powerful pedagogical tools in their own right (Berquist & Widders, 2011). Study-abroad experiences have been linked to the concept of self-efficacy, since they provide a variety of challenges that students must negotiate, from transportation systems to language and new cultural norms (Gardner, Gross, & Steglitz, 2008). There is also a link between study-abroad programs and economic development. Advocates for education abroad argue it is essential for increasing both economic and homeland security since the economic well-being of the United States depends increasingly on global engagement (Conway, 2004).

Colleges and universities today are in competition to claim leadership in preparing students for a global world through participation in international experiences. Given its long history in international engagement, MSU is recognized as a leader in this competition (Gardner et al., 2008). With more than 275 programs in more than sixty countries around the world, the university led the nation in study-abroad enrollment among public universities during 2004–2011. Thirty study-abroad programs at MSU include a community engagement component, around 10 percent of the catalog (Berquist, 2012). Despite the many start-up challenges facing study-abroad programs with a community engagement component, advocates argue that these programs add both student and community benefits to the international learning experience (Crabtree, 2008; Parker & Dautoff, 2007).

The growing popularity of experiential/service-learning and community-engagement pedagogies is part of the larger outreach and engagement movement in U.S. universities that as began in the 1990s (Parker & Dautoff, 2007).[1] There is a growing public sentiment that universities should inform problem-solving processes through responsible community engagement rather than solving problems themselves (Amey, 2002; Votruba, 1997). As a land-grant university, MSU has long recognized that outreach and engagement for the benefit of external audiences are significant aspects of a university's responsibilities (Church et al., 2003). Conversations in the late 1980s led to a successful grant from the Kellogg Foundation to redefine lifelong education (Fitzgerald, 2016). In the early 1990s, MSU revisited its outreach mission, prompted in part by Boyer's landmark monograph, *Scholarship Reconsidered: Priorities of the Professoriate* (1990), which called on faculty members to rethink their notion of scholarship so universities could become responsive to the needs of society. Relying heavily on Boyer's work, a 1993 faculty committee formally defined outreach at MSU as "a form of scholarship that cuts cross teaching, research, and service. It involves generating, transmitting, applying, and preserving knowledge for the direct benefit of external audiences in ways that are consistent with university and unit missions" (Church et al., 2003, pp. 142–143). Fear, a former senior associate dean in the College of Agriculture and Natural Resources at MSU, is of the view that outreach takes place when the faculty members use their academic expertise to meet the knowledge needs of others in the context of fulfilling their institutional mission, whether in teaching, research, or service.

Since 1993, MSU has devised ways to become a more engaged university and more deliberate and purposeful in understanding and measuring outreach and engagement activities.[2] MSU has devised a faculty outreach and engagement classification scheme to account for all university faculty outreach and engagement scholarship. Under the current classification system, academic service learning that uses community engagement as a course component is one of several types of experiential/service-learning activities regarded as faculty outreach and engagement. In addition to experiential service-learning activities, other types of outreach and engagement performance include applied research, technical assistance, policy analysis, impact evaluations, organizational and community development, program development, and outreach instruction, which include credit and noncredit courses as well as public events and information (Doberneck, Glass, & Schweitzer, 2009; Amey, 2002).

Innovations to account for outreach activity, as well as advances in its scholarship and ways to evaluate it, have strengthened outreach and engagement scholarship at MSU (Lunsford, Church, & Zimmerman, 2006). The current administrator of the Office of University Outreach and Engagement at MSU, Associate Provost Fitzgerald, distinguishes between campus-based (inreach) and community-based research (outreach) approaches to make the point that the same criteria for evaluating faculty is applicable regardless of where the research takes place. He helped create the Developmental Science Model about Applied Developmental Science, which measures outreach research across five product domains: (1) stakeholder needs assessment, (2) capacity building, (3) knowledge generation, (4) information dissemination, and (5) resource generation (Fitzgerald, 2000).

In summary, experiential service learning, as a form of community engagement that recognizes there is more to learning than reason alone, has become an established and highly valued pedagogy in institutions of higher education in the United States and worldwide. It continues to grow as a learning approach for a variety of reasons, including the learning benefits to students from using a community engagement pedagogy and growth in the study-abroad programs and the outreach and engagement movements at U.S. universities since the early 1990s. The latter movement has brought greater appreciation for the scholarship of engagement, and within that literature, community-engagement pedagogy has evolved into a branch of study. The transition to embracing community-engagement pedagogies is one way universities have responded to Boyer's challenge to rethink their notion of scholarship so they can better respond to the needs of society. The growing scholarship of engagement has also brought forth the cry for a faculty stance, as compared to an administrative stance, on defining standards for community engagement practice in American higher education.

The Engagement Interface Framework as a Critical Stance on the Scholarship of Engagement

There is often acknowledgement of the significant and tangible impact of Boyer's work on the outreach and engagement movement at MSU and across American higher education (Church et al., 2013; Fear et al., 2006; Thomson, 2008). Because of Boyer (1990), many campuses recognize outreach and engagement as a legitimate form of scholarship, and administrators are aligning institutional obligations and practices with outreach and engagement in mind. As at MSU, many colleges and universities across the country have been trying to put into practice what Boyer called "the scholarship of engagement." This academic approach calls on institutions of higher education (IHE) to engage with community by connecting their teaching and research to the outside world. Although IHEs have long been engaged in community life, arguably since the colonial era (Ross, 2002), today there is an undeniable emphasis nationwide on recognizing and affirming outreach and engagement as a legitimate form of scholarship (Fear et al., 2001). Colleges and universities are broadening their view of scholarship by applying it to critical issues and problems that threaten the quality of life in local communities, in the United States and abroad. There is increasing recognition of the tangible benefits to IHEs from this broader view of scholarship: better-educated students, better-trained professionals, increased grant funding, and increased financial, academic, and social benefits to communities from the investment of university resources where the outreach takes place (Thomson, 2008).

Boyer's work has helped institutionalize outreach as scholarship at U.S. universities through innovations that reframe faculty reward processes and reorganize undergraduate curricula around service-learning themes. These types of changes at universities to accommodate the engagement and outreach movement are part of a larger and more significant "administrative discourse" in engagement, which Fear and colleagues characterize as "instrumental, reformist, and structural in rhetoric and practice" (Fear et al., 2006, p. 17). The reformist agenda, in particular, enables the university "to occupy, if not own, the engagement space" (p. 17). Such discourse and way of thinking are part of an epistemology where even participatory development is a form of corporatism, directed by university administrators for administrative and university gains.

As an alternative to this dominant administrative discourse in engagement, Fear and his colleagues (Fear et al., 2001) challenge faculty to be a stronger voice in the discourse on scholarly engagement in American higher education. They invite scholars to engage in "outreach as scholarly expression"—the quest associated with understanding outreach work more completely and deeply, by writing about the work faculty members do in the name of scholarly engagement and outreach.

A key concept to understanding scholarly engagement is what Fear and his community of scholars call the "engagement interface," defined as the setting where the work of engagement takes place. "It is the dynamic, evolving and co-constructed space—a collaborative community of inquiry," where collaborators from the academy and society engage each other to address pressing social issues and problems (Fear et al., 2006, p. 68). The concept is one of several unifying frames of reference proposed by the authors to advance outreach as scholarly expression. Central to their engagement model is the concept of "engaged learning," a practice outcome in the engagement interface that emphasizes shared learning and an ethos of mutuality, respectfulness, and stewardship. It relies on dialogue and inclusive well-being to guide engagement work (p. 62). Fear and his colleagues include the following among the distinctive essential features of engaged learning practice in the engagement interface: (1) joint construction of purposes, (2) developing shared norms, (3) bringing unique perspectives and skills to bear in practice, and (d) engaging in the shared appraisal of outcomes (p. 71).

The engagement interface framework introduced by Fear and friends that I use here to assess the engagement work I did as a faculty leader of the Peru study-abroad program in the summer of 2012 represents a critical reframing of core understandings of the scholarship of engagement. As much as Fear has applied Boyer's work, his framework represents a rejection of Boyer's interpretation of scholarship conceived in multiple distinct forms: as discovery, learning, engagement, and integration. The Fear community of practice prefers to see all those forms of faculty work as forms of "scholarly expression" (Fear et al., 2001). Rather than speak in terms of the scholarship of engagement, for example, Fear and his colleagues prefer to focus their attention on a particular form of engagement they refer to as "scholarly engagement."

The engagement interface framework also represents a critique of traditional scholarship interpreted as an idealized process (Fear et al., 2006, p. 60), where work is undertaken in a controlled or otherwise stable environment with those responsible in control. This image of engagement work challenges Fear and his community of scholars since engagement for them is "a participatory and collaborative process as expert and local knowledge systems merge to address compelling issues located in time and context." According to the authors, "embracing such a stance involves, first and foremost, respect for people and place, followed by understanding one's responsibilities as a participant-collaborator in an engaged relationship" (p. 62).

Rather than view engagement scholarship in strictly process terms, the engagement interface framework views engagement as a "collaborative inquiry." Using Bray, Lee, Smith, and Yorks (2000, p. 6), Fear and company (2006) define collaborative inquiry as "a process consisting of repeated episodes of reflection and action through which a group of peers strives to answer a question of importance to them" (p. 62). According to the authors, the concept of collaborative inquiry goes beyond the instrumental role of answering questions of mutual importance. It is also a stance that takes seriously the concept of "peers," where "participants are colleagues in a jointly defined and undertaken enterprise," with power distributed equitably among partners, open transactions, and the sincere, authentic desire to learn from and with each other. A third quality of engagement as collaborative inquiry is that, for its participants, it "holds the prospect of personal transformation" (p. 62), as engagement can affect them deeply, provided there is authentic reflection on the interests that motivate their participation.

The outcome that emerges from the view of faculty work in community engagement as collaborative inquiry is a practice Fear and his colleagues refer to as "engaged learning." The conventional approach to scholarship of engagement speaks to a technical rationality perspective on scholarship grounded in the techno-development paradigm of modernity and its associated techno-scientific discourse, whereas engaged learning is a practice associated with an alternative to this historically dominant paradigm. According to the authors of *Coming to Critical Engagement*, it represents a form of Schön's "New Scholarship." The authors define it thus: "Engaged learning is grounded in an ethos of mutuality, respectfulness, and stewardship; it proceeds through dialogue, and fosters inclusive well-being. It is an approach; an expression of being; a leadership and management ethic; and a way for scholars to connect otherwise diverse activities thematically, coherently, and meaningfully" (Fear et al., 2006, p. 63).

There are four different and interrelated ways to analyze and interpret engaged learning in practice. As a thematic, connective expression of scholarly work, engaged learning is a cross-cutting function and transcendent stance and approach that embrace participatory processes with emancipated outcomes. Embracing engagement as an ethos, on the other hand, is seeing engaged learning as a deeply personal stance on the felt and relational dimensions of engagement, which are characterized by a set of "norms of engagement" (Fear et al., 2006, p. 64). These include "respectfulness, collaboration, mutuality, and dedication to learn with emphasis on the values of community, responsibility, virtue, stewardship, and mutual concern for each other" (Fear & Sandmann, 2001–2002, p. 31). Engagement as action-based learning raises the question of why engage. Fear and colleagues answer, "to enhance understanding and the capacity for action through learning" (Fear et al., 2006, p. 65), which for them is best captured through the image of people engaging each other and learning together.

The final way to consider engaged learning is as a scholarly stance toward practice. Engaged learning as a stance is informed conceptually by a situated learning context and through dialogue, which reflects a respectful stance: people engaged for the purpose of understanding and taking action. Matters of importance to recognize in this participatory framework include listening, rather than promoting one's agenda, and being mindful of who comes to the table and why: how they prefer to interact, and how willing they are to put their beliefs (and themselves) "out there" for consideration. Philosophically, as with many forms of participatory inquiry, engaged learning champions inclusivity and is grounded in a participatory worldview characterized by collaborative inquiry, collaborative learning, and participatory and action research. Beyond process and participation, another element of the scholarly stance embedded in engaged learning is recognition of its normative intent, characterized by its alignments with the reality of a postmodern world in which there is the explicit recognition of the importance of "ecological responsibility, ethical comportment, cultural respectfulness, and spiritual attentiveness" (Fear et al., 2006, p. 68).

In summary, the engagement interface is a unifying frame of reference for a critical interpretation of scholarly work on engagement that is useful in advancing community engagement as practice and as an academic field of study. The educational and developmental endeavor that constitutes engaged learning practice in the engagement interface emanates from engagement scholarship as collective inquiry. As such, it has the following aforementioned essential features: (1) joint construction of purposes, (2) developing shared norms, (3) bringing unique perspectives and skills to bear in practice, and (4) engaging in the shared appraisal of outcomes (Fear et al., 2006, p. 72). This approach to the scholarship of engagement, which adheres to a participatory and emancipatory worldview, is a contribution to the "New Scholarship" school of engagement. As such, it constitutes an alternative scholarship to the historically dominant paradigm.

In concluding this section, I owe it to the readers to explain my choice of the engagement interface framework to guide this inquiry into my own work as program leader of the Peru study-abroad program. Like the authors of the engagement interface framework, I too take a stance methodologically in favor of "collaborative forms of action inquiry." That is because community engagement work is accomplished principally through human relations that require care to establish and maintain (Schatzman & Strauss, 1973). I appreciate that the framework represents propositional knowledge grounded in the researchers' own experiential knowledge. What they share from the field of engagement as collaborative inquiry resonates with me because of what I do that works in community economic development, my field of study and practice. Community economic development is one of various fields where the inclination by the faculty to engage the community—the individuals, community-based institutions, and local businesses and institutions—in the search for solutions has long been considered necessary to achieve community improvements. In general, there is increased recognition that concepts concerning community participation offer one set of explanations of why the process of community engagement might be useful in addressing the social and physical long-term aspects of an individual's environment (Centers for Disease Control and Prevention, 1997).

The Peru Study-Abroad Program

In recent decades, study-abroad programs have proliferated and overall numbers of U.S. overseas study participants have increased steadily. Each year, study-abroad programs become more attractive as a recruiting tool for colleges and universities so such increases in participant numbers are likely to continue. The choices for students are becoming more complex with the proliferation of program types, as these programs vary by focus, destination, duration, participant preparation, and outcomes (Engle & Engle, 2003).

In 2010, the MSU Office of Study Abroad operated around twenty-five study-abroad programs with some type of community engagement component. That number is currently around thirty. The Peru community-engagement program, as implemented in the summer of 2012, had much the same purpose and structure as the Peru study-abroad program first implemented by Widders in 2009 and 2010, although there were some important variations, particularly in the number of faculty available to assist students with their action research projects in Huamachuco. Like in its previous rendition, however, the primary goal of the 2012 program was to use cultural, language immersion, and community engagement projects to enhance the quality of the interdisciplinary learning experience for students and address the social and economic development goals of the Andean highland community of Huamachuco, Peru.

Widders chose the community of Huamachuco as the site for the community engagement study-abroad program for a number of reasons. These included the receptivity of the Huamachuco community to the MSU Peru program, the development challenges in the city of Huamachuco and the region of Sanchez Carrion, which faces 80 percent poverty rates and 60 percent malnutrition rates in children, and the fact that Spanish was the native language of the region (Berquist & Widders, 2011). According to Widders, the program created in 2009 itself represents the evolution of a program first offered by MSU professors in Cusco, Peru, during the first part of the decade (Berquist & Widders, 2011). When Widders added the community engagement component, he included three critical components, which remain in the program today. These are Spanish language competency and understanding of Peruvian history; culture, community structure, social norms, and development challenges (through home stay, local residents, visits to natural, archeological, and cultural sites, and classes in Spanish from Peruvian professors); and opportunities for both service-learning and active-learning community-engagement projects in partnership with nonprofit organizations and public-sector agencies in Huamachuco. The first two components of community engagement are considered essential prerequisites for students to effectively participate in the community-engagement project opportunities in Huamachuco.

As in previous years, a set of seven principles governed the 2012 program. These were the following: (1) to be a platform for university-wide engagement with highland communities in Peru (i.e., Huamachuco and surrounding area); (2) to commit to interdisciplinary scholarship by participating faculty members and undergraduate and graduate students; (3) to create opportunities for students and faculty members to be co-learners with individuals in the community; (4) to respect culture, traditions, and norms of the community of Huamachuco; (5) to support community organizations and institutions and their priorities in Huamachuco and not promote different agendas or initiate new programs; (6) to create community relationships that are mutually beneficial for the community and Michigan State University; and (7) to support initiatives that contribute to sustainable improvements in the welfare and livelihoods of the community members, giving special priority to gender.

The Peru program has four academic components and is structured as a twelve-week program with the opportunity for student to earn a minimum of thirteen credit hours. These elements help the students selected for the program meet their academic program needs and prepare them for their community engagement experience in Huamachuco. The first component consists of a set of three one-and-a-half- to two-hour-long predeparture meetings for students participating in the program. At these meeting, we revisited the program objectives, structure, activities, and expectations as related to activities at MSU, Cusco, and Huamachuco. Predeparture issues were also discussed, such as ticket purchases, assignments and arrangements for home stays in Cusco and Huamachuco, passport information, appropriate course enrollments, visiting the travel clinic, and risks and codes of conduct to ensure a safe and enjoyable experience by students in Peru. We also assisted students with the development of their field research project proposals. The meetings also provided students with information and advice on working with organizations in Huamachuco. Students from pervious program were invited to share their experiences, and the incoming students had an opportunity to ask them practical questions.

The second academic component requires the completion of a four-credit course, the focus of which is on the origin and history of Andean cultures, social and political organization, impact of the La Conquista Española on Andean societies, literature, Andean traditions and religious practice, and the impact of globalization on modern-day communities. The course has an MSU component and a Cusco component. The MSU component consists of twenty hours of instruction over five days, and the Cusco component that followed comprised forty-five to sixty hours of instruction over a five-and-a-half-week-long period.

The MSU component of the course in 2012 covered many of the same topics addressed in in the classes of 2009 and 2010, such as an introduction to the social capital paradigm and to the social, economic, environmental, health, and political development challenges of Latin America, Peru, and particularly Huamachuco. Other class topics included poverty and the challenges of overcoming it, principles and challenges of community development, participatory development, the ethics of community engagement, and an introduction to quantitative, qualitative, and community action-based research. In addition to lectures by MSU faculty members and staff, there were also presentations by members of the DeWitt Rotary Club and our coordinator in Huamachuco, Lucho. We were able to use Skype to introduce the students to Lucho and to share the students' career and research interests. Lucho talked about Huamachuco and shared information on the various private and public agencies and the community engagement opportunities available. A particular focus of the class during the first week was also to help students complete their research project proposals. In many instances, the students knew the sector they wanted to work in and the type of research they wanted to do, based on information about the needs in Huamachuco. Most of the students had worked with Lucho and me since being accepted into the program earlier in the semester, so when we met in May, they had a very good idea of what they wanted to do for their community-engagement research projects.

The second part of the four-hour class taught in Cusco consists of five weeks of lectures by Peruvian scholars, complemented by guided field trips to archeological sites and museums in Cusco and the Sacred Valley, an indigenous community, and an NGO engaged in community development in the region of Cusco. A one-day guided tour to Machu Picchu is also scheduled. The lectures consist of twenty hours of formal instruction involving a series of presentations and discussions based on readings related to Andean history, culture, traditions, community structure, and social issues. Faculty members from the Pontificia Universidad Catolica del Peru in Lima and from the Academia Latinoamericana de Español in Cusco, Peru, where students enrolled in Spanish classes, offered the lectures to the students.

The program's third academic component is language acquisition to enable the students to develop adequate Spanish proficiency to complete their community service and action field research projects in Huamachuco in a satisfactory manner. Students receive eighty hours of intensive formal Spanish instruction at the Academic Latinoamericana de Español, a certified Spanish language institute in Cusco. Spanish language acquisition is further enriched through lectures in Spanish, homestays with Spanish speaking families, completing reports in Spanish, and the use of Spanish while working on the community development project in Huamachuco.

The three components of the program just described are invaluable in achieving the pedagogical and community development goals of the Peru study-abroad program. In combination, these program components provide opportunities for students to develop valuable skills necessary to succeed in the fourth and final academic element of the program, which consists of the community engagement component in Huamachuco. It is in Huamachuco that all elements of the study-abroad program come together. Huamachuco is ground zero for the community engagement phase of our program. In terms of our analytical framework, it represents the engagement interface, where members of the community of Huamachuco and MSU faculty members and students in the Peru study-abroad program engage in a collaborative inquiry that informs the development needs of the residents and organizations of Huamachuco.

As noted earlier, the Huamachuco component is six weeks long and the community engagement pedagogy involves two elements: a community service-learning element and an active research-learning element. The latter element usually involves the completion of independent research projects identified as a priority for the community and of interest to the student as well as the host organization where the student interns. To complete their community service projects and achieve their service-learning objectives, students work under the supervision of an NGO or a governmental agency. As program leader, I identify the community service projects and the placement of students, via consultation with the students, and with Lucho, who arranges with public and private agencies to facilitate the service and research projects the students plan to undertake in Huamachuco. I make the placement of students in the various agencies in Huamachuco in advance of their departures for Peru. Also finalized in advance of the students' departures are decisions on housing arrangements, internship locations, and action research projects.

The most significant change in the Peru program in 2012, from how the program operated in 2009 and 2010, occurred in the Huamachuco component of the program. The change had to do with the way MSU faculty and staff members administered the community research projects while on site in Huamachuco. In the 2009 and 2010 renditions of the program, faculty mentors joined the program during the spring semester and students worked with these mentors to develop a learning plan and research projects. The number of mentors was high compared to other study abroad programs, prompting resistance from the MSU administrators representing the various colleges sponsoring the program. To them, the program model that required multiple MSU faculty members on site in Huamachuco at various times during the six-week period to supervise individual student projects was inefficient and unsustainable. Additionally, it did not appear that a large pool of faculty members had interest in supervising in-country projects. More importantly, these leaders felt strongly that costs associated with multiple faculty members on site should not be borne by the students or the various college sponsors.

It was this disagreement over program staffing that led to the cancelation of the Peru program in 2011. When I took over the program in 2012, both college representatives and the Office of Study Abroad supported the traditional model of a program leader and an on-site assistant, which I reconfigured into four- and two-week stays in Huamachuco for two faculty mentors, respectively. The plan was for me to spend the first four weeks in Huamachuco with the students to help place them with local organizations and help them get started in their community engagement research projects. My colleague arrived before my departure, to spend the last two weeks of the program with the students and help bring closure to their projects and the program.

As in previous years, the community service projects took the form of internships, where local organizations supervised student work. We grouped the students into teams of two. An organizational staff assigned to each team provided direct oversight of daily activities and facilitated coordination of project activities in the target community. In addition, my faculty colleague and I were on site to mentor the students on the implementation of the community development projects and to assist with field research as needed. In consultation with Lucho, we had helped the students identify research topics and develop proposals for research projects during the week-long Michigan component of the program. Students were also encouraged to call on MSU faculty members in their major units to get disciplinary help with their projects. Lucho facilitated assistance from local experts, and the organization staff person provided direct oversight, facilitation, and coordination of student project activities in the community.

The overall goal of the Huamachuco component of the Peru program is to enrich the learning experience of students from diverse disciplines and interests by providing them a five-and-a-half-week-long opportunity to work on community engagement projects that address the complex social, economic, environmental, and health and nutrition challenges facing Huamachuco. The program enables students to apply their academic and cultural knowledge, and their language and professional skills, in partnership with local community organizations, to contribute directly to the community development goals of Huamachuco. The students who took and met the Peru 2012 summer program challenge represented a diverse group from across the university, whose projects addressed a variety of community and organizational needs:

- Educational Programs for Special Needs Children (Colegio Santa Ana, Huamachuco)
- Educational Programs for Working Children and Adolescents (Proyecto Amigo, Huamachuco)
- Nutrition Education in Primary Schools (Jardin 100, Huamachuco)
- The Needs of Single Mothers of Young Children (Jardin 100, Huamachuco)
- Development and Marketing of Peruvian Textile Products (Los Laureles Cooperative, Huamachuco)
- Institutional Capacity and Resource Analysis of a Local Public Hospital (Hospital Leoncio Prado, Huamachuco)
- Survey Assessment of Diseases of Miners Working in the Informal Mining Sector (Hospital Leoncio Prado, Huamachuco)

Recruiting students from diverse academic backgrounds who have the skills to conduct outreach research projects that address the needs of the community is an annual challenge for the program I anticipate having in the future. It will also be a challenge to sustain continuity in the research efforts from one year to the next. However, those are challenges for the future. As far as the summer 2012 program is concerned, it met the challenges it faced.

Program Implementation in the Huamachuco Engagement Interface

The Fear et al. (2001) concept of engagement interface serves to draw out the characteristics and appraise scholarly engagement work in any type of context, including a study-abroad program context, where community-engagement pedagogy is employed to address both student learning and community action goals. In this section, I apply the framework to the Peru study-abroad community engagement program I reinstated in 2012. My approach focuses attention on the elements of the Peru program, the Huamachuco community engagement component in particular, and the use of key concepts and characteristics of the engagement interface model to explain my work and thinking as leader of the community-engagement study-abroad program.

Engagement as Collaborative Inquiry

Chief among the concepts in the Fear model of community engagement is the view of the scholarship of engagement as collaborative inquiry, defined earlier as "a process consisting of repeated episodes of reflection and action through which a group of peers strives to answer a question of importance to them" (Fear et al., 2001, p. 62). In our case, this definition immediately raises the questions "What was the question of importance?" and "Who was in the group of peers striving to answer it?"

As program leader and organizer in my first year, the object of my immediate inquiry was to determine the best way to implement the program to capitalize on the learning and career interests of the students in the program to advance the development goals of the residents of Huamachuco. As such, for me, the key question was as follows: How could the program serve as a pedagogical tool and a community development intervention, where students can apply their academic and cultural knowledge, their language and professional skills, and their partnership with the Rotary Club of Huamachuco and other local community organizations, to implement community development projects consistent with the priorities of the community?

In answering this question as collaborative inquiry, readers need to appreciate the fact that my situation was not one of starting the Peru study-abroad program from scratch. There was no need to establish relations and enter into first-time understandings and commitments. Indeed, there was already in place strong program support from both the community and the university. After the MSU suspension of the 2010 summer program, letters of support for the program from the DeWitt Rotary Club and from NGOs and public agencies in Huamachuco began to arrive at the MSU president's desk. The letter from the DeWitt Rotary Club, in particular, regretted deeply the loss of the program, and conveyed a shared vision of the program and its instrumental role in addressing community development goals of Huamachuco. On the MSU side, program support was equally as strong, except for the expectation that the faculty to student ratio be sustainable. MSU valued the community engagement model as a pedagogical tool, and so did the Huamachuco, where there was solid community support for the program.

When I committed in the fall of 2011 to lead the twelve-week study-abroad program and learned about the infrastructure already in place at MSU, Cusco, and Huamachuco, I realized I would not be alone in figuring out how to best implement the study-abroad program's many activities, which were wide-ranging. Among the program's many facets are the following: gain approval from MSU Office of Study Abroad and other MSU stakeholders to implement the program, market the program, recruit and select students, negotiate the learning activities and arrangements for students in Cusco, meet with students to prepare ourselves for their international experience, hire additional faculty, develop and teach the MSU component of the College of Social Science

ISS 330 course, make the arrangements for students to be in Huamachuco for six weeks, identify community engagement projects, place students in various agencies, and get them back to the United States safely. I also knew I would be spending four weeks in Huamachuco, assisting with and facilitating the students' community engagement projects, making logistical plans with Lucho, dealing with emergencies and attending to personal and health issues of the students, getting to know the agency directors and host families, and representing MSU in Huamachuco in numerous ways. However, I also knew that planning and implementing the scholarly program would be a collaborative effort. At my disposal were communities at MSU, in Cusco, and in Huamachuco, to help me achieve the goals of the program.

So who, in retrospect, was in the group of peers who shared my concern of reinstating the Peru study-abroad program? Who, in other words, made up my university and non-university "community of practice" engaged with me in collective inquiry to discover the best way to reinstate the community engagement intervention in Huamachuco, Peru, that constituted the study-abroad program?

From my point of view as program leader and organizer, the structure of the community of practice to reinstate the community engagement study-abroad program in Peru consisted of not just one group of peers, but of multiple groups of peers, separated by function and location. Rather than seen as one group of peers, the collaborative community committed to reinstating the Peru study-abroad program in all it entailed consisted of the MSU community, the Cusco community, and the Huamachuco community of peers working collaboratively from distinct locations in distinct aspects of the Peru program. The community group or groups in each location together comprise the larger community of practice of university and non-university community entities and individuals committed to the reinstatement and success of the Peru program. Each group has a different motivation for being involved with the program, and each contributes in its own way to helping me decide the best ways to design and implement the Peru program for the benefit of both the students and the community of Huamachuco.

When considering the university community of peers involved in reinstating the program, aside from the students, three groups of MSU colleagues and peers informed and facilitated the design and setup of the program. One group consisted of the previous program leader, Irv Widders, and some of the faculty and staff members who had participated with him in the program. This group supported my leadership of the program and assisted me in many ways. Widders, in particular, who had invited me to take leadership of the program, met with me early on and shared his ideas. He later shared program files with report documents from previous years, as well as some of the research project reports completed by the students. He also shared information about his Peruvian contacts and introduced me to members of the Lansing–DeWitt Rotary Club.

Another MSU supporting group consisted of the three sponsoring colleges of the program and the MSU Office of Study Abroad. Representatives from these units, led by the College of Agriculture and Natural Resources and the Office of Study Abroad who committed financial resources to help with the program. These representatives were experienced administrators of study-abroad programs and curricula and were responsible for providing the final clearance for the program to go. This supporting group greatly facilitated my ability to navigate the university and learn what was necessary to design an academically acceptable study-abroad program that would meet the approval of my MSU peers. As a novice study-abroad program leader, I had plenty to learn about the important MSU study-abroad program quality and safety standards in support of students' academic programs at reasonable costs.

A third group of MSU colleagues consisted of my own immediate team that helped me with recruitment and predeparture activities, including developing and teaching twenty hours of the ISS 330c course that met for four hours the week before the students departed to Peru. This group consisted of doctoral students and colleagues from campus who assisted me in teaching the weeklong class.

In planning the Cusco component of the program, I relied largely on Irv Widders's work. He had used a collaborative study-abroad program model of community engagement (Office of Study Abroad, 2011), in which Spanish and history courses are specifically designed for our program students and taught by Peruvian professors. MSU and Academia Latinoamericana de Español, a Peruvian school of languages in Cusco, enter a legal agreement for the provision of formal instruction to the students in language, history, and culture, guided tours to important natural and historical sites, and homestay with Cusco residents. The relationship between MSU and the school is largely a market exchange relationship, where services are exchanged for money. As part of the agreement, the school identifies host families and places the students according to their needs, based on student survey information I provide in advance. As the principal collaborator in Cusco, the Academia Latinoamericana de Español was also our lead contact on matters of safety and student well-being.

When I visited Peru for the first time in November 2011, I spent two days in Cusco and met with the administrators of the school and some of the teaching staff. I also visited the school and toured the city to learn more about the students' learning and living environments and their safety. Irv Widders had established an understanding with the Academia, which I knew had been acceptable to MSU, and I was interested in making similar arrangements. Although my stay in Cusco was short, it met my immediate needs. I left Cusco feeling comfortable with the people from the Academia, who had been wonderful hosts, and satisfied with the understanding that we would finalize our plans and make arrangements once we recruited the students. My communication with the administrators from the Academia continued after my return to the United States and through the spring semester. We finalized a contractual agreement with Academia in April of 2012.

The Cusco component is critical to the success of the Peru program because it prepares the students linguistically and culturally to effectively conduct their community engagement projects in Huamachuco. Cusco is also an important consideration when recruiting students for the program because it is an attraction to students as a study-abroad program destination. The Cusco component is also crucial in meeting the academic needs of students, in terms of both their general university requirements and their college and program requirements. While in Cusco, students earn ten of the thirteen MSU academic course credits they can net through the program. The time spent in the Inca capital is also very important for personal growth. It helps the students to bond as a group and to develop their self-efficacy, as they navigate the Peruvian experience on their own.

The Huamachuco Community of Peers in the Engagement Interface

Unlike the Cusco component of the program, which employs a collaborative model (Office of Study Abroad, 2011) of community engagement, the Huamachuco component operates under a faculty-led model, which means the faculty member leading the program is in charge of the on-site operation. As program leader, it was my responsibility to engage with the people of Huamachuco to decide on the best way to implement the various elements of the program. The community offered an elaborate network of residents, community groups, and local nonprofits and government agencies in support of the program. The key to penetrating this rich network of people and organizations, and gaining their trust and collaboration, was Lucho, whom I had met in November 2011, through Mario Diaz, the MSU alumnus native of Huamachuco who was a founding leader of the Huamachuco Rotary Club and the Peru study-abroad program in Huamachuco. Lucho had secured the cooperation of the NGOs and governmental entities that supported the students' outreach projects and of the host families where the students could stay. He also helped me identify some of the needs and community action goals of the local NGOs and the local government, and assisted in designing appropriate outreach projects.

During Lucho's tenure as president of the Rotary Club of Huamachuco, the club has largely functioned as a community development organization. During Widders's tenure as program leader, Lucho entered into partnership with MSU to act as an on-site program coordinator, which also made him the Peru program's leader and champion in Huamachuco. His leadership role as president of the local Rotary Club facilitated his ability to access the community resources necessary to fulfill his responsibilities as coordinator of the study-abroad program. Lucho's coordinator responsibilities were vital to the actualization of the community engagement experience for the students, and essential to the success of the program. Among these responsibilities were the following: to identify and get nonprofit-sector agencies and public agencies to agree to host the students, to assist in identifying research projects suitable to the students and the local organizations, and to compensate the families with whom the students could stay for six weeks. In addition, Lucho made the hotel accommodations for the faculty, arranged and paid for weekly field trips, coordinated welcome and farewell receptions, attended to the health and safety of both faculty and students, and facilitated the execution of their community engagement projects.

As was the case with me and my peers in Cusco and MSU, Lucho was compensated for assisting with the program in his role as on-site coordinator in Huamachuco. However, Lucho's motive for accepting the responsibility of the program coordinator role was less monetary gain and more reciprocity. He saw the Peru study-abroad program as a community-building effort for Huamachuco, with an opportunity to focus on strengthening the social capacity of Huamachuco residents through their interactions with Americans. He had been instrumental, as early as July 2010, in facilitating formal agreements between the community and the university to promote international academic cooperation. These voluntary draft agreements, although never formally signed by the university and the municipality, indicated commitment by members of both parties to the following activities: (1) development and implementation of research projects involving MSU students, staff, and faculty members appropriate to the needs of the Huamachuco community, and (2) technical assistance.

Even though the university did not sign these agreements, the fact that they were drafted speaks volumes about the instrumental intent of the Huamachuco component of the Peru program—another critical element in the scholarship of engagement interpreted as collaborative inquiry. Service learning, coupled with research projects, which involved MSU students, staff, and faculty, targeted the needs of the Huamachuco community. This instrumental role of the program has always been the signature quality of the Peru program. Indeed, its community engagement pedagogy is what distinguishes the Peru program from other study-abroad programs offered at MSU.

The instrumental character of the Peru program, Lucho's leadership role as president of the local Rotary Club, which facilitated his ability to access the community resources necessary to fulfill his responsibilities as coordinator, and the community support for the Peru program were important program context features beneficial to the community-building effort to establish the study-abroad program in Huamachuco. I maintain, however, that an equally important factor was Lucho's qualities as a community leader. Paul Mattessich and Barbara Monsey (1997), researchers with the Amherst H. Wilder Foundation, have linked the characteristics of community-building organizers to the success of community-building initiatives. Among the characteristics of community-building organizers of successful community-building initiatives that I witnessed Lucho possess were his sincerity of commitment, relationships of trust with community residents, understanding of the community, organizing and administrative experience, and social standing in the community. I am sure the residents of Huamachuco where aware of Lucho's link to the local Rotary Club. However, it was his qualities as a human being and community leader that facilitated his ability to get local agencies and local residents, many dealing with foreigners for the first time, to commit as host families or accommodate the students and facilitate their service-learning and community research projects.

I had the opportunity to witness Lucho's leadership qualities and high social standing in the community during my first visit to Huamachuco in November 2011, as he and I met with leaders from various public and nonprofit agencies and as residents of the community came to his home. Although I was in Huamachuco a short period during my first visit, I was so impressed with Lucho that I remember thanking him for being an example of what it was to be a model public servant.

Lucho and I would meet nearly daily during the four weeks I spent in Huamachuco. He invited me wherever he went and he accompanied me wherever I needed to go, if I so desired. Over the course of the four weeks, we engaged in "repeated episodes of reflection and action," to figure out how to facilitate the work of the students, deal with the daily issues that arose, and engage in dialogue over the long-term challenge of improving the program. Meetings with particular students, their supervisors, and host families took place as needed, although I saw the students nearly every day, since they usually spent some time in Lucho's house, where the Internet signal was the strongest.

The daily dialogue that transpired between Lucho and me was often done in the company of others, rather than in isolation, removed from the input of the students, other stakeholders, and the network of organizations and people who also were part of the community of practice vested in the success of the program. These second-tier members of the Huamachuco community of practice included the students, the host families, the NGOs and public agency organizations where we placed the students, and the individuals overseeing the students' work. Our discussions with the students about their work and home arrangements were particularly useful in helping me think through what could be accomplished by students during five to six weeks, what could be learned by addressing the community development issues in Huamachuco, and what types of skills would be needed in students of the program in the future. Residents of Huamachuco, particularly those who were involved in the program, recognized the importance of the study-abroad program and were motivated to do their part to make it succeed. The families hosting the students and the agency supervisors of the students had shown flexibility with the students and were adaptive to their service-learning and research interests. In addition to Lucho's leadership, a social cohesion existed in Huamachuco, which in hindsight was evidence of the fact that the community had previously come together and collaborated on projects involving international characters, like MSU students and faculty members.

A third tier of members of the Huamachuco community of practice included Huamachuco Rotary Club members and other individuals, local associations, and all of the other more formal institutions located in Huamachuco that welcomed the students and facilitated completion of their work. An important member of this group included the mayor of Huamachuco, who gave the students and the program faculty a welcome reception and signed proclamations in recognition of their good work. Another important individual was Mario Diaz, the MSU alumnus I met when I first assumed leadership of the program. He and other MSU alumni, as members of the DeWitt Rotary Club, had sponsored community engagement projects in Huamachuco for many years. Mario met me in Lima and accompanied me to Huamachuco in November 2011, when I first met Lucho and some of the local agency leaders. Like Lucho, he too has been a source of support and inspiration.

Inasmuch as there existed a mutually negotiated entrée between MSU and the Rotary Club of Huamachuco, as program leader, it is good practice to remember, and to remind the students, that we are invited guests. Huamachuco, as the host community, and the Huamachuco Rotary Club, as the partnering organization, hold the option to prevent continuous entry and to terminate MSU access to Huamachuco at any time. Being mindful of this potentiality is necessary to focus not only on accomplishing the tasks associated with community development outcomes, but also on establishing and developing relationships to promote mutual support and trust. This is necessary, not only with Lucho, the chief host, but with a variety of less powerful persons at the subsite level, like the directors of the different NGOs and public agencies where our students do their community engagement projects, or the heads of the host families. Given my long-term interest in the program's sustainability, and despite our excellent collaborating partner in Lucho and the Huamachuco Rotary Club, I deemed it necessary to spend as much time as I could getting to know subsite-level community leaders to nurture trust and reaffirm the instrumental intent of the program.

Respectful Engagement and Engaged Learning

Having a community of practice to "interact collaboratively and deliberatively for the purpose of creating and enacting a shared learning agenda" (Doberneck, 2009) is a critical element in the scholarship of engagement interpreted as collaborative inquiry. In addition to its instrumentality, another characteristic of this new scholarship of engagement is its stance on the importance of "respectful engagement" and the co-ownership of the community engagement process and outcome.[3] This stance situates community participants and MSU faculty and students as colleagues and co-learners in a jointly defined enterprise, which in our case was reinstating the study-abroad program in Huamachuco with benefits to MSU students and the community of Huamachuco. In the program in 2009 and 2010, the community engagement projects of MSU students had benefited the students and enabled community development programs. Thus, it was our goal to emulate prior renditions of the program and generate similar benefits for MSU students and residents of Huamachuco.

As stated in the program's description, the Peru program in Huamachuco is governed by a set of principles that speak of the program as an intervention grounded in a philosophical stance that supports a participatory worldview in which the research needs of the residents are given priority and where the generation of knowledge is a shared responsibility. Of the set of principles for the Peru program, Principle 5 in particular resonates with me the most, given its commitment to supporting community organizations and institutions and their priorities through a participatory approach focused on the needs of the community of Huamachuco. To that end, our effort to reinstitute and implement the 2012 Peru study-abroad program as a university intervention and community development initiative was very much a social product. It represents a coupling of student research skills and interests with organizational resources in Huamachuco to address the needs of the community. Students interested in going on a study-abroad program knew about the community-engagement focus of the program from the start of the program. The students who joined the program welcomed the opportunity to collaborate with an NGO working on bettering the community. They embraced the process of identifying outreach research projects and internship opportunities with NGOs and public agencies. The ISS 330c course I taught on campus helped reinforce the concept of participatory action research, collaborative learning, and respect for the host country and its people.

As noted earlier, in a variety of fields, including my own, the inclination by the faculty to engage communities in the search for solutions has long been popular. In community economic development, in particular, participation by individuals, community-based institutions, and local businesses and institutions is essential to achieve community improvements. Indeed, concepts concerning community participation provide one set of explanations of why the process of community engagement might be useful in addressing the social and physical long-term aspects of an individuals' environment (Centers for Disease Control and Prevention, 1997). As a faculty member teaching and conducting outreach and research for the last twenty years in the field of community economic development, I had long embraced this approach to my work and found it indispensable to the work students and I were doing in Huamachuco.

As such, the MSU–Huamachuco Rotary Club collaboration to implement the MSU community-engagement study-abroad program, as collaborative learning for development, represents an alternative to the traditional development model in the sense that the university did not dictate or direct its operations in Huamachuco, at least not entirely. Just as the community of Huamachuco has the power of invitation, MSU has the power of separation from Huamachuco, which it chose to exercise in 2010 by discontinuing the program. Inasmuch as the college sponsors endorsed Huamachuco as a site suited for a study-abroad program, the program also had to make sense administratively and financially. From the perspective of college representatives who had the final say on the continuation of the program, the pedagogical approach to engagement embedded in the study-abroad program as originally designed, which relied on a low student–mentor ratio to provide technical assistance to the student in their projects, was deemed unsustainable, cost-ineffective, and therefore unacceptable. When I assumed leadership of the program in the fall of 2011, I had to adhere to a traditional study-abroad model that had a higher student–faculty ratio than was required by the mentor model used by my predecessor in 2009 and 2010.

Aside from the MSU debate over the number of faculty members who could participate in the program, the Peru program represented the making of what is a collaborative effort. The Huamachuco component, in particular, was executed on the basis of participatory principles and collective discourse, between myself, as program leader, and Lucho, our key coordinator and community representative in Huamachuco. Although the students in the study-abroad program did not arrive in Huamachuco until mid-July of the summer of 2012, the efforts to plan the program and their community outreach projects began much earlier—in November 2011, when I first visited Huamachuco and spent time with Lucho and Mario. The "joint talk" Lucho, Mario, and I had over the four days I visited Huamachuco envisioned a program much like before. Our discussions produced a joint understanding of the purpose for the program and reaffirmed our joint vision, governed in principle by earlier visions of the program under Irv Widders's leadership.

The community and organizational needs I identified through my dialogues with Lucho, Mario, and others I met through acquaintance while in Huamachuco served to market the program and recruit students when I got back to MSU. The marketing of the research and service opportunities in Huamachuco also helped us with the student application since the students who signed up for the program had to write an essay describing their research interests and career plans. The interviews with the students that followed helped us determine the suitability of the program for the students before granting admissions.

The integration of student interests with community needs initially took the form of written research project proposals on topics of mutual interest to students and the community. Students worked on their research proposals while taking ISS 330c at MSU during the first week of the program before they departed for Peru. To facilitate the proposal writing process and engage the students in a meaningful way, students made contact with Lucho via Skype, who provided a better understanding of the community, its needs, and detailed information about the various agencies where the students would intern. To give the students a clear idea of what was expected for their research papers, students were also asked to review and discuss research papers of students who had participated in the program in prior years. The last day of the class was devoted to presentations and discussion of their own research proposal plans. While the research proposals provided them with a concrete idea of what they could undertake as a research project in Huamachuco, students were reminded of the need for flexibility, in both research methods and topics.

Students traveled from the United States to Cusco before traveling to Huamachuco, so six weeks would transpire from the time the students drafted their research proposals to the time they would be on site in Huamachuco to undertake their research projects. I joined the students in Lima after their stay in Cusco. We met up with Lucho in Trujillo in Northern Peru two days later, and he accompanied us the next morning on our six-hour bus ride to Huamachuco. It was cold, wet, and late the Saturday night we arrived, and the host families had been waiting at the bus station several hours, so Lucho quickly paired students with preselected host families, who helped the students with their luggage and took them to their houses.

I met with the host families on numerous occasions over the course of my four weeks in Huamachuco. However, to honor the relationship between the students and their host families, I kept a respectful distance. Only in one case did an incident occur where Lucho and I had to intervene to resolve a matter between a student and her host family. I later learned that after I departed Huamachuco, problems between the student and her host family reemerged, and the student took advantage of the opportunity to move in with the host family of another student.

That incident is a reminder of how easily matters can derail and how fragile relationships can be in the engagement interface. The host family involved in the incident had been a host family in the 2010 Peru Program. The head of household, who made the host family arrangements with Lucho, was a nurse and Lucho highly regarded the host family. It was an unfortunate situation for the student, but also for Lucho, who wanted to keep the family as a host family in the future. Lucho had lost host families in the program before, and he wanted to hold on to those he had. Housing, he explained to me, was a real problem in Huamachuco because of the growth in the mining industry and the increased demand for housing by miners. Because of this increased demand for housing, the rent for a single room was extremely high.

Lucho and I met up with the students on Monday after arriving in Huamachuco, and we escorted each student to the organization where they were going to do their service-learning projects. We met the NGO personnel and student supervisors, received an orientation of the facility, and discussed their service-learning projects. Surprisingly, these service-learning assignments went relatively smoothly for the students. For the most part, the students and their supervisors handled the issues associated with these placements.

In my role as program leader, interested in the effective execution of the Peru program in Huamachuco, I was observer, listener, questioner, encourager, and facilitator. My approach and system of inquiry generally involved getting answers to questions about situations and events I saw in Huamachuco that could affect the program, or about the range of community development options and opportunities that the students could engage in over the long term. There were two occasions in which Lucho and I intervened directly to address some student concerns, but for the most part, students handled things on their own, often after talking things over themselves and/ or with Lucho and me. We gathered each Friday night as a group and shared weekend excursions, so we maintained frequent interaction with the students. At these reflection sessions, I often encouraged journal writing for students to reflect on their experiences. I also reminded them of the norms of engagement and their role as both MSU and U.S. ambassadors of our program.

In the majority of service-learning projects, the service-learning activities consisted of a teaching role, in Spanish, by the MSU students. Two students, with career interest in studio art and theater, respectively, teamed up and used their theater and art techniques to teach middle school students at a local alternative school about self-esteem. Two other students with interest in nutrition, history, and culture, respectively, did their community service project at a prekindergarten school, where they prepared lesson plans in Spanish for preschoolers on eating healthy, being patriotic, and improving social behavior. A third student, with interest in working with children with disabilities, worked at a local primary and secondary school helping a teacher instruct in a classroom of handicapped children. In addition, the MSU student helped teachers of English at the school with their English pronunciation. Another student, of fine arts, with an academic and career interest in textile products, took photos of textile products made by students at a local alternative school as part of career training, and then compiled an electronic catalog of all the products and put them on the Internet. Two other students, with interests in health issues, were assigned to a local hospital to help in various capacities, from assisting nurses with patients to putting on workshops for children.

The students and I had consulted with Lucho and his network of organizations in selecting and planning their research projects before departing for Peru; thus, in the majority of instances, the students' research proposals served as their guide to their research project activities. Only in one instance did an initial research proposal prepared before the students departed not match the final research project completed. All the projects were organized around issues that mattered to the people of Huamachuco.

Students were encouraged to take ownership of their outreach projects, in consultation with their supervisors, for the benefit of community. My role in helping the students with their research projects was as an encourager and facilitator, but also as an educator. Most students had methodological concerns, although a couple of students needed better understanding of the problem they wanted to research. One student needed help with survey development, another needed help identifying interview clients, and a third needed help with the formation of focus groups. Two other students needed help with data collection, data access, and dataset development. The students and I mostly addressed these matters, but Lucho was always a nearby resource.

The research projects produced some tangible results. Each student made a presentation of their findings to the community as planned, and all but one student submitted their research project papers. The teachers and agency directors kept the lesson plans, needs assessments, and research findings for them to consider.

Regrettably, I did not spend the last two weeks of the program with the students due to prior commitments. However, Lucho and the students' supervisors were pleased with the contributions of the students. My faculty colleague had this to say about the students and their work on those final weeks of the program in Huamachuco, as I was preparing their final grades:

> So, one thing that I forgot to mention is my recommendation that the students—all—get a 4.0 as grades for their work in their courses. I am sure that you will agree with me that the group was simply unbelievable. This group of students had no slacker whatsoever . . . All of them were working hard in challenging conditions and except for a few things here and there, all of them were real troopers. They certainly adapted, contributed, and learned from Peru. (e-mail from M. Chavez, August 20, 2012)

Although we did not formally evaluate student outcomes, we did spend a considerable amount of time with the students and had the pleasure of reading their reflective essays. It is clear the students had a transformative experience. As one student states in her reflective essay, "This was definitely a life experience I will always hold close to me, cherish, and never forget. As my friend Will from the trip stated, 'youth, money, life well spent'" (Bassman, 2012).

It also appears that the community leaders of the program were equally satisfied with the students and program overall. I conclude this section with a letter I received from Lucho after the program was over. It summarizes the benefits to the community that he saw accrue because of the community engagement component of the program. His letter is his personal assessment of how the program went. It is not meant to be a comprehensive assessment of the program's impact. According to Lucho, the benefits of the community engagement program positively affected four constituencies:

- Benefits for the sectors (governmental and nongovernmental organizations) of the area were principally the exchange of understanding; the help provided by each student in their research project was invaluable, as was the teaching of English to students and teachers a beautiful experience.
- Benefits for the host families, primarily the exchange of culture, the experience of assuming responsibility for a new son in the family, getting used to and close to the students, and being deeply saddened by their departure.
- Benefits to the children, the families, were excellent, as exemplified by public demonstration of satisfaction and respect for MSU students in the streets and in public forums.
- Benefits to the community of Huamachuco, primarily the exchange of culture, the assistance to arts and crafts production and marketing of textile products abroad, the teaching of English to children, as well as the physical therapy for adults and children in the hospital, teaching the parents about food nutrition for their children, and teaching children to eat healthy.

MSU colleagues speak in terms of the need to "interact collaboratively and deliberatively for the purpose of creating and enacting a shared learning agenda" (Doberneck, 2009). There is no denying the fact that the outcomes of the Peru program were the result of collaborative efforts of many groups of people at MSU, in Cusco, and in Huamachuco. As diverse as we were, we functioned as a cohesive collaborative community of interest, bound by our commitment to see the program succeed. In the Huamachuco engagement interface, in particular, Lucho and I were keenly aware of the need to work collaboratively and for me to learn more about the needs and assets of the community. I also realized that to effectively capitalize on the strengths of the MSU students and the community's readiness to accept the program, I needed to strengthen my relationships not just with Lucho and his fellow Rotarians, but also with a variety of less powerful persons at the subsite level. This included people like the directors of the NGOs where our students did their community engagement projects, the host families, and other community leaders, like the local bishop, the mayor, and members of his administration.

Summary and Conclusion

This chapter began with a brief overview of the outreach and study-abroad movements in higher education. It linked these developments to the growth in the use of community engagement pedagogy in study-abroad programs to promote both student learning and community goals. We then explained the engagement interface framework we used to describe the work we did through the Peru program in Huamachuco in the name of engagement as collaborative inquiry.

What did the MSU Peru study-abroad program accomplish in Huamachuco in the name of community engagement? The service-learning literature suggests that student development takes different forms, including students' academic learning, sense of civic responsibility, and life skills (Gray et al., 1999). Although a formal assessment of student development outcomes resulting from this program is not part of this analysis, our study suggests Huamachuco was an excellent setting to facilitate these learning outcomes. As a community, Huamachuco was ready to move forward with the MSU Peru study-abroad program and was very accommodating to the students. Lucho certainly recognized the importance of the community engagement projects in facilitating student learning and reflection. The organizational staff of the agencies where students worked engaged in daily dialogue with the students and was sensitive to their needs. The students interacted with Lucho and me on a regular basis, often sharing their highs and their lows of what they were learning. Personal and group discussions with the students, written commentary, the strong commitment shown by the students to their community engagement projects, and the respect and appreciation they showed their NGOs and host families all suggest to us significant outcomes in student development.

There were also tangible outcomes for the community and the university from our engage-ment. In Huamachuco, each of the eight students in the program contributed at least forty hours a week for five and a half weeks, in direct services to NGOs, schools, a cooperative, and a regional hospital. This resulted in a variety of outputs, including electronic catalogs of products produced by nonprofits, and lesson plans for the centers to use. The students also committed considerable amounts of time to their research projects in support of community and organizational action goals, the findings of which were shared with their supervisors and members of the community. Our discussions with the staff members who coordinated or oversaw volunteer programs in the various agencies suggest that the contributions of our students were significant. Lucho was certainly pleased and urged us to bring a larger number of students in 2013. Institutionally, the success of the program expanded the capacity of MSU to operate a study-abroad program where community-engagement pedagogy is its distinguishing feature. By supporting the program, MSU demonstrates its commitment to student learning, international collaboration, and community development.

This chapter also demonstrates how the engagement interface framework of engaged learning can be used to understand what it takes a program leader to make the Peru program a teach-ing and learning strategy that integrates meaningful community service with instruction and reflection to enrich the students' learning experience and strengthen communities. As a unifying frame of reference for scholarly work in engagement, the framework embraces engagement as a collaborative form of action inquiry, which stands in sharp contrast to the historically dominant paradigm where control of the engagement process resides with university experts. As such, the analysis brings recognition to the multiple university and community groups that were vested with me in figuring out the best way to implement the program. It also facilitates recognition to Huamachuco as a community with the leadership and community readiness necessary to implement the Peru program. The importance of the enterprise as collaborative inquiry was particularly evident in the way the students and I worked in collaboration with Lucho to design and implement the students' community outreach projects.

Engagement as collaborative inquiry resonated with me as sound propositional knowledge because of what I do that works in community economic development, which embraces a participatory approach as best practice. Hence, from the start, I was respectful of the need to engage the community—the individuals, community-based institutions, and local businesses and institutions—in the search for solutions to ways that resembled "essential practices of engaged learning" in the execution of the duties associated with implementing the Peru study-abroad program.

There are a couple of key takeaways I would like to emphasize from my assessment of my experience as a first-time program leader of the community-engagement project that is the Peru study-abroad program. First, it is important to recognize that I was fortunate to step into a situation that had the support of the both the university and the community. Multiple groups from MSU, Cusco, and Huamachuco were vested in the successful reinstatement of MSU's Peru study-abroad program in Huamachuco, and this support needs to be recognized as a key factor in the program's successful reentry into the community. Entering in Huamachuco had been and continues to be mutually voluntary but negotiated, with key principles to guide our participation. I was particularly fortunate to collaborate with the Huamachuco Rotary Club and Lucho, its president, who willingly assumed major responsibilities as the program's on-site coordinator and champion. These responsibilities were key to the program's success because even though we were welcomed and granted permission to enter the community and share in their lives, in actuality, it was Lucho and the local Rotary Club who had been granted permission. It was they who secured the support of the community and created the conditions necessary to facilitate acceptance of the study-abroad program in the community. Gaining access into the community of Huamachuco certainly would have been much more difficult if the Huamachuco Rotary Club and Lucho had not been our collaborators or if we had started from scratch. Although all elements of the program are important in its successful implementation, perhaps the most important component is having a competent and respected partner and community leader you can depend on as on-site program coordinator. It is perhaps the most important requirement in the implementing a study-abroad program using a community engagement pedagogy.

The other main takeaway from this case study is the importance of recognizing the scholarship of engagement as contested terrain in the way we learn, which suggests the need for researchers to be mindful of taking a personal stance on the matter. Part of the discourse in engagement as a field of study is about whether engagement scholarship should be seen as the functional equivalent of laboratory research, an idealized scientific process, controlled by experts and grounded in the positivist tradition. The new scholarship of community engagement stands philosophically in conflict to this historically dominant paradigm and prevailing ethos of technical rationality found at American research universities. The alternative to this, which I embrace, is to identify with scholarship that is grounded in a participative worldview and places an emphasis on experiential encounter as the ontological basis for knowing and being. This view of engagement and way of knowing, in my opinion, is the pragmatic stance to take in context of a study-abroad program reliant on community engagement pedagogy for the benefit of both students and community.

NOTES

1. Education brought recognition to service learning as an academic field. Another catalyst for the outreach and engagement movement within higher education was passage of the National and Community Service Act of 1990, which provided funding to develop and implement service learning curricula (Ross, 2002).

   It should be noted, however, that the benefits from community engagement have been recognized in fields other than education. Over the past three decades, researchers have provided evidence to support the notion that community engagement is a powerful vehicle for bringing about environmental and behavioral changes that will improve the health of the community and its members. In the early 1990s the Centers for Disease Control and Prevention developed a working definition of community engagement as "the process of working collaboratively with and through groups of people affiliated by geographic proximity, special interest, or similar situation to address issues affecting the well-being of those people" (Centers for Disease Control and Prevention, 1997).

2. Bob Church, who once served as Vice Provost for University Outreach at MSU, explains that they chose to identify this type of scholarly activity as outreach to distinguish it from "public service," "service," and "extension" but that they could have just as well call it "engagement" (Church et al., 2003).

   The year 1990 was a watershed year for the outreach and engagement movement in American universities. Among the most significant events was the publication of Ernest Boyer's landmark study *Scholarship Reconsidered: Priorities of the Professoriate,* which called on faculty members to rethink their notion of scholarship so universities could become responsive to the needs of society. The year 1990 was also the year Campus Compact initiated its flagship Project on Integrating with Service with Academic Study, which helped universities incorporate community service into their teaching and research. The National Society for Experimental Education published a three-volume set on service learning that year.

3. These concepts were borrowed from *Coming to Critical Engagement* (Fear et al., 2006, pp. 26 and 62).

REFERENCES

Amey, M. J. (2002). Evaluating outreach performance. *New Directions for Institutional Research, 114,* 33–42.

Bandy, J. (2012a). What is service learning or community engagement? Retrieved from http://cft. vanderbilt.edu/guides-sub-pages/teaching-through-community-engagement.

Bandy, J. (2012b). A word on nomenclature. Retrieved from http://cft.vanderbilt.edu/ guides-sub-pages/a-word-on-nomenclature.

Bassman, E. (2012). Reflection essay. Unpublished manuscript for Michigan State University course ISS 330 C Community Engagement and Interdisciplinary Study of Global Issues in the Peruvian Andes.

Bawden, R. J. (2001). Life beyond economics: Learning systems and social capital. In I. Falk (Ed.), *Learning to manage change: Developing regional communities for a local-global millennium.* (pp. 23–30). Kensington Park, Australia: National Center for Vocational Education Research Ltd. and the University of Tasmania.

Berquist, B. (2012, November 2). Office of Study Abroad 2012 student conference presentation. East Lansing, MI.

Berquist, B., & Widders, I. (2011). Liderazgo en la internacionalización: Un compromiso comunitario. *Educación Global, 15,* 87–97.

Boyer, E. T. (1990). *Scholarship reconsidered: Priorities of the professoriate.* San Francisco: Jossey-Bass.

Bray, J., Lee, J., Smith, L., & Yorks, L. (2000). *Collaborative inquiry in practice: Action, reflection, and making meaning.* Thousand Oaks, CA: Sage.

Brown, W., & Mondol, H. (2010). Re: Huamachuco, Peru Study Abroad Program. Received by Lou Anna K. Simon, December 31.

Centers for Disease Control and Prevention. (1997). *Principles of community engagement.* Atlanta, GA: CDC/ATSDR Committee on Community Engagement, Public Health Practice Program Office.

Church, R. L., Zimmerman, D. L., Bargerstock, B.A., & Kenny, P. A. (2003). Measuring scholarly outreach at Michigan State University: Definition, challenges, tools. *Journal of Higher Education Outreach and Engagement, 8*(1), 141–152.

CIC Committee on Engagement. (2005). *Engaged scholarship: A resource guide,* Champaign, IL: Committee on Institutional Cooperation.

Conway, C. (2004). An economic development perspective on education abroad. *International Educator,* April, 34. Retrieved from http://highbeam.com/doc/1P3-772375901.html.

Crabtree, R. D. (2008). Theoretical foundations for international service learning. *Michigan Journal of Community Service Learning, 15*(1), 18–36.

Dewey, J. (1919). *Democracy and education: An introduction to the philosophy of education.* New York: Macmillan.

Doberneck, D. M. (2009). Community engagement in rural Ireland, a lecturer's perspective. In L. McIlrath & A. Farrell, (Eds.), *Mapping civic engagement within higher education in Ireland* (pp. 58–81). Kildare, Ireland/Dublin, Ireland: All Ireland Society for Higher Education/Network for the Promotion of Civic Engagement in Irish Higher Education.

Doberneck, D. M., Glass, C. R., & Schweitzer, J. H. (2009, September). *Scholarly outreach and engagement reported by successfully tenured faculty at Michigan State University 2002–2006.* East Lansing: National Center for the Study of University Engagement, Michigan State University.

Engle, L., & Engle, J. (2003). Study abroad levels: Toward a classification of program types. *Frontiers: The Interdisciplinary Journal of Study Abroad, 9,* 1–20.

Fear, F. A., Bawden, R. J., Rosaen, C. L., & Foster-Fishman, P. (2002). A model for engaged learning: Frame of reference for scholarly underpinnings. *Journal of Higher Education Outreach and Engagement, 7*(3), 55–68.

Fear, F. A., Rosaen, C. L., Bawden, R. J., & Foster-Fishman, P. (2006). *Coming to critical engagement: An autoethnographic exploration.* Lanham, MD: University Press of America.

Fear, F. A., Rosaen, C. L., Foster-Fishman, P., & Bawden, R. J. (2001). Outreach as scholarly expression: A faculty perspective. *Journal of Higher Education Outreach and Engagement, 6*(2), 21–34.

Fear, F. A., & Sandmann, L.R. (2001–2002). The "new" scholarship: Implications for engagement and extension. *Journal of Higher Education Outreach and Engagement, 7*(1 & 2), 29–39.

Fitzgerald, H. E. (2000). From inreach to outreach: Innovations in higher education. *Journal of Higher Education Outreach and Engagement, 6*(1), 61–70.

Fitzgerald, H. E. (2016). RE: University engagement defined. Received by the author, December 5.

Freire, P. (1970). *Pedagogy of the oppressed.* New York: Herder and Herder.

Gardner, P., Gross, L., & Steglitz, I. (2008, March). *Unpacking your study abroad experience: Critical reflection for work competencies* (Research Brief 1). East Lansing: College Employment Research Institute, Michigan State University.

Gray, M., Ondaatje, E. H., Fricker, R., Geschwind, S., Goldman, C., Kaganoff, T., Robyn, A., Sundt, M., Vogelgesang, L., & Klein, S. (1999). *Combining service and learning in higher education: Evaluation of the Learn and Serve America, Higher Education Program.* Santa, Monica, CA: RAND.

Lunsford, C. G., Church, R., & Zimmerman, D. L. (2006). Assessing Michigan State University's efforts to embed engagement across the institution: Findings and challenges. *Journal of Higher Education Outreach and Engagement, 11*(1), 89–104.

Mattessich, P., & Monsey, B. (1997). *Community building: What makes it work: A review of factors influencing successful community building.* St. Paul, MN: Wilder Research Center, Amherst H. Wilder Foundation.

Michigan State University, University Outreach and Engagement. (2012). Outreach & Engagement Measurement Instrument (OEMI). Retrieved from http://oemi.msu.edu/Default.aspx?ReturnUrl=.

Office of Study Abroad, Michigan State University. (2011). Models. Retrieved from http://studyabroad.isp.msu.edu/program_development/steps/framing/models.htm.

Parker, B., & Dautoff, D. A. (2007). Service-learning and study abroad: Synergistic learning opportunities. *Michigan Journal of Community Service Learning, 13*(2), 40–52.

Rosaen, C., Foster-Fishman, P., & Fear, F. A. (2001). The citizen scholar: Joining voices and values in the engagement interface. *Metropolitan Universities, 12*(4), 10–29.

Ross, L. M. (2002, August). Lasting engagement: American higher education and community engagement: A historical perspective. In M. Martinez (Ed.), *Lasting engagement: Building and sustaining a commitment to community outreach, development, and collaboration* (pp. 1–17). Washington, DC: U.S. Department of Housing and Urban Development.

Schatzman, L., & Strauss, A. L. (1973). *Field research: Strategies for a natural sociology.* Englewood Cliffs, NJ: Prentice Hall.

Schön, D. A. (1983). *The reflective practitioner.* New York, NY: Basic Books.

Thomson, J. S. (2008). Finding my voice to make democracy work. *Journal of Higher Education Outreach and Engagement, 12*(2), 113–116.

Votruba, J. C. (1997). Strengthening the university's alignment with society's challenges and strategies. *Journal of Public Service and Outreach, 1*(1), 29–36.

CHAPTER 8

Reexamining University–Community Partnerships in a Civic Engagement Study-Abroad Program

Vincent Delgado and Scot Yoder

I t is no secret that strong university–community partnerships are essential to successful domestic service-learning and civic-engagement programs.[1] However, while there is an increasing desire to incorporate service learning or civic engagement into international study-abroad programs, relatively little attention has been paid to the nature of the university–community partnerships in this context. In this chapter we explore how our experience with a study-abroad program in Costa Rica has led us to rethink our model of university–community partnerships and its implications for student learning. This program involves civic engagement as a central component. We describe the program and thinking that led to its construction, clarify the nature of our university–community partnerships as we initially developed them, identify particular challenges that have arisen from these partnerships, and discuss the implementation of an alternative model of university–community partnerships designed to better meet the needs of students, faculty, and community partners.

The Program

"Ethics in Tourism and Sustainable Development—Costa Rica" is a study-abroad program sponsored by the Residential College in the Arts and Humanities (RCAH) at Michigan State University (MSU). The RCAH is a unique interdisciplinary arts and humanities program with a mission to "weave together the passion, imagination, humor, and candor of the arts and humanities to promote individual well being and the common good." The college emphasizes world languages and cultures, critical thinking, creativity, ethics, and engaged learning to accomplish this mission. Civic engagement is included not as an option, but as a central and required element of the core curriculum.

In 2008, we began planning a study-abroad program that would meet the curricular needs of RCAH students while taking advantage of our professional backgrounds and personal experience. We decided to develop a program in Costa Rica, as we both had significant experience and established connections in the country. Given the RCAH curriculum and our own professional backgrounds (Yoder, philosophy/ethics; Delgado, civic engagement), we decided to develop a program around the core RCAH themes of ethics and civic engagement.

The program focuses on the ethics of development and the important role that tourism plays in Costa Rica's sustainable development strategy. With natural beauty, incredible biological diversity, a high rate of literacy, and a stable democracy, Costa Rica has become a popular destination for international tourists. Many large resorts have been built and tourism has grown into one of the leading sectors of the Costa Rican economy. While the country is famous for ecotourism, several forms of alternative tourism, including volunteer tourism, educational tourism, and community rural tourism, have also rapidly developed. The program objectives related to tourism and sustainable development involve helping students to:

- explore the concept of sustainable development;
- consider relevant forms of alternative tourism (e.g., ecotourism, community rural tourism, volunteer tourism, and educational tourism) as sustainable development strategies; and
- develop an understanding of how these forms of tourism have been implemented in Costa Rica and the impact they have had at both the national and local levels.

The program also focuses on developing student understanding of what Mitchell, Visconti, Keene, and Battistoni (2011) refer to as the knowledge, skills, and attitudes required to be active and engaged citizens. The program includes courses from the college-level civic engagement curriculum, which is based on the RCAH Model of Civic Engagement. This model identifies four critical components:

1. Insight—increasing an awareness of ourselves, communities, and the world.
2. Practice—developing our relationships to communities and the world.
3. Action—affecting positive social change in the community.
4. Passion—cultivating a sense of wonder and joy in our relationships with others (Delgado & DeLind, n.d.).

The model is not linear. For instance, while the civic engagement curriculum begins with an emphasis on insight as preparation for practice and action, the process of engaging with communities further deepens insight, which in turn leads to still deeper forms of engagement. Thus, the process is both developmental and recursive.

This particular program, then, was designed specifically to meet the following educational goals related to the civic engagement curriculum:

- Gain a better understanding of civic engagement as it connects to the broader context of the arts and humanities.
- Understand the roles that self-reflection, inner growth, and personal commitment play in civic engagement.

- Develop the skills and passion necessary for engaging in community partnerships, including colearning, building trust, capacity building, forming partnerships, and networks.
- Apply the RCAH generative model of civic engagement in a specific community context.
- Synthesize academic, community-based, and other methods/sources of knowledge and expertise in defining problems, researching issues, and proposing projects.
- Understand civic responsibility as driven by a sense of personal commitment.

While the goals provided the foundation of the ethics and civic engagement curriculum, we also identified several additional principles to guide us in the development of the program. These principles were intended to ensure that the program was both mutually beneficial to our Costa Rican partners and a rich, culturally immersive, and holistic student experience:

- Do not transport the culture of MSU to Costa Rica. We want students to be immersed in Costa Rican culture. For this reason, we keep the program small (i.e., we try to limit enrollment to fifteen students) and make homestays a central element.
- Make the length of the trip longer rather than shorter. Eight weeks is the minimum.
- Consider ethical issues every step of the way. Ethics is one of the cornerstones of the RCAH curriculum, and we keep it in the forefront of everything we do in the program. At the most basic level, the content of the program is about the ethics of tourism and sustainable development. However, we also want students to reflect on the ethics of our engagement with Costa Rican communities and on our role as tourists in the country. Finally, we try to model ethical behavior in our community partnerships.
- Focus on skills and tools. To help our students engage, we help them develop certain basic skills and tools. These include, but are not limited to, Spanish language skills, collaboration skills, and self-assessment skills. After working with our communities for a few years, we added basic training in teaching English as a foreign language.
- Make experience a text.[2] It is tempting to treat the study-abroad program as a set of on-campus courses with learning objectives focused on certain content areas. However, we had learned from previous experience that loading students with "academic" work leaves little space to incorporate learning that emerges from the immersion experience itself. By thinking of the experience as text we hope to bring this sort of learning to the forefront.
- Keep the program partner-driven. Our community partners are absolutely essential to the success of the program. We are successful only to the extent that We collaborate with our partners to develop a program that is co-generative and mutually beneficial.

These principles shaped both the content and structure of the course, which has run five times since 2009, with groups ranging from six to sixteen students. (We made changes prior to running the program in 2015 that are discussed later.) During the first four weeks, students live with families in Santa Ana and take intensive Spanish classes taught by Costa Rican instructors,[3] as well as two courses taught by the RCAH faculty. One is an ethics course focused on tourism and sustainable development (Special Topics in the Arts and Humanities) and the other is a course that explores the principles, methods, and meaning of civic engagement and prepares students to work collaboratively in communities (Engagement and Reflection). Civic engagement and ethics are thus given equal weight. The program uses civic engagement to teach ethics and ethics to teach civic engagement. We also plan group excursions and assignments to progressively prepare students to travel independently in Costa Rica.

At the end of this period we divide the group into smaller teams of two to four students and disperse them to small communities throughout the country, where they live with families and work with community partners on a variety of rural tourism projects for the next four weeks. To date, we have worked with nine different communities at various stages in the development of community rural tourism—El Yüe (located in Province of Talamanca), Palmichal (Province of San Jose), San Pablo (Province of San Jose), Cedral de Mirimar (in the Montes de Oro in the Province of Puntarenas), Santa Rosa (Province of Limon), Cartagena (Province of Limon), Tres Rios de Coronado (Province of Osa), Cañas (Province of Puntarenas), and San Luis (Province of Puntarenas). These are all very small communities, and some do not even appear on maps of Costa Rica. During this time, we visit each community at least twice to work with students and nurture relationships with our community partners. Finally, we bring the students back to a single location for a few days at the end of the program to debrief and work on their final projects before returning to the United States.

The Importance of Partnerships

In a program that requires students to study civic engagement and engage deeply in rural communities that are often isolated physically and economically from the rest of the county, our community partnerships are essential to the program. Indeed, much of our work in-country—beyond teaching—is spent ensuring our infrastructure of community partnerships is robust, highly communicative, and informed by the latest research on university–community partnership development. Because much of our course content focuses on helping students consider, and in some cases develop, the knowledge, skills, and the attitudes required for engaged citizenship, our partnerships are more than a necessary infrastructure; they are critical pedagogical elements of the program.

Understanding what is needed for these partnerships has not been a simple task. Little research has been conducted specifically on service learning and civic engagement partnerships for international study. This has required us to rely on past experience with study abroad and to adapt scholarship on domestic service learning and civic-engagement partnerships to guide the development of our partnerships and programming abroad. During the past several decades, scholars, for instance, have increasingly pointed to the power dynamics between university and community institutional and organizational partners, suggesting that too often the focus is on student pedagogical outcomes and university research rather than on community impact (Afshar, 2005; Cruz & Giles, 2000; Ferman & Hill, 2004; Leiderman, Furco, Zapf, & Goss, 2003; Stoecker & Tyron, 2009). Still other researchers have focused on the partnership factors that influence positive student, university, and community outcomes (Holland & Gelmon, 1998). Ferman and Hill

(2004) suggest partners reach consensus on desire and incentive for the partnership, as well as on capacity and physical space issues. Some call for practitioners to spend significant time building reciprocal relationships (Weerts & Sandmann, 2008), identify mutually beneficial tasks (Karasik & Wallingford, 2007), consider issues of power and authority (Prins, 2005), and map the dimensions of partnership relationships (King & Baxter Magolda, 2005) and multilevel trust (Rousseau, Sitkin, Burt, & Camerer, 1998). We have focused closely on these dynamics, engaging in frequent discussions with our partners about who they are, what they want out of our collaboration, and how we can work together toward mutually reciprocal outcomes.

Still, much of the research on partnerships for service learning and civic engagement resides at the level of partnerships between institutions and organizations, which is where we have focused our energies and other resources in the development of our infrastructure of partnerships across Costa Rica. Rogge and Rocha (2005), for instance, suggest that universities and their partners establish common goals, financial incentives, and an understanding of differences in time management. In our program, we develop memoranda of understanding with our partners and have ensured that they are fairly compensated for their collaboration with our program. For instance, we often pay higher rates for homestays than do other institutions running programs in Costa Rica.

Others scholars recommend acknowledging differences between university and community institutions in elite power (Boyle & Silver, 2005), culture (Bringle & Hatcher, 2002), and dialogic practice (Miller & Hafner, 2008). On each visit to our communities, we spend many hours with the leaders of our partner organizations discussing many of these issues, followed by frequent periods of reflective practice, in an attempt to build authentic relationships that reflect an understanding of these differences in power, culture, and dialogic practice.

Finally, we have focused much of our work on considering the specifics of our partnerships—following what in the literature is often comprised of frameworks and best practices recommended for successful university–community partnerships. We have considered the elements that Baum (2000) suggests: continued organization, flexibility, time and resources, continued learning, compensation for mistakes, consideration of identities, and the ability to change directions. We've attempted to address the ideas that show up in Martin, Smith, and Phillips's (2005) list of best practices: proper funding, communication, partnership synergy, measurable outcomes, visibility, dissemination of knowledge, technology and organizational compatibility, and simplicity in goals and outcomes. Indeed, a robust literature has been developed often saturated with exhaustive lists of factors necessary to develop effective partnerships between universities and communities (Clayton, Bringle, & Hatcher, 2013; Eddy, 2010). We consider as many as we can in working out the practicalities as faculty in our relationship with our community partners.

How We Build Partnerships

Most of our partners are nonprofit community organizations, with many having developed explicitly with the goal of stimulating community development through the promotion of small-scale rural tourism. As our primary contacts in the communities, they not only guide the work of the students, they also arrange for homestays, manage funds received from the university, and in many ways frame the experience for students. We establish these partnerships long before students are in the country, and in doing so, we have come up with our own informal list of factors and practices to guide our collaboration with them. We visit communities to identify potential partners and begin a conversation about establishing a long-term partnership. We explain our program, our educational goals, the type of students we have, and our expectations regarding what communities will need to provide in order for us to be able to work with them. For instance, they need to be able to assure the safety and security of our students, arrange for homestays, and have a community organization (rather than an individual) to which our university can make payment.

We listen to what organizational leaders and community members say about their vision of how tourism fits sustainably within their community and what they need to move it forward. Only if we both decide that we can benefit from placing students in the community do we move forward. Once we establish the partnership and place students in the community, we continue to nurture and assess the relationship. As mentioned earlier, we visit each site at least twice while students are present to make sure that both our expectations and those of the community are being met; at the end of the program, we assess the experience, drawing on feedback from both students and our community partners.

Finally, transparency and the open sharing of information are critical for making the partnership work. We prepare students by describing the communities in which they will work and our history of working with them. We prepare communities by describing the students who will be placed there, indicating their particular skills, interests, and level of Spanish competency. We also translate the instructions for the students' final assignment and share them with our community partners. They know what type of questions students may be asking, why they are asking them, and what information they may be asked to provide. This gives our partners the opportunity to critically reflect with the students. After the program, we provide communities summaries of the student projects translated into Spanish.

This sharing of information is not only vital to student development, but also extremely valuable to communities as well. The very presence of students in the community provides the impetus to focus on issues related to tourism and how they are affected by it. Our community partners consistently tell us that while the actual work that students do is helpful, the most important contribution that students make comes through the questions that they ask. When students ask, for instance, about the environmental, social, and economic impacts of tourism on the community, community members are led to think carefully about these impacts, to examine their tourism practices, and to articulate their goals and concerns. Moreover, we often hear that as they engage students in these conversations, community members engage with one another and, in the process, identify shared goals and concerns.

The Need for a New Approach

While we developed strong and mutually rewarding relationships, we still had reason to believe that, as structured, they were inadequate to help us meet our objectives for the program. At a general level, because the partnerships had been developed largely between organizational leaders and faculty/administrators over the course of more than five years, they often appeared mysterious and difficult for students who were in the communities for only four weeks to unpack, analyze, and consider critically. More specifically, feedback we received from students suggested that our current framework for university–community partnerships did not adequately help students make sense of their experience.

Two frequent complaints were symptomatic of this inadequacy. First, students often reported that they did not get adequate direction from either the faculty or our community partners, or that they felt misled as to what they would be doing. Though we provided them with extensive information on the communities and the histories of our partnerships, the gap between what some expected and what they experienced frustrated them and gave them the sense that information was being withheld. Second, some students frequently claimed that the story we and the community partner told about the community and the community's experience with rural community tourism was not accurate. In many cases they came to this conclusion upon finding that their host families or residents not directly associated with the community partner had quite different stories to tell. Both types of experience led to breakdowns of trust among the students, faculty, and community partners that required considerable discussion.

Our first reaction to both of these symptoms was twofold. First, by providing more information we tried to prepare students for the fluidity of working in small communities with informal patterns of organization. Second, we sought to strengthen our relationships with community partners so that we could better match the experience with student expectations. These efforts, however, were less than successful, and upon further reflection, we came to the conclusion that the symptoms stemmed not from a lack of information or the strength of the university–community partnerships, but from employing an inadequate model of university–community partnerships to underlie the engagement experience. More specifically, a model of partnership focused on the relationship between faculty and a community organization did not adequately incorporate the roles, needs, and perspectives of either students or other community members. We needed a broader model of university–community partnerships.

Including Students as Partners

Recent studies on international partnerships, civic engagement partnerships, and community–university partnerships suggest a reinvestigation into the critical and multiple moving parts of partnerships—the people and the complicated and multiple narratives they bring to collaboration. Until recently, many researchers on international partnerships grounded their work in exchange theory, bargaining power, knowledge differentials, and instability (Beamish, 1995; Inkpen & Beamish, 1997). More recently, however, studies have looked more closely at individual cultural backgrounds (Sakar, Echambadi, Cavusgil, & Aulakh, 2001), individual learning (Johnson & Wilson, 2006), and both collective and individual identities (Ybema, Vroemisse, & Marrewijk, 2012). Similarly, theorists on community–university partnerships have shifted from a view that held the university at the center to one emphasizing the generative cocreation of knowledge and community change that is highly localized, inclusive, and multidirectional (Musil, 2003; Saltmarsh & Hartley, 2011). For example, Saltmarsh and Hartley (2011) suggest the university be seen "as part of an ecosystem of knowledge production addressing public problem solving" (p. 22).

The limitations of the traditional university–community partnership model have been noted by Bringle, Clayton, and Price (2009). As a remedy, they developed a more complex structural model, what they call the SOFAR model. Rather than look at the university–community partnership in terms of two constituencies or stakeholders, the SOFAR model differentiates the campus into three categories—administrators (A), faculty (F), and students (S)—and the community into two categories—organizational staff (O) and residents (R). Relationships can develop between constituencies or stakeholders in any of these five categories, allowing for ten dyadic relationships. These authors also distinguish between "relationships" and "partnerships," using the former to refer to all types of interactions between persons, and the latter to refer only to "relationships in which the interactions possess three particular qualities: closeness, equity, and integrity" (Bringle et al., 2009, p. 3). In other words, relationships can develop into partnerships, but they need not.

This model allows for a more nuanced understanding of the university–community partnership in several ways, particularly in international study abroad. First, by more explicitly identifying a broader range of stakeholders and acknowledging the differences between them, it recognizes the complexity of many civic engagement experiences. For instance, the differentiation between students and faculty acknowledges that students and faculty have different knowledge, goals, resources, and levels of power, and that as a result they may relate to communities in very different ways. Likewise, the differentiation between organizational staff and residents acknowledges that they too may have different knowledge, goals, resources, and power, and that their representations of the community may be very different. Second, the model recognizes that these relationships can differ qualitatively, with some developing into partnerships while others do not.

We hypothesized that using the SOFAR model to help frame the civic engagement component of our program might improve the student experience. First, it would help students anticipate, and thus negotiate, the complex network of relationships that they encounter during the program. This is particularly salient in study-abroad contexts in which students participate in private homestays that require the negotiation of close, community- and family-based relationships. This experience is rarely encountered by students engaging in domestic communities. Second, by clearly identifying students as stakeholders distinguishable from faculty or administrators, the model would validate the unique perspective of students and help them consider how their experience may substantially differ from the experience of the faculty. Third, recognizing students as independent stakeholders would encourage them to take responsibility in developing relationships with other stakeholders, thus encouraging student agency. Our hope was that they would develop partnerships, rather than seeing their relationships only as an extension of an already established university–community partnership. Finally, the model would help students understand how the various relationships between different stakeholders account for the different representations of the host community that they inevitably encounter. We say more about this later.

At a more practical level we believed that using the model would help address the two concerns raised by students mentioned earlier. The first complaint from students was that they did not get adequate direction from either the faculty or our community partners, or that they felt misled as to what they would be doing. The SOFAR model would help students understand that the information we give them emerges from our—that is, the faculty—relationship with the staff from the community organization and is a description of what we anticipate the relationship of student to the organization will entail. However, it would be up to the organizational staff and particular students to develop their own relationships and to fill in the details of activities based on this new relationship. This would empower students to develop more mutually beneficial partnerships with the organizational staff.

The second concern frequently raised by students is that the story that we and the community partner told about the community, the community organization, and the community's experience with rural community tourism was inconsistent with the narrative provided by their host families or other residents not directly associated with the community partner. The following example from our program illustrates this situation vividly.

In one area we partner with a nonprofit community development organization that works with two communities, which we will call Community A and Community B for the sake of anonymity. The communities are located along the same river and connected by a rough unpaved road, with Community A located several kilometers downstream from Community B. The distance between the two, however, is more than physical. Members of Community A have greater access to financial, educational, and political resources. There are a large coffee company, both an elementary school and a high school, and a paved road connecting the town to other towns and cities. A bus route to the town makes it possible for some people to travel and work in the capital city of San Jose, an hour away. Several members of the community are fairly well connected politically and, as a result, have been able to access regional, national, and international resources. In contrast, Community B is accessible only by the rough unpaved road (and an often washed-out bridge) and is more socially isolated. There is a small elementary school, but to attend high school, students must walk approximately thirty to forty-five minutes down the mountain to Community A. While some members of the community are traditional landowners, many are what might be called squatters with more tenuous property rights. Compared to Community A, members of Community B have little political voice at the regional level, much less national or international levels.

The community organization with which we officially work is comprised primarily of members of Community A. With the help of international funding, the organization started a significant community rural tourism project several years ago. To protect the watershed they purchased a large parcel of wooded land upriver, on the other side of Community B, to operate as a forest reserve. In addition to the reserve, they built a small ecolodge, restaurant, and visitor center to host tourists and provide environmental education for local schools and religious groups. While our students work under the supervision of this organization from Community A, they often live with families in Community B because of the proximity of those families to the ecolodge and reserve.

One result of this arrangement is that students hear quite contrasting narratives about the project. Members of Community A depict the project as a model example of sustainable development, one that uses income from tourism in support of both environmental protection and local economic development. Moreover, they argue that it has benefited Community B in tangible ways. The road, while still rough and unpaved, has been improved, a bridge connecting two parts of the community has been constructed, and children have been provided with better educational opportunities. The organization has also obtained funding to relocate several homes that are built right next to the river and pose an environmental threat to the watershed. However, members of Community B tell a much different story. Their story is one of appropriated land, unfulfilled promises of economic development and employment, and coerced displacement from homes in the name of promoting tourism. To get to know the communities in which they live and work, students need to sort through these stories and weave together a fuller narrative for themselves. They must also carefully negotiate the social environment so as not to alienate either group.

Programmatic Implications—Moving Partnerships to the Center

In November 2014, with these challenges in mind, a group of MSU partners from across MSU and Costa Rica met at Conversa for a student-organized summit on sustainable partnerships sponsored by the MSU Office of Study Abroad and the RCAH (Cooper, Delgado, Krueger, & Yoder, 2014). The catalyst paper prepared for the summit introduced the SOFAR model and proposed the following key questions: (1) How can we continually grow and nurture our partnerships with each other? (2) How can we create an information network that has impact for all of us? (3) How can we better integrate the RCAH's goals with those we are working with? (4) With all of these new discoveries in community–university partnerships, student learning abroad, and co-generative engagement and impact, what improvements can we make to our current programming together? After three days of dialogue, appreciative inquiry, and visioning, the following recommendation, noted in the summit results paper, was made:

> MSU needs to take itself out of the center and allow for community partners to play a more significant role in designing, developing and leading this program. Partners suggested a host of new ideas, or solutions to the program's current structural constraints. Yet, in many ways they all led back to the idea of decentralizing the university as a means to developing more sustainable programs in these communities. When this conversation regarding structure took place, most groups envisioned a vast network of stakeholders in the community that includes students, community residents, community leaders, and associations from neighboring areas. This suggests a restructuring in the way the program is envisioned by all parties—a change that requires all to re-examine how stakeholders interact with one another. Most appeared to favor a network of communities throughout Costa Rica engaging in their own individual projects while collaborating with each other and with the university. (Cooper et al., 2014, p. 5)

The participants thus envisioned a relationship model between MSU and Costa Rican partners that is co-generative with all partners—students, community members, community organizations, faculty members, and MSU administrators—at the center.

The impact of the summit soon became apparent. By spring of 2015, our Costa Rican partners had begun to meet together without MSU's involvement—developing a capacity-building and information-sharing network of rural communities that now spans the country. Several of the partners engaged in technical assistance and took best-practice tours of each other's locations. The RCAH ran a well-attended study-abroad program in 2015 that included early introductions of students and partners and the implementation of community participatory research projects at each location.

By fall of 2015, the partners had begun proposing more significant colearning relationships and research, including a proposal organized by Conversa for low-cost, semester-long programming, leveraging MSU's valuable existing assets in Costa Rica. The proposal called for a focus on first-year transitional learning, use of colearning pedagogies, and community-based research between new and existing partners, all of whom support and struggle with the challenge of Costa Rica's commitment to sustainable development and pledge to become carbon neutral by 2021. As of this writing, the RCAH is sponsoring the creation of a new hub for community partnerships in Costa Rica it is calling the Program on Sustainable Development in Costa Rica. Slated to open in November 2016, the program is designed to promote innovation of new models of global education in collaboration with this network of multidisciplinary, multisector, and multigenerational partners across Costa Rica. By developing a hub for this developing network, the new program offers the intellectual, infrastructure, and research capacity for significant additional opportunities, including research on engaged international learning and sustainability, technological enhancement, and the further development of campus-wide, international and community partnerships.

Pedagogical Implications

Understanding student relationships and community engagement in terms of the SOFAR model has critical implications for pedagogy, partnerships sustainability, and community impact that require further exploration.

First, by emphasizing the student role in our partnerships via the SOFAR model, we may be able to help students learn through the multiple narratives they encounter. We have found that students often interpret these multiple narratives as an obstacle to learning. They often believe that there is a single true narrative, so that when they encounter more than one narrative, someone must be wrong, perhaps even deceiving them. And because they are likely to form a partnership with their families who often offer a dissonant narrative, they may come to distrust the faculty and community organization. The model may help them to see that multiple and often conflicting narratives are a normal part of having multiple relationships with stakeholders who hold different perspectives. They can then develop a deeper understanding of themselves and the community by moving from asking "What is the true story?" to "What do these different stories tell me about the relationships in the community?"

Second, we should expect students to more easily develop partnerships with host families. This is an unusual structure, not commonly found in domestic service learning or civic engagement courses. However, the program's homestays naturally lead to a situation in which students are prone to form partnerships with the residents of a community. Here, thinking about the movement from relationship to partnership is important. There is not a formal agreement to become a partner with the host family, nor is there shared work around an objective. However, sharing living space and meals increases the likelihood that students and families will establish close relationships that may lead to partnerships.

Third, this suggests that further research is required to understand what pedagogical methodologies are required to help students involved in civic engagement understand their relationship to the multiple narratives they encounter. What is the relationship of critical reflection to this more nuanced understanding? What collaborative and critical thinking skills should be prioritized here? How does knowledge about power, privilege, social justice, culture, and systems of inequity come into play here? And, finally, what is the relationship between multinarrative thinking and student agency and psychosocial development?

Finally, rethinking the nature of student relationships and partnerships in their communities is shifting the emphasis in our program—from an exploration of the ethics of tourism and sustainable development that utilizes engaged partnerships, to an emphasis on engaged partnerships that use the subject of sustainable development more generally to help students ground their work. Such a shift brings both the impact and scope of critical self-reflection in the civic engagement experience into question. Commonly, well-designed self-reflection is recommended both for students who study abroad and for those engaged in service-learning and civic engagement. It is less commonly recommended for faculty members and rarely discussed in the literature for organizational partners. It is practically unheard of for community members. But if civic engagement in an international context becomes the focus of inquiry, it seems logical that all involved—from students to faculty to community leaders to residents—should engage in critical and well-conceived self-reflection. The nature of partnerships and relationships may demand it.

NOTES

1. We use the term "university–community partnership" throughout this chapter to refer to partnerships between communities and institutions of higher education. Some authors use the term "campus–community partnerships." The advantage of this terminology is that it does not distinguish between different types of institutions of higher education—for example, between colleges and universities. However, in the context of study abroad using a term that seems to imply a specific place seemed less appropriate.

2. See (Varlotta, 2000) for an interesting discussion of how to use the metaphor of "service as text" to operationalize a pedagogy of service learning.

3. We work with Centro Linguistico Conversa, a language school located just outside of Santa Ana. Conversa provides language instruction (for which students receive university credit), arranges all homestay accommodations, provides transportation to and from the school, and provides other services as needed. For more on Conversa see http://www.conversa.com.

REFERENCES

Afshar, A. (2005). Community-campus partnerships for economic development: Community perspectives. *Public and Community Affairs Discussion Papers.* Boston: Federal Reserve Bank of Boston.

Baum, H. S. (2000). Fantasies and realities in university-community partnerships. *Journal of Planning Education and Research, 20*(2), 234–246.

Beamish, P. W. (1995). Keeping international joint ventures stable and profitable. *Long Range Planning, 28*(3), 2–3.

Boyle, M. E., & Silver, I. (2005). Poverty, partnerships, and privilege: Elite institutions and community empowerment. *City & Community, 4*(3), 233–253.

Bringle, R. G., Clayton, P. H., & Price, M. F. (2009). Partnerships in service learning and civic engagement.

Partnerships: A Journal of Service Learning & Civic Engagement, 1(1), 1–20.

Bringle, R. G., & Hatcher, J. A. (2002). Campus-community partnerships: The terms of engagement. *Journal of Social Issues, 58*(3), 503–516.

Clayton, P. H., Bringle, R. G., & Hatcher, J. A. (Eds.). (2013). *Research on service learning: Conceptual frameworks and assessment.* Sterling, VA: Stylus.

Cooper, E., Delgado, V., Krueger, E., & Yoder. S. 2014. *Summit catalyst paper and program.* Unpublished manuscript. Michigan State University.

Cooper, E., Delgado, V., Krueger, E., & Yoder, S. 2015. *Summit results paper.* Unpublished manuscript.

Cruz, N. I., & Giles, D. E. (2000). Where's the community in service learning research. *Michigan Journal of Community Service Learning, 7*(1), 28–34.

Delgado, V., & DeLind, L. B. (n.d.) *The RCAH model for civic engagement.* Retrieved from http://rcah.msu.edu/sites/default/files/RCAH%20Engagement%20Model.pdf.

Eddy, P. (2010). Partnerships and collaborations in higher education. *ASHE Higher Education Report, 36*(2).

Ferman, B., & Hill, T. L. (2004). The challenges of agenda conflict in higher-education-community partnerships: Views from the community side. *Journal of Urban Affairs, 26*(2), 241–257.

Holland, B. A., & Gelmon, S. B. (1998). The state of the "engaged campus": What have we learned about building and sustaining university-community partnerships. *AAHE Bulletin, 51,* 3–6.

Inkpen, A. C., & Beamish, P. W. (1997). Knowledge, bargaining power, and the instability of international joint ventures. *Academy of Management Review, 22*(1), 177–202.

Johnson, H., & Wilson, G. (2006). North-South/South-North partnerships: Closing the "mutuality gap." *Public Administration and Development, 26*(1), 71–80.

Karasik, R. J., & Wallingford, M. S. (2007). Finding community: Developing and maintaining effective intergenerational service-learning partnerships. *Educational Gerontology, 33*(9), 775–793.

King, P. M., & Baxter Magolda, M. B. (2005). A developmental model of intercultural maturity. *Journal of College Student Development, 46*(6), 571–592.

Leiderman, S., Furco, A., Zapf, J., & Goss, M. (2003). *Building partnerships with college campuses: Community perspectives.* A publication of the Consortium for the Advancement of Private Higher Education's Engaging Communities and Campuses Grant Program. Washington, DC: Council of Independent Colleges.

Martin, L. L., Smith, H., & Phillips, W. (2005). Bridging "town & gown" through innovative university-community partnerships. *The Innovation Journal: The Public Sector Innovation Journal, 10*(2).

Miller, P. M., & Hafner, M. M. (2008). Moving toward dialogical collaboration: A critical examination of a university-school-community partnership. *Educational Administration Quarterly, 44*(1), 66–110.

Mitchell, T. D., Visconti, V., Keene, A., & Battistoni, R. (2011). Educating for democratic leadership at Stanford, UMass, and Providence College. In N. V. Longo & C. M. Gibson (Eds.), *From command to community: A new approach to leadership education in colleges.* (pp. 115–148). Medford, MA: Tufts University.

Musil, C. M. (2003). Educating for citizenship. *Peer Review, 5*(3), 4–8.

Prins, E. (2005). Framing a conflict in a community-university partnership. *Journal of Planning Education and Research, 25*(1), 57–74.

Rogge, M. E., & Rocha, C. J. (2005). University-community partnership centers: An important link for social work education. *Journal of Community Practice, 12*(3–4), 103–121.

Rousseau, D. M., Sitkin, S. B., Burt, R. S., & Camerer, C. (1998). Not so different after all: A cross-discipline view of trust. *Academy of Management Review, 23*(3), 393–404.

Sakar, M., Echambadi, R., Cavusgil, T. S., & Aulakh, P. S. (2001). The influence of complementarity, compatibility, and relationship capital on alliance performance. *Journal of the Academy of Marketing Science, 29*(4), 358–373.

Saltmarsh, J., & Hartley, M. (2011). Democratic engagement. In J. Saltmarsh & M. Hartley (Eds.), *To Serve a Larger Purpose: Engagement for Democracy and the Transformation of Higher Education.* (pp. 14–26). Philadelphia, PA: Temple University.

Stoecker, R., & Tyron, E. A. (Eds.). (2009). *The unheard voices: Community organizations and service learning.* Philadelphia: Temple University.

Varlotta, L. (2000). Service as text: Making the metaphor meaningful. *Michigan Journal of Community Service Learning, 7*(1), 76–84.

Weerts, D. J., & Sandmann, L. R. (2008). Building a two-way street: Challenges and opportunities for community engagement at research universities. *The Review of Higher Education, 32*(1), 73–106.

Ybema, S., Vroemisse, M., & Marrewijk, A. V. (2012). Constructing identity by deconstructing differences: Building partnerships across cultural and hierarchical divides. *Scandinavian Journal of Management, 28*(1), 48–59.

CHAPTER 9

Civic Engagement's Challenges for Study Abroad: An Ethical and Political Perspective

Stephen L. Esquith

S tudy abroad invariably is applauded for its life-changing impact on students from the United States who study in other countries. It changes how they think about themselves, about the people they have lived and worked with abroad, and about the cultures they come home to (Lewis & Niesenbaum, 2005; Dwyer & Peters, 2004). They are more aware of their own cultural assumptions, more understanding of cultural differences, and more prepared to think critically about their own ways of life. Incorporating civic engagement into study abroad promises to make these good things even better (Klein & Lawver, 2007). But making them better is an uphill climb. This essay is about some of the challenges that civic engagement poses for study abroad and how to recognize these challenges. It is a rough guide to reflection from an ethical and political perspective for study-abroad students and faculty members who wish to incorporate civic engagement projects into study abroad. It also lays the groundwork for a more general discussion of global responsibility and the political education required to recognize it.

The Michigan State University (MSU) Residential College in the Arts and Humanities (RCAH), from its beginning in 2007–2008, has stressed the importance of civic engagement (http://rcah. msu.edu/student-life/civic-engagement). Our students have worked in local schools, art studios, community centers, private companies, and public agencies to teach and learn through collaborative projects as familiar as a neighborhood garden and as unusual as an interactive 40- by 200-foot collage. They have done this in the university's own backyard, the mountains of West Virginia, the neighborhoods of Detroit, the desserts of Israel, the rain forests of Costa Rica, and the villages of Mali. We call this kind of experiential and hands-on engaged learning civic engagement, because we believe that the arts and humanities should contribute to the common good. It is the way that RCAH brings the arts and humanities to life.

All RCAH students and many of its faculty members participate in civic engagement courses and projects. Some faculty members teach courses in the civic engagement sequence that all RCAH students are required to take on the history and theory of civic engagement, as well as its practice. Other faculty members integrate creative civic engagement projects into other courses, for example, using photography in a community development photovoice project as part of an introductory seminar or using ceramics in a peace studies course with young people enrolled in a court diversion project. As civic engagement has become one of the signature elements of RCAH, its importance for our study-away and study-abroad programs has also grown.

Student responses to RCAH civic-engagement study-abroad programs support the general self-reported findings on student satisfaction just referred to. RCAH students have reported greater confidence in their ability to relate to citizens of very different cultures. They feel they have made a difference, albeit a modest one, in a manner that they want to pursue in the future. In fact, several of them have cited this experience as a primary reason for pursuing a career in teaching or another service profession. They also say that they are more critical of what they believe are the excesses of their own lifestyles and levels of consumption. One might describe these changes as greater self-awareness and a sense of greater responsibility.

This chapter concentrates on three challenges that study-abroad programs may face as they embrace civic engagement. I call these challenges perplexities, dilemmas, and illusions. All three affect the achievement of the values of self-awareness and responsibility that RCAH civic-engagement study-abroad programs strive to embody. It is not that self-awareness and responsibility cannot be realized because of the perplexities, dilemmas, and illusions students and faculty encounter. It is rather that self-awareness and responsibility are harder to realize than one might imagine because of the particular perplexities, dilemmas, and illusions that may arise in this kind of program. Once we understand these challenges, greater self-awareness and responsibility through a civic-engagement study-abroad program become possible. Not all study-abroad programs that seek to incorporate civic engagement will do it the way we have in RCAH. The challenges outlined in this essay are fairly daunting ones, but that is because, done right, civic engagement sets a high bar for students, and we believe it makes study abroad even more meaningful and worthwhile.

Perplexities: Multilingual Education

I use the word "perplexity" to mean the same thing that Jane Addams meant in her 1902 book *Democracy and Social Ethics*. Addams did not apply this term to anything like today's academic study-abroad programs, but the neighborhoods of Chicago at the turn of the twentieth century were truly global villages. She worked with immigrant and refugee communities in which class, gender, racial, and ethnic conflicts were often divisive and spilled out onto a wider political stage. It was no accident that toward the end of her life, Addams was awarded the Nobel Peace Prize. It was through her increasingly sophisticated advocacy for democracy at home that she became a voice for peace abroad (Hamington, 2009; Fischer, 2004; Knight, 2010).

According to Addams, perplexity is the initial stage in practical inquiry. It refers to the puzzlement she and other social reformers often experienced when their assumptions did not allow them to transform a troubling situation into a less harmful and violent one. For example, Addams argued that "charity workers" at the turn of the century in Chicago were often perplexed by the habits of dress, the early marriage customs, and the child labor practices that they found among immigrants and refugees, which ran contrary to their bourgeois assumptions about proper living.

Civic engagement in RCAH is not charity work, but it generates its own perplexities, sometimes more intractable and not as easy to identify as the dissonance between bourgeois values and working-class and immigrant customs that perplexed Addams and her coworkers.

Perplexities such as these cannot be dissolved or overcome through careful analysis. They persist, and they have to be worked through over and over again. Let me briefly cite one example from my own experience as a coleader of our Ethics and Development in Mali Study Abroad Program. The most obvious perplexity that has arisen for us in the context of our work with the K–9 Ciwara community school in Kati, Mali, is that of appropriate language of instruction. The native language of the students in the Ciwara school is Bamanakan, the language of the Bamana people. Some of our Malian students knew a few words in French, the colonial language. None of the students or the teachers spoke English. The directors of the school want the youngest students to begin learning in Bamanakan and then gradually use French and English as they progress through the higher grades. This multilingual curriculum requires that the Ciwara school (and its parent Malian nongovernmental organization [NGO], the Institute for Popular Education) produce its own teaching materials; the directors are eager to have our RCAH students assist them in the classroom as they compose these materials and introduce English to their students and teachers. Since 2014, we have helped them produce several new picture books in Bamanakan, French, and English that address conflicts and issues Malian students and their families have faced because of the coup d'état and occupation in 2012–2013.

It is difficult, however, to find Malian teachers who are both willing and able to participate in this multilingual curriculum. Few have the language skills, and most are seeking better paying teaching positions in public schools where they teach only in French. This skepticism toward instruction in the native language is even more common among the parents of the Ciwara students. They worry that their children will be at a disadvantage when they take the national exams to enter high school and college if instruction in French is delayed.

Our RCAH students were dependent upon the young Ciwara school teachers to help them communicate with the Malian students in Bamanakan and French, but the Ciwara school teachers have been trained to teach in French and sometimes do not see the value of multilingual education for themselves or for their young Malian students. They also felt some pressure from the parents to concentrate more heavily on French. Our RCAH students were perplexed by their counterparts' resistance to multilingual education when it seemed only natural that a child's education should begin in the language in which the child thinks and should include French as well as English only later in order to increase the student's opportunities for higher education abroad.

Our RCAH students on this study-abroad program encountered other situations that challenged their tolerance for different cultural traditions. They were generally appalled at the pervasiveness of female genital cutting among young girls in Mali. They were troubled by the commercialization of traditional fabric arts. They were uncomfortable watching traditional dances performed just for the sake of tourists. But these concerns are not the same as the feeling of perplexity they experienced in the multilingual civic-engagement program at the Ciwara school. As tourists, they did not want to damage Malian cultural traditions or remain oblivious to the suffering of innocent children. As collaborators at the Ciwara school, they faced a different set of questions. It was not just a matter of doing no harm. They were in a position to contribute to the education of young Malian students, but they soon discovered that there is no simple road to higher education for these students. There are costs as well as benefits to a multilingual program that may impact their collaborating Malian teachers as well as their students. If RCAH students choose not to teach in English, they really do not have much to contribute to the education of the Ciwara students. If they choose to teach in English, they may be helping some of their students and collaborating teachers but also making it harder on others. Young students who do not catch on to English may lose ground. However, young Ciwara teachers who wish to help their struggling Malian students may feel like the introduction of English into an already challenging bilingual curriculum (Bamanakan and French) is only making their job harder. The RCAH assumption that multilingual is better, just like Addams's assumption that purchasing inexpensive clothing makes economic sense for poor immigrants, proves to be more perplexing than RCAH students initially realized. It was in working side by side with young Malian teachers their own age who were struggling to find a career in education themselves that our RCAH students felt perplexed, as they should have and as their Malian teaching partners did.

Dilemmas: Linkage Agreements and Child Labor

Just as perplexities are not merely logical contradictions, the dilemmas that arise through civic-engagement projects on study-abroad programs are also practical challenges. One type of dilemma involves the tension between trust and truth.

Both trust and truth are necessary for a civic-engagement study-abroad program to have the proper impact. Students must establish trust between themselves and their community partners in order to understand the needs of the community and play a useful role in addressing them. Students also must be willing to tell their partners the truth when they feel it is necessary, to listen to their partners however hard it may be to hear the truth, and to be truthful with themselves about their own skills and competencies. Trust and truth should complement each other. Trust without truth will be hollow. Truth without trust will be useless. Where's the dilemma?

The reason that there is more going on here than just a mutual dependence between trust and truth is because of the difference between truth and truthfulness. In the context of a study-abroad civic-engagement program from a relatively rich country to a poorer one, building trust and telling what one thinks is the truth (i.e., being truthful) never reach a stable equilibrium. This happens at the program level and also on a one-to-one level between students and their community partners.

The tension at the program level involves the uncertainty of the future. For example, if asked by a poor community partner when the study-abroad program will be returning, the study-abroad program leader has to be very careful. Budgets and politics are unpredictable, and one does not want to create unrealistic expectations. However, to be effective, civic-engagement projects must have strong continuity from year to year. The more effective they are, the more they become built in to the operations of the host community organization, as they provide necessary training, labor, and resources for the organization. Doubts about that continuity may lead the host partner to look elsewhere and possibly make other arrangements that will not be in the host partner's interest if the program continues and those alternative arrangements prove to have been unnecessary.

Insurance like this is expensive. For this reason, the study-abroad program leader is tempted to hold out hope and make promises that may not be entirely true in order to sustain the relationship. This tension between trust and truth sometimes takes the form of a linkage agreement between the visiting university and its host institutions that has little binding power. On paper, a linkage agreement seems promising, but often it is not a good predictor of actual behavior. Being truthful about the binding force of such a linkage agreement may weaken the trust necessary for building a strong partnership, and it may not be in the interest of the host-country partner. But more likely, the host-country partner will be well aware of the force of the linkage agreement and will be content to go along with the charade because it can be used to convince a different future partner to create a new program; thus, one linkage agreement can lead to another. Both sides know the truth, but in order to maintain the trust between them, neither side is entirely truthful with the other.

On a one-to-one level, truthfulness can also undermine trust. For example, the more truthful a study-abroad student is with herself about what she is capable of doing and why, the more difficult it is to maintain a trusting relationship with individual community partners. Then, once she realizes that she may be creating false hopes among some community partners, she may begin to suspect that she is not being honest with herself or her partner in other ways. Indirection, subtlety, and even ambiguity may be necessary to convey the relevant part of the truth in a graduated way in order to build and sustain trust. Truthfulness involves judgments about what it may take to sustain trust, not just one's sincere belief in what constitutes the whole truth. Truthfulness involves what Addams called a "sympathetic understanding" of how one's partner sees things, not just a cold calculation of facts and probabilities from the perspective of an outside impartial observer.

Rather than bemoan the fact that civic-engagement study-abroad programs face this unavoidable dilemma, I believe this is precisely what makes them so valuable for RCAH and for its students. How much can and should we promise our community partners? How truthful are we being with them and with ourselves? These questions require a level of self-awareness and sense of responsibility that cannot be reduced to a rule or principle. "Always tell the truth," for example, can only get you so far if you are discussing the value of a linkage agreement. What part of the truth you emphasize will be just as important as any budget spreadsheet you can provide. What I hope our students are learning when they report greater self-awareness and responsibility is that as precarious as their positions are in these programs, they have a better sense of what it takes to maintain their balance in situations in which "sympathetic understanding" or compassion is just as important as any principle of truth-telling.

To see this dilemma clearly requires a better understanding of the sources of distrust that exist in poor countries and the contested nature of what students and study-abroad leaders might have previously thought was the truth of the matter. For example, students and faculty members who have had to confront the realities of child labor in poor countries in a face-to-face way realize that trust is much more difficult to build; also, once you create that trust, what once looked like the simple fact of the matter is no longer so simple. A clear example of this dilemma involves the problem of what to do when confronted with children working in the fields or performing household domestic labor in support of the study-abroad program. At the Ciwara school, should RCAH students object to the harsh working conditions of the very children they may be teaching or children in the surrounding village who are not allowed to attend school but instead provide services for RCAH students? Should the elimination of child labor be a condition of the partnership? The child laborers may be working in the kitchen and cleaning up after meals. They may be washing clothes for the study-abroad students instead of attending school. They may be working in the fields, harvesting the food that the study-abroad students are eating. And many of these children may be far from their own home village, hoping to save a little money and send it back to their families. Is this exploitative child labor, is it vocational training, or is it a form of migrant labor that is not unlike the migrant labor that RCAH students only dimly attend to back in Michigan when they are purchasing their own food (Dougnon, 2011)?

There may not be any simple answers to these questions. If the RCAH study-abroad program demands that children not be employed during their time at the Ciwara school, this may make the lives of the families of these children much harder. Can the RCAH students take time off to provide some instruction for these child laborers? This is a creative solution, but it may not be accepted by the other Malians who will then have to do the work the children had been doing, with no additional compensation. Like any dilemma, one feels caught on one horn and then the other. You can either be honest and tell the community partner that child labor is morally unacceptable and risk losing the trust of the community partner who may feel you do not really understand the situation. Or you can be less than honest with yourself and say that these children are actually better off than they would have been without the child labor that the program has created. You may not be able to be fully honest and fully trusted at the same time.

Illusions: NGOs and Democracy

Unlike perplexities and dilemmas that study-abroad students face as integral parts of their civic engagement work, illusions are a more diffuse problem, potentially the most serious, yet also the most enlightening if they can be confronted. Once again, I use examples from my own experience in Mali.

I have wondered whether my inability to recognize the warning signs of the military coup of March 21, 2012, in Mali and the violence that quickly followed was simply a result of my own lack of in-depth knowledge of Malian history and society. However, I was not the only one taken by surprise as the coup and its after-effects spread throughout the country. As our partners in Mali struggled with the economic consequences of the rapid exodus of expatriates and the cancelation of government and private development contracts, it seemed to me that many experts and Malians themselves were also caught by surprise. One article by eight scholars with an intimate knowledge of Malian history and culture begins with this surprising statement:

In 2012, the political landscape in the Republic of Mali transformed rapidly, drastically, and unpredictably. The formation of a new Tuareg political movement—the National Movement of Azawad—in October 2010 and the return to Mali of Tuareg with military experience from the Libyan conflict in August 2011—bringing along heavy weapons and logistical supplies—made speculation on renewed violence on the part of separatist Tuareg inevitable. Indeed, Tuareg separatists launched attacks on

Malian garrisons in the Sahara in January 2012. Mali had experienced such rebellions before. *What nobody foresaw* was that this renewed conflict would lead to a coup d'état by disgruntled junior officers; the near total collapse of Mali's army and most of its democratic institutions; the seizure of all of northern Mali by Tuareg rebels and foreign and local *mujahideen*; the precocious proclamation of an independent Azawad Republic; and the effective occupation of the north of the country by an alliance of Jihadi-Salafi movements who imposed their form of shari'a law on a suffering and largely recalcitrant population. Those events happened very quickly, and their effects will be felt for years. (LeCoco et al., 2012)

The 2012 military coup in Bamako, the capital city, initially did not seem to have strong support among the military or the civilian population. The coeval opportunist advances of Tuareg separatists and their newfound extremist allies in the North appeared to be equally unpopular, especially where they were coupled with violations of human rights. United Nations resolutions condemning the coup and the separatist violence also were moderately encouraging. I was told by our Malian partners in Bamako and in nearby Kati (where, coincidentally, the military coup originated) that they were waiting to see what would happen. I took that too as an encouraging sign. When French forces intervened to repel the advances of extremists into the central part of the country and new elections were set for July 2013, I continued to believe that it was just a matter of time before things returned to normal. My confidence that the situation would be quickly and peacefully resolved proved to be optimistic. A new government was formed in 2014, regular terrorist attacks continued, and fifteen thousand international peacekeeping forces were still stationed throughout the country in 2016. What explains the illusion in 2013 that things would return to normal quickly?

Since 1991, Mali has enjoyed a relatively positive reputation as a democratic country in Africa that has avoided the tragic, violent conflicts that have occurred in many other West African countries. Its elected presidents have abided by the new constitutional term limits, and its rich cultural traditions, especially in music and fabric arts, have been applauded and emulated in Europe and North America. Admittedly, agricultural production and manufacturing were not keeping pace with the needs of a young, growing population, and dissatisfaction among ethnic groups in the northern parts of Mali led to periodic clashes with government forces. But despite this failure to decentralize political power and address poverty, disease, and famine in more effective ways, over the past twenty years Mali attracted new donors, new investors, and a new generation of enthusiastic expatriates and visitors. I count myself among them.

From 2002 until 2012, I was a co-leader of our study-abroad program four times and spent the 2005–2006 academic year as a Fulbright Scholar teaching ethics and development to Malian students at the University of Bamako. Also during this period, through a U.S. State Department grant, I was able to host two sets of Malian academic and religious leaders in RCAH and take two sets of MSU faculty and community leaders to Mali as part of an exchange program on democracy and religion. All of these experiences were gratifying. My Malian students and colleagues were eager to learn about the work of scholars such as Amartya Sen, Martha Nussbaum, Jeffrey Sachs, and others. My American study-abroad students quickly discovered how eager Malians were to befriend them and share their culture. The participants in our State Department exchange program seemed to delight in their experiences, despite the cool Michigan temperatures and the hot Malian climate.

In summer 2010, the Ciwara school built a small residence for us in Kati, with healthy food and Internet access, within safe walking distance of the school. My next set of plans included organizing an international ethics and development conference on democracy, education, and development in Kati and raising money to bring Malian university students to RCAH as part of a reciprocal study-abroad program between RCAH, the Ciwara school, and the University of Bamako. Funds for the conference were tentatively committed by USAID and a January 2013 date was scheduled. Our partners at the Ciwara school planned to include a proposal for the reciprocal study-abroad project in their next grant renewal request to their major funding agency, the Hewlett Foundation. March 21, 2012, put all of these plans on hold, many of them permanently.

At the risk of hyperbole, I will call my optimism "living within a lie." I borrow this phrase from Vaclav Havel (1986), the last president of Czechoslovakia (1989–1992) and the first president of the Czech Republic (1993–2003). He was an articulate dissident and leader of the opposition after the suppression of liberal reforms in Czechoslovakia in the Prague Spring of 1968. From 1968 until 1989, he was arrested and harassed repeatedly by the secret police, spending four years in prison between 1979 and 1983. Havel coined the phrase "living within a lie" to describe the situation of Czech citizens living under communist domination in a post-totalitarian society. While there are many obvious differences between Czechoslovakia during this period and post-authoritarian Mali between 1991 and 2012, there is an important similarity that I think is worth bringing out to explain what I mean by the challenge of illusion and my particular optimistic version of it.

First, let me review Havel's account of post-totalitarian Czechoslovakia (1986). "Living within a lie" is not the same as lying. One need not consciously tell a lie, with the intention to mislead, to live within one.

> The post-totalitarian system touches people at every step, but it does so with its ideological gloves on. This is why life in the system is so thoroughly permeated with hypocrisy and lies; government by bureaucracy is called popular government; the working class is enslaved in the name of the working class; the complete degradation of the individual is presented as his or her ultimate liberation . . .
>
> Individuals need not believe all these mystifications, but they must behave as though they did, or they must at least tolerate them in silence, or get along well with those who work with them. For this reason, however, they must live within a lie. They need not accept the lie. It is enough for them to have accepted their life with it and in it. For by this very fact, individuals confirm the system, fulfill the system, make the system, are the system. (p. 45)

Havel introduces us to one such individual who is "living within a lie" by posting a seemingly innocuous sign in the window of his small grocery story.

> The manager of a fruit and vegetable shop places in his window, among the onions and carrots, the slogan: "Workers of the world, unite!" Why does he do it? . . . Has he really given more than a moment's thought to how such a unification might occur and what it would mean?

Havel says no: "The overwhelming majority of shopkeepers never think about the slogans they put in their windows, nor do they use them to express their real opinions" (p. 41). What is more significant is the web of relationships and collective state of mind that such individual actions constitute.

The greengrocer and the office worker have both adapted to the conditions in which they live, but in doing so, they help to create those conditions. They do what is done, what is to be done, what must be done, but at the same time—by that very token—they confirm that it must be done. They conform to a particular requirement; in so doing, they themselves perpetuate that requirement. Metaphysically speaking, without the greengrocer's slogan, the office worker's slogan could not exist, and vice versa. Each proposes to the other that something be repeated and each accepts the other's proposal. Their mutual indifference to each other's slogan is only an illusion: In reality, by exhibiting their slogans, each compels the other to accept the rules of the game, and to confirm thereby the power that requires the slogans in the first place. Quite simply, each helps the other to be obedient. Both are objects in a system of control, but at the same time they are its subjects as well. They are both victims of the system and its instruments (Havel, 1986, pp. 51–52).

This notion of the "illusion" of "mutual indifference" is deeply troubling. Despite their belief that in posting meaningless signs they are having no effect on one another, that is, that they can live and let live, in fact they are "helping the other to be obedient."

The greengrocer's sign reminds me of my own illusions about ethics and development in Mali in 2002–2012, embedded as I was among others telling a similar story, posting, if you will, a sign in the window, thereby perpetuating an illusion of mutual indifference. In my case, it was the illusion of mutual indifference not just toward the expressed beliefs of others but toward democratic politics.

One symbol of such indifference is the abbreviation "NGO." NGOs (local, national, and international) have a certain aura about them in a country like Mali. "NGO" represents on the one hand the promise of aid and assistance, but on the other it undermines political responsibility. As clients of NGOs, individuals and groups do not have a strong connection to the state. They are not dependent upon state tax revenues for their survival, and they have less of an incentive to hold the state accountable through electoral process for what it does with the tax revenues it collects. Political participation is disconnected from the common wealth of society when NGOs become the primary source of wealth, employment, and services. In this situation, there is a strong "disappointment" in democratic politics that can mask the fragility of the political system.

According to an *Afrobarometer* public opinion survey:

> In a striking result, Malians express disappointment in the performance of state institutions. Almost everyone interviewed (96 percent) say that "the crisis" has changed their perceptions of "the institutions of the Republic" in a negative direction. (Coulibaly & Bratton, 2013)

To call this "living within a lie" seems like a harsh judgment. Many of Mali's problems come from a colonial past that still casts a long shadow over the transportation infrastructure, the organization of government ministries, and the professions, especially education. The struggle against French colonial rule culminating in independence in 1960 was followed by thirty years of one-party rule that was overturned in favor of a multiparty democracy in 1991. This is a much different path to democracy than Eastern European countries such as Czechoslovakia have taken. I do not want to suggest that the cruelty of slavery and exploitation of African peoples by Western Europeans (Bingen, Robinson, & Staatz, 2000; Mamdani, 2012) were the same as the Soviet domination of Eastern Europe during and after World War II (Snyder, 2010). The multiple, lasting effects of slavery, genocide, and ethnic cleansing on such massive scales cannot be reduced to common denominators. The comparison I want to make is a very limited one on the level of social consciousness. Specifically, I want to suggest that in Czechoslovakia in 1977 until the fall of the Soviet empire, a form of denial was present regarding the tacit support that citizens gave to their post-totalitarian regime and that a similar denial ("indifference") has occurred in Mali since the fall of Moussa Traoré's dictatorship in 1991. Until the collapse of their democracy in 2012, many Malians and expatriates like myself did not recognize how clientelism had replaced democratic citizenship in Mali. Our study-abroad program was not officially an NGO, but it functioned the same way a small one does in Mali. We provided training and employment for Malians willing to develop a new model of active teaching and learning as an alternative to the state-run public school system.

Still, one might object that Czechoslovakia during this period was a one-party dictatorship while, whatever its shortcomings, Mali was a democracy during 1991–2012, at least in form if not in substance. This is certainly true. However, the legacies of colonialism and one-party dictatorship until 1991 in Mali have had a continuing impact on the level of democratic political participation in Mali. This has been exacerbated by corruption and political mismanagement (Wing, 2013). Malians have had one of the lowest voter turnouts in Africa, and this is in part due to disaffection with the corruption of the central government, the lack of coordination between local government and traditional village authority structures, and primarily the short-circuiting of electoral politics in general by the ubiquity of NGOs of all stripes (Afrobarometer, 2008). Politics in Mali remain identified with the "French system" of bureaucratic rule and the personal corruption of the Moussa Traoré era. There have been exceptional moments when democratic politics have prevailed (Poulton & Youssouf, 1998). But until the coup of 2012, Malians preferred to take for granted their new credentials as a constitutional democracy in order to maintain the flow of Western aid and loans through NGOs that rarely benefited the people they were designed to reach.

Conclusion

There are, of course, many ways to characterize the challenges that civic engagement creates in a study-abroad program. I have described these challenges in ethical and political language, in part because the study-abroad program I have used to illustrate these challenges is itself focused on ethical issues in development. Students and faculty leaders came prepared to reflect upon the moral assumptions they brought with them, the difference between the truth itself and the difficulty of being truthful all the time, and the temptation to believe that the best thing to do is not question the political status quo. This kind of critical reflection is not easy. However, when it happens, it can make study abroad a more lasting experience and prepare students for the future challenges that they will undoubtedly face as global citizens, both at home and abroad.

The general goal, then, of this kind of study-abroad program is political education in a dual sense, one positive and one negative. First, it is an education in the harsh realities of democratic politics: the unavoidable perplexities, dilemmas, and illusions that democratic citizens, wherever they are, will face. This is the challenge of democratic politics, not just the challenge of an academic civic engagement project. One must be prepared for perplexities, dilemmas, and illusions because this is how one learns to use political power for humane common purposes and limit its devolution into violence.

The second way in which civic engagement offers study-abroad students a political education is in a negative sense. Civic engagement through study abroad should not strive to cultivate a responsibility for all peoples, in place of a responsibility for one's particular community back home. That kind of sweeping utilitarian ethic is unrealistic at a motivational level and also runs roughshod over the moral ties that do bind people to one another as members of particular communities. However, civic engagement can and I believe should provide students with a recognition of the limited cosmopolitan responsibilities they have.

What these limited cosmopolitan responsibilities are is a matter for another occasion. For the moment, let me simply assert that students can return from study abroad with a clearer view of their own responsibilities at home and abroad if they first recognize the global origins of the benefits they enjoy at home and the risks their own political society imposes on other societies abroad (Vernon, 2010). They are not innocent bystanders to the problems they encounter through study abroad, nor are they entirely powerless to change those things that place them within a complex network of causes and benefits (Esquith, 2010). The challenges that stand in the way of this greater self-awareness and sense of responsibility are not trivial. How one responds to them is a matter of choice.

ACKNOWLEDGMENTS

I am grateful to Tabor Vits for his research assistance and to the students in my RCAH 292B Reflection and Engagement and PHL 850 Injustice and Global Responsibility courses for their comments on earlier drafts of this essay.

REFERENCES

Addams, J. (2002). *Democracy and social ethics.* Urbana and Chicago: University of Illinois Press.

Afrobarometer. (2008). *Afrobarometer Round 4: The quality of democracy and governance in Mali.* Retrieved from http://www.icpsr.umich.edu/icpsrweb/ICPSR/studies/34006.

Bingen, J., Robinson, D., & Staatz, J. M. (Eds.). (2000). *Democracy and development in Mali.* East Lansing: Michigan State University Press.

Coulibaly, M., & Bratton, M. (2013). Crisis in Mali: Ambivalent popular attitudes on the way forward. Briefing Paper 113, Afrobarometer. https://afrobarometer.org/publications/bp113-crisis-mali-ambivalent-popular-attitudes-way-forward.

Dougnon, I. (2011). Child trafficking or labor migration? A historical perspective from Mali's Dogon Country. *Humanity,* Spring, 85–105.

Dwyer, M. M., & Peters, C. K. (2004). The benefits of study abroad. *Transitions, 37,* 5. Retrieved from http://www.transitionsabroad.com/publications/magazine/0007/index.shtml.

Esquith, S. L. (2010). *The political responsibilities of everyday bystanders.* University Park: Pennsylvania State University Press.

Fischer, M. (2004). *On Addams.* Louisville, KY: Wadsworth.

Hamington, M. (2009). *The social philosophy of Jane Addams.* Urbana and Chicago: University of Illinois Press.

Havel, V. (1986). *Living in truth,* ed. J. Vladislaw. London: Faber & Faber.

Klein, C., & Lawver, D. (2007). Community based ecotourism design studio in the Yucatan Peninsula: Enhancing study abroad with a service learning component. *Journal of International Education and Extension Education, 14*(3), 97–107.

Knight, L. W. (2010). *Jane Addams: Spirit in action.* New York: W. W. Norton & Co.

LeCoco, B., Mann, G., Whitehouse, B., Badi, D., Pelckmans, L., Belalimat, N., & Lacher, W. (2012). One hippopotamus and eight blind analysts: A multivocal analysis of the 2012 political crisis in the divided Republic of Mali. Extended editors' cut. Retrieved from http://bridgesfrombamako.com.

Lewis, T., & Niesenbaum, R. (2005). Extending the stay: Using community-based research to enhance short-term study abroad. *Journal of Studies in International Education, 9*(3), 251–264.

Mamdani, M. (2012). *Define and rule: Native as political identity.* Cambridge, MA: Harvard University Press.

Poulton, R. E., & Youssouf, I. (1998). *A peace of Timbuktu: Democratic governance, development and African peacemaking.* New York: United Nations.

Snyder, T. (2010). *Bloodlands: Europe between Hitler and Stalin.* New York: Basic Books.

Vernon, R. (2010). *Cosmopolitan regard: Political membership and global citizenship.* New York: Cambridge University Press.

Wing, S. D. (2013). Mali's precarious democracy and the causes of conflict. Special Report 331, United States Institute of Peace. Retrieved from www.usip.org.

Conclusion

Pat Crawford, Frank A. Fear, and Robert Dalton

ach of the contributors brings a unique voice to the discussion of community engagement abroad. For many, engagement is considered primarily as an activity, something to do, and (with that) a means to an end, having instrumental value. The ends include (among other things) providing undergraduate students with rich, field-infused experiences; building local capacity, perhaps enabling community transformation; increasing the prospects that scholarly innovations will be transferred and used in community settings; and providing practice opportunities in conjunction with professional education programs. When expressed this way, engagement has extrinsic value: It is a tool or approach to put into action, one that yields valued outcomes.

There are others who are drawn to engagement for values-based, normative reasons. For them, it is not just what engagement "can deliver," it is about what engagement means (and represents) in deeply personal terms. When interpreted in that way, engagement is an ethos—a way of being in the world—as one engages professionally. It is a highly relational, connective experience, enabling local people to take greater control over their lives and circumstances. It also offers opportunities for self-growth, perhaps to be transformed by engagement experiences. When thought of in this way engagement has intrinsic value: It is valued for what it means and represents.

And there are those, irrespective of perspective and approach, who want to contribute to the scholarship of engagement. They analyze and evaluate engagement experiences, studying them and writing about them, for the purpose of sharing learning with the community of scholars and practitioners. There are multiple foci associated with learning and understanding. Some of the learning involves culling field experiences for the purpose of declaring principles of good practice. This is especially robust in engagement because many of the challenges/issues are not specific to a single discipline, field, or profession; instead, they are cross-cutting in nature, such as establishing relationships with local people and working out collaborative routines. This means that learning in the health-related fields can be relevant for those working in other fields, such as urban planning or the arts. Learning this way—and the understanding emanating from it—comes from studying engagement as an object of attention.

There is also the matter of enhancing our understanding of engagement as a unique expression, as a nuanced and complex phenomenon. Learning that way—with the understanding emanating from it—comes from studying engagement as subject of attention. With so many and different actors drawn to engagement—from different fields and for different reasons—sense-making is required, not just to do engagement better, but to get a better handle on answers to a foundational question: "What do we have here?" An example of engagement as subject of attention is when a scholar studies personal experiences autobiographically—or studies others' work—as a means to understanding how engagement influences academic thinking and practice.

A common thread in our stories is a focus on education as engaged and transformative learning in an international context. As a group, we engaged with each other. At the onset we agreed to define engagement at a broad and multifaceted concept: from "big E to little e," community-driven to experience of place. We did not want a singular definition of "engagement" to be a deciding factor on who was in and who was out. The author perspectives, and lenses through which the authors see the world, ranged from administration to faculty to students. In the chapters we shared how we engaged with people, places, ideas, and values. The group also agreed to let each author define their own style of how to tell their story. In the spirit of big E engagement, the community drove the process and outcomes of our learning journey. Weaving together the voices is challenging and exciting. Is it like a painter's palette, where the individual colors come together to create a unified image? Or more like a symphony, where the tones and notes are composed on a linear structure, sometimes a blend of instruments and at others a solo? Our minds finally rested on the image of a three-dimensional form—a triangular pyramid, a tetrahedron with four sides and a common vertex. Because the sides are of equal length and area, any side can be the "bottom" plane. Each of the chapters has a unique tetrahedron, with its core framework components forming the sides. The framework forms the lens through which these tell their story. The vertex is the "focus point" where the core of the story comes together, creating lessons learned and integrating the framework components into a transformational experience. Individually the stories, and the tetrahedrons, are useful objects. When they are brought together a greater structure can be realized—a geodesic dome (figures 1a and 1b). Compression and tension are balanced to create a structure with the strength to span greater distances (than stacked and cantilevered objects) and the refraction to see through multiple sides (lenses) simultaneously.

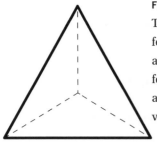

FIGURE 1A.
Tetrahedron form chapter analogy with four sides and a common vertex.

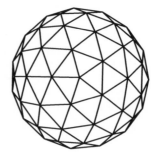

FIGURE 1B.
Geodesic dome form bringing chapter tetrahedrons together analogy in a composite form.

For the summary, the case stories are grouped and explored from their value approaches of extrinsic, intrinsic, object, and subject, as explained earlier. The stories are told in the authentic voices of the authors. Summarizing their stories to fit into the analogy of the pyramid assists with understanding the volume as a whole. Key aspects are diagramed as pyramid faces (keeping in mind that any face can be the "bottom") and key learnings (the vertex) are highlighted in italicized text. Readers are encouraged to study the full chapters to appreciate the nuances and richness of their experiences. Individual writing style and chapter organization are reflective of their personal and disciplinary epistemology (ways of doing), ontology (world view), axiology (values and preferences), and methodology (ways of doing).

Extrinsic Value

The first two chapters set the stage and are authored from an administrative lens focusing on the extrinsic value of outcomes. Fear and Casey set an institutional framework of engagement and study abroad at Michigan State University. One of the takeaways (their vertex) is the importance of unearthing and understanding the context and influence of institutional assumptions and priorities. The relational aspect of engagement is described as a disruptive experience at the faculty and institutional scales. Their "making sense of a cluttered landscape" provides a system for organizing the different value approaches to community engagement abroad. The pyramid faces in their system represent values as an extrinsic expression of the outcomes, as intrinsic personal and community meaning, for good practice and principles (as an object of attention), and for sense making (as a subject of attention).

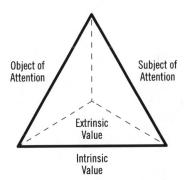

FIGURE 2. Fear and Casey lenses representing extrinsic value and institutional framework.

The second chapter, by Berquist and Milano, frames the literature around service learning, international service, and university engagement. The authors propose an adaptation of Engle and Engle's 2003 typology as a framework to analyze community engagement abroad programs. The sides of their pyramid include interaction through length of stay, language immersion, and housing types; reflection as a learning tool to enhance deep learning and cultural competencies; recognition of roles and self-determination by faculty, students, and the community; and sustainability of the relationship. An extrinsic system of analysis for comparing programs and program components assists future administrators and program leaders to make better informed choices.

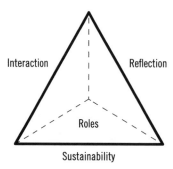

FIGURE 3. Berquist and Milano lenses representing extrinsic value and program analysis framework.

Intrinsic Value

Intrinsic value stories focus on what the experience means and represents to the participants, for personal or professional growth. In a program for leadership in medicine for the underserved, described by Schnuth and Celestin, an international immersion experience is embedded in the curricular structure. These authors explore "who do I want to be" within a professional choice context and use evidence of achieving professional standard goals as a measure of learning outcomes. The authors note the importance of institutional culture and faculty composition on impacts of medical student choice of specialty and their views toward working as agents of social change. The program outcomes and impacts focus on career choice, global citizenship, disciplinary growth, and interdisciplinary teamwork.

FIGURE 4. Schnuth and Celestin lenses representing intrinsic value for the participants.

Object of Attention

A focus on good practice and cross-disciplinary perspectives represents exploring community engagement abroad as an "object of attention" to achieve better results. Dutkiewicz and Dutkiewicz identify principles of good practice to expand the impact of short term programs. The idea of an "extended learning horizon" challenges the traditional academic structures of class and semester. When seeing engagement as a learning and knowledge ecology, partnerships are more sustainable through continued engagement over time, interdependencies, deepening connections, and evolving engagement structures.

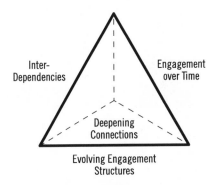

FIGURE 5. Dutkiewicz and Dutkiewicz lenses representing an object of attention focus on the practice of study abroad.

A thirty-plus-year international partnership is presented by Kotval, Ziegler-Hennings, and Budinger that integrates real-world experience with disciplinary theory for planning students in the United States and Germany. Subject skills, techniques, and theory provide a solid intellectual foundation, but experiential learning provides the soft skills (communication, teamwork, self-management) that are required for professional practice and addressing contemporary societal issues. Supporting long-term relationships, building trust between the institutional faculty members, attention to group work skills in program delivery, and fostering transferable skills are essential elements of success.

FIGURE 6. Kotval, Ziegler-Hennings, and Budinger lenses representing an object of attention focus on the practice of study abroad.

A new model of university–community partnerships, the foundation of the relationship, is proposed by Delgado and Yoder. By putting the engaged rethinking partnership at the forefront and the disciplinary content as the supporting character, their model emphasizes the transactions that occur and development of critical thinking and interpersonal skills. Students move from dissonant narratives being seen as obstacles to finding comfort in holding multiple narratives simultaneously, to craft a deeper understanding of themselves and the community. The multiple stakeholder perspectives embrace student narratives, faculty narratives, community leader narratives, and resident narratives.

FIGURE 7. Delgado and Yoder lenses representing an object of attention focus on the practice of study abroad.

Subject of Attention

Sense-making is an expression of studying community engagement abroad as a "subject of attention" to understand the experience of engagement. Dokter and Willyerd explored global health and osteopathic students learning using a phenomenological study design. Multiple observation and assessment techniques included journaling, interviews for critical incidents, and interpretation of longitudinal patterns of change. Motivation and commitment to the work (and the international experience) are identified as key for transformative learning to occur. The authors' lens combined theories of transformative learning, self-reflection, motivation, and identity development.

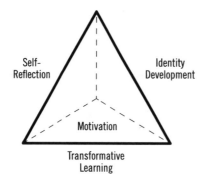

FIGURE 8. Dokter and Willyerd lenses representing a subject of attention focus for sense making.

Rosenbaum's collaborative inquiry is grounded in his personal ethics and principles of community based participatory work. With a candor that is achieved through extended personal reflection, he shares twenty years of experience of in South America. He approaches his story with insights of a personal journey, as a scholar-activist, mindful of social justice and the importance of community relationships. The process of engagement requires a personal commitment by the faculty member and shows that working in the contested terrain of the scholarship of engagement can be transformative for the faculty member as well as the students and the community.

The challenges of civic engagement and study abroad are explored by Esquith through critical self-reflection. Self-awareness, perplexities (a logical contradiction when assumptions are challenged), dilemmas (such as the tension between trust and truth), and illusions ("living within a lie") are the structure within which the reflections are composed. The challenge is to embrace

FIGURE 9. Rosenbaum lenses representing a subject of attention focus for sense making.

the positive and negative aspects of global political and economic understanding, through self-aware choices—especially, in making informed domestic decisions.

FIGURE 10. Esquith lenses representing a subject of attention focus for sense making.

Wrapping Up

Through the stories, the authors have shared their passion for education as real-world, engaged, transformative learning in an international context. As Delgado and Yoder write, the challenges are to find comfort in the dissonance, hold the multiple narratives simultaneously, and explore how each tells a piece of the overall story: how they all fit together. The chapter lessons and pyramid framework are combined into table form as a way of seeing how the pieces fit together (table 1).

We learned about the importance of understanding the context and influence of assumptions and priorities in our work, and how to use that as a tool for organizing and making transparent our perspectives (Berquist and Milano; Crawford, Dalton, and Fear; Fear and Casey). Creating external frameworks for evaluation allow us to engage others in the conversations, whether they be for assessing program design or using professional standards as a measures of student learning and growth (Berquist and Milano; Esquith; Dokter and Willyerd; Schnuth and Smith). Sometimes community engagement abroad work requires thinking "outside the box" to extend the learning horizon, to knowingly grapple with the contested terrain of the scholarship of engagement to become a scholar-activist, and to challenge students and ourselves with uncomfortable questions (Dutkiewicz and Dutkiewicz; Esquith; Rosenbaum). Community-engaged work in an international context creates an elevated platform for transformative learning, bringing together theory and

Table 1. Summary of Chapter Lessons and Framework

	AUTHORS	LESSONS	PYRAMID FRAMEWORK
EXTRINSIC VALUE	Fear and Casey	Importance of unearthing and understanding the context and influence of institutional assumptions and priorities.	Extrinsic value Intrinsic value Object of attention Subject of attention
EXTRINSIC VALUE	Berquist and Milano	An extrinsic system of analysis for comparing programs and program components assists future administrators and program leaders to make better informed choices.	Interaction Reflection Roles Sustainability
INTRINSIC VALUE	Schnuth and Celestin	Importance of institutional culture and faculty composition on impacts of medical student choice of specialty and their views toward working as agents of social change.	Career choice Global citizenship Disciplinary growth Interdisciplinary teamwork
OBJECT OF ATTENTION	Dutkiewicz and Dutkiewicz	The idea of an "extended learning horizon" challenges the traditional academic structures of class and semester.	Engagement over time Interdependencies Deepening connections Evolving engagement structures
OBJECT OF ATTENTION	Kotval, Ziegler-Hennings, and Budinger	Subject skills, techniques, and theory provide a solid intellectual foundation, but experiential learning provides the soft skills (communication, teamwork, self-management) that are required for professional practice and addressing contemporary societal issues.	Long-term relationships Building trust Group work skills Transferable skills
OBJECT OF ATTENTION	Delgado and Yoder	Students move from dissonant narratives being seen as obstacles to finding comfort in holding multiple narratives simultaneously to craft a deeper understanding of themselves and the community.	Student narratives Faculty narratives Community leader narratives Resident narratives
SUBJECT OF ATTENTION	Dokter and Willyerd	Motivation and commitment to the work (and the international experience) are identified as key for transformative learning to occur.	Transformative learning Self-reflection Motivation Identity development
SUBJECT OF ATTENTION	Rosenbaum	The process of engagement requires a personal commitment by the faculty member and shows that working in the contested terrain of the scholarship of engagement can be transformative for the faculty member as well as the students and the community.	Personal journey Scholar-activist Social justice Community relationships
SUBJECT OF ATTENTION	Esquith	The challenge is to embrace the positive and negative aspects of global political and economic understanding, through self-aware choices—especially, in making informed domestic decisions.	Self-awareness Perplexities Dilemmas Illusions

practice, expanding personal development, and exploring our roles as agents of social change (Kotval, Ziegler-Hennings, and Budinger; Schnuth and Smith).

At the end of the day, we have learned much by starting this conversation with our colleagues. We have more to learn and our horizons will broaden as we lay the foundation with informed dialogue, scholarly work, and scholarship.

Contributors

As director international, **Brett Berquist** leads the international strategy and operations at the University of Auckland after working in Europe, Asia, and the United States as academic staff and administrator leading international recruitment strategy, transnational education, English as a second language provision, campus-wide internationalization strategy, and credit mobility. Prior to Auckland, he led one of the largest study abroad programs among U.S. public universities with more than three hundred programs on seven continents and three hundred dedicated faculty program leaders, with more than forty offering a community-engagement component. He also launched the first U.S. study abroad doctoral fellowship, served as co–principal investigator on GLEO, a research project on graduate education abroad, and led a Big Ten benchmarking project that advanced the field's understanding of noncredit education abroad, including service learning. As a first-generation student himself, he has sought to increase access for underrepresented students by collaborating with Diversity Abroad; serving on the Forum on Education Abroad Council and study-abroad provider advisory boards; and co-chairing the content committee for the Global Internship Conference. He holds degrees in music, French, and linguistics. His most recent publication, coedited with K. Moore and J. Milano is *International Internships: Mission, Methods & Models, a Collection of Papers from the Global Internship Conference* (2018).

Anne Budinger, née Hoffmann, obtained a PhD (2012) in spatial planning at Dortmund University of Technology (TU Dortmund). From 2006 she worked as a research scientist and lecturer at the TU Dortmund, School of Spatial Planning, Chair of Landscape Ecology and Landscape Planning. She was involved in the joint student workshops between MSU und TU Dortmund for more than ten years. In March and April 2011 Budinger was a guest lecturer and visiting scholar at the School of Planning, Design, and Construction at Michigan State University. Her professional interests are open space and green space planning in urban areas, the effect of open spaces on the value of real estate and on the quality of the housing environment, and the effects of garden exhibitions on urban development. Since 2015 she has worked for the Ruhr Regional Association as a team leader in the field of park management and development for the Emscher Landscape Park.

Karen McKnight Casey is director emerita of the award-winning Michigan State University (MSU) Service-Learning and Civic Engagement initiative. During her tenure as director (2000–2013), Karen was responsible for facilitating endeavors that provided academic, curricular and cocurricular, service-based learning, and community and civic engagement opportunities for MSU constituencies. She worked closely with faculty, university administrators, students, and community partners to ensure that opportunities were offered that met academic, personal, professional, and civic development goals, while simultaneously addressing the community-generated requests related to service and capacity building. In addition to her role as director, Karen was credentialed as a field instructor in the MSU School of Social Work, of which she is an alumna, and served as an adjunct with the Department of Human Development and Family Studies. Her background also includes that of specialist and director of the nationally recognized Young Spartan Program partnership with schools, work as an academic advisor and resident director, extensive professional experience managing and directing in community nonprofit organizations, and service with the Peace Corps. She has presented extensively, and is published in the areas of university–community partnerships, the integration of service-learning into the curricula, and civic engagement pedagogy. While at MSU, Karen presented at national and international conferences and was active with a variety of national and state networks and committees and community boards.

Cheryl Celestin, EdD, joined Michigan State University College of Human Medicine as an academic and diversity specialist for the Leadership in Medicine for the Underserved Program (LMU) and Center of Excellence. She enjoys working with community resources in developing curriculum and local and international service-learning experiences for medical students in the LMU program. She serves as staff development and faculty advisor for unconscious bias courses. She holds certifications as facilitator and trainer in unconscious bias, cultural intelligence and poverty simulations experiences. Cheryl is a proud graduate of two historically black colleges and universities: Grambling State University and Xavier University of Louisiana. Her doctoral degree is from Western Michigan University.

Pat Crawford, PhD, RLA, is currently the director of the School of Design at South Dakota State University. She is a past associate director of the School of Planning, Design and Construction (SPDC), and past senior director of the Bailey Scholars Program at Michigan State University (MSU). Bringing together the MSU community delivering engaged study abroad began in 2012 through a dialogue with Brett Berquist and Frank Fear. A faculty learning community, hosted through the Bailey Scholars Program, created the foundational discussions for this volume. The process combined two of her passions, international study and community engagement. Her approach to teaching and learning embraces active, engaged, and experiential pedagogies. As a constructivist at heart, her experiences create the foundation for learning and build the scaffold for integrating new knowledge and deconstructing assumptions. Her interests in study abroad focus on the transformative learning impacts for students, how international experiences enhance employability skill development, and the use of field sketching as a way of understanding place in new environments. Peer-reviewed publications have been one avenue for sharing her scholarship in teaching and learning, study abroad, and community engagement. Her articles have been published in the *Journal on Excellence in College Teaching, Journal of Faculty Development, Journal of Higher Education Outreach and Engagement, Town Planning Review, Current Urban Studies, National Association of College Teachers in Agriculture*, and the *Landscape Research Record*. Through her work she has had experiences in the United Kingdom, Germany, Italy, France, Poland, Greece, Spain, Estonia, the Netherlands, South Africa, China, Australia, and New Zealand. Her education includes a PhD in environmental design and planning from Arizona State University, a master of landscape architecture from Kansas State University, and a BS in horticulture from the University of Missouri–Columbia.

Robert Dalton, PhD, is a landscape designer and estimator working in private practice in Metro Detroit, Michigan. He has a PhD in planning, design, and construction as well as a Bachelor of Landscape Architecture from Michigan State University. His research and practice interests include integrative learning in built environment education, community engagement, and successful student transition from theory to practice.

Vincent Delgado is the founding director of the MSU/RCAH Program on Sustainability in Costa Rica. Cofounder of the Refugee Development Center, past cochair of the Power of We Consortium and a former MSU associate dean for Civic Engagement, he works in international and immigrant contexts, innovative civic engagement projects, and large systems change networks. Initially a print journalist covering humanitarian issues in Central America, labor in Mexico, and politics and local government in the United States, Delgado is published in major newspapers, travel magazines, and academic journals. As resettlement director at St. Vincent Catholic Charities, Delgado led resettlement of Afghan families and the Lost Boys of Sudan following 9/11. Fluent in Spanish he has taught English, community college political science, and served as a Lansing City Council member. His areas of interest include nonprofit management, international partnership ecosystems, and civic engagement curriculum development and assessment. He wrote the documentary cookbook *A Taste of Freedom: A Culinary Journey with America's Refugees* (2003) and was International Humanitarian of the Year for the American Red Cross Great Lakes Region (2005/2006).

Christina Dokter, PhD, is a faculty member in the Department of Pharmacology and Toxicology at Michigan State University. She is an instructional designer and an educator. Her research areas include study-abroad courses, academic integrity, team leadership, and instructional technology. She has been researching medical students' participation in medical service trips to Guatemala and Peru since 2009. Her original research question targeted the transformational power of such trips for identity and career development toward primary care. She has been serving on a local board of health for several years and was president of the National Association of Local Boards of Health in 2018. She now resides in Georgia and teaches courses about leadership and team development and courses about academic and research integrity. In Georgia, she is involved in mitigating the opioid crisis through various kinds of work on state public health committees.

Daniel Dutkiewicz (MA, MS) holds degrees in history and epidemiology from Michigan State University. He has been instrumental in the design and development of numerous international programs. Dutkiewicz has also supported experiential-based leadership programs and been the in-country faculty host for Chinese students studying abroad at MSU. In collaboration with student leaders, he supported the development of MSU Students Advancing International Development. He is currently completing his dissertation in the Department of Epidemiology at Michigan State University, where he is working to better understand the connections between group identity and parental decision-making about childhood vaccinations in order to implement public health policies that will better protect communities from preventable diseases.

Keri Dutkiewicz, PhD, currently serves as the director of Faculty Learning at Davenport University in Grand Rapids, Michigan, where she facilitates professional development opportunities, mentors faculty and administrators, and designs innovative and engaging learning experiences. She also partners with the Cultural Intelligence Center to help build inclusive, equitable, and diverse educational communities. Dutkiewicz has more than twenty-five years of teaching and administrative experience in higher education at large research institutions, liberal arts colleges, and career-focused universities. She served as senior leader in a highly successful e-learning startup and continues to bring an entrepreneurial creativity to her work in education. A certified Equine Experiential Learning facilitator, she leverages her love for horses to help leaders at all levels build congruency and communication skills. She has developed and led international programs in China, India, and Mongolia. Dutkiewicz also leverages her creativity to design engaging online and blended professional development programs, including a Green Zone Training to help faculty and administrators understand the perspectives and needs of military students and colleagues. She holds degrees in comparative literature and English from Michigan State University.

Stephen L. Esquith has been working on ethical problems in developing countries since 1990, when he was a senior Fulbright scholar in Poland. His research and teaching since that time have focused on democratic transitions in post-authoritarian countries. He has written on the rule of law, the problem of democratic political education, mass violence and reconciliation, and moral and political responsibility. He is the author of *Intimacy and Spectacle* (1994), a critique of classical and modern liberal political philosophy, and *The Political Responsibilities of Everyday Bystanders* (2010), on mass violence and democratic political education. He has been involved in numerous civic engagement projects in the public schools and has led a study-abroad program focusing on ethical issues in development in Mali in summer 2004, 2006, 2008, 2010, and 2014. He spent the academic year 2005–2006 teaching and working with colleagues at the University of Bamako, Mali, as a senior Fulbright scholar. He has coedited a volume of critical essays on the capabilities approach to development, and has recently written on children's human rights, the problem of self-sacrifice, the role of film in democratic political education, and dialogue and reconciliation in postconflict situations. As the recipient of an MSU Alliance for African Partnership award in

2016–2018, he has worked with partners in Mali to build a network for peace education. He serves on the advisory board of the International Development Ethics Association. After serving as chair of the Department of Philosophy for five years, he returned to Michigan State University in fall 2006 to become dean of the new Residential College in the Arts and Humanities (RCAH). Central to the mission of the RCAH is the importance of civic engagement, peace education, and global justice.

Frank A. Fear is professor emeritus and senior fellow in Outreach and Engagement, Michigan State University. In addition to academic roles, Fear served MSU over the years in various administrative roles: as Department of Resource Development chairperson, acting associate director of MSU Extension, director of The Liberty Hyde Bailey Scholars Program, and senior associate dean, College of Agriculture and Natural Resources (CANR). He was the first person to be named to the Bailey Scholars and CANR administrative posts; units under his direction won the MSU Phi Kappa Phi award for Interdisciplinary Scholarship and the MSU Excellence in Diversity Award. A sociologist, Fear works in the fields of community and organization development. His primary interest is citizen engagement in public affairs with special reference to how social institutions—higher education in particular—enable citizen activism. His is the lead author of the book *Coming to Critical Engagement*, and has published in a variety of journals, including the *Journal of Higher Education Outreach and Engagement*, the *Journal of Leadership Studies*, *About Campus*, and the *Higher Education Exchange.* A scholar-practitioner in approach, Fear has received service awards from the Greater Lansing Food Bank and MSU's Community Volunteers in International Programs. He is the 2013 recipient of the Charles A. Gliozzo Award for International Public Diplomacy.

Zenia Kotval is a fellow of the American Institute of Certified Planners. She is also a Fulbright scholar and a former Lilly Teaching Fellow. Kotval currently serves as a member of the Planning Accreditation Board and as an ex officio member of the Association of Collegiate Schools of Planning Governing Board. As a professor of urban and regional planning in the School of Planning, Design and Construction, she regularly teaches courses in economic development and planning practicum. Kotval's scholarship interests are in community-based development, economic policy and planning, the changing structure and characteristics of local economies, and the impacts of community development strategies. With a strong, structured research, teaching, and engagement agenda, she focuses on linking theory and practice with a special emphasis on local economic development, industrial restructuring, and urban revitalization. As director of MSU Extension's Urban Collaborators, Kotval's service continues to be dedicated to making academic and professional expertise available to meet the needs of Michigan's core cities. Throughout her years at MSU, she has integrated the world scale and the land-grant mission into her scholarship. Kotval is an internationally recognized expert on economic development and community engagement, speaking frequently at national and international venues.

Joy Milano has spent the majority of her career as a writer, editor, teacher, administrator, and researcher at the post-secondary level. She holds a BA in English from Michigan State University, a MEd in adult and higher education with an English specialization from Grand Valley State

University, and a PhD in higher, adult, and lifelong education from Michigan State University. She currently manages a federal grant for the Michigan Department of Education related to improving the state's early childhood care and education system in the State of Michigan, while also working as a contract editor and academic coach.

Rene Rosenbaum, PhD economics, 1985, University of Notre Dame, is an associate professor of community and economic development in the School of Planning Design and Construction and a senior faculty associate with the Julian Samora Research Institute at Michigan State University. He has research interest in and has published in heterodox economics, community economics, and labor economics, and he specializes in community economic development as it relates to the U.S. Latinx population. He currently teaches a class on poverty and inequality in America and leads a modified version of the study-abroad program to Peru that he writes about in his chapter. Before joining the school in 2016, Rosenbaum taught and conducted research and outreach in community economic development in the Department of Community Sustainability, where he worked for more than twenty-five years. His current research on Latinx community development focuses on Hispanic-serving institutions and their roles as higher education anchors for local economic development in host communities that are increasingly Latinx.

Rae Schnuth, PhD, is retired after working for nineteen years at Michigan State University. She was assistant dean in the College of Human Medicine and was the director of the Leadership in Medicine for the Underserved Certificate Program. Her career has focused on teaching medical students, nursing students, and other health care providers to understand and develop effectiveness and skill in caring for vulnerable populations in urban, rural and international settings.

Gary Willyerd, DO, is an associate dean for the Michigan State University College of Osteopathic Medicine, Detroit Medical Center. He also has eighteen years of experience as Director of Medical Education and has organized and participated in more than twenty medical missions to Central and South America with medical students, interns, and residents. Willyerd for the past five years has offered medical service electives to medical students and takes students to Guatemala and Peru. Willyerd also served as the president of the Association of Directors and Medical Educators (AODME) and as the chair of the American Osteopathic Association (AOA) Internship Evaluating Committee. He is currently a member of the AOA's Council of Osteopathic Training Institutions and a board member/treasurer of DOCARE, Intl., a medical outreach organization founded by osteopathic physicians dedicated to providing needed health care to indigent and isolated people in remote areas around the world.

Scot Yoder is associate dean of students and associate professor of philosophy at Michigan State University. His research focuses on health care and environmental ethics, American pragmatism, and the philosophy of religion.

Christiane Ziegler-Hennings is a former research scientist and lecturer at the Chair of Landscape Ecology and Landscape Planning, Department of Spatial Planning, Dortmund University of

Technology (TU Dortmund). Her teaching and research areas are in the fields of urban ecology, open space planning, and brownfield redevelopment. She has taught in the postgraduate course for planners from Africa and Asia at TU Dortmund and at the European Business School. From 1986 to 2011, she was responsible for the organization of the student exchange, faculty exchange, and joint study abroad between Dortmund and Michigan State University. She currently works as a private consultant on urban economic development and open space planning. She has numerous publications and presentations on brownfield redevelopment, children and urban nature, sustainable development of commercial areas, and open space planning.

Index

Page numbers in italics refer to figures and tables.